PRAISE

MAPLE AND VINE

"Mr. Harrison's clever fantasy teases out the reality of moving back to the past more completely, making a sneaky, compelling case for the seductions of living the Ozzie and Harriet life full time, as opposed to just dipping into it via the DVR . . . Piquantly funny, cleverly executed and darkly playful."

—NEW YORK TIMES

"Funny and trenchant . . . a wickedly satiric and sympathetic portrait of twenty-first-century angst and the desire to escape into the past."

—BACKSTAGE

AMAZONS AND THEIR MEN

"The life of Leni Riefenstahl, the filmmaker who made movies for Hitler, has been examined and critiqued aplenty, but rarely so entertainingly as in *Amazons and Their Men*, a brash play by Jordan Harrison."

—NEW YORK TIMES

"*Amazons and Their Men* is chillingly affecting—and surely unforgettable."

—WASHINGTON POST

DORIS TO DARLENE, A CAUTIONARY VALENTINE

"*Doris to Darlene* is that rare thing: a rarefied theatrical experiment that has the glow of pure entertainment and the warmth of a folktale . . . Harrison's teasing, rapturous chamber opera of a play spins and crackles like a beloved old 78 under a bamboo needle."

—NEWSDAY

THE AMATEURS

MAPLE AND VINE
& OTHER PLAYS

MAPLE AND VINE

& OTHER PLAYS

JORDAN HARRISON

THEATRE COMMUNICATIONS GROUP   NEW YORK   2025

Maple and Vine & Other Plays is published by Theatre Communications Group, Inc., 520 Eighth Avenue, 20th Floor, Suite 2000, New York, NY 10018-4156

Special thanks to Judith O. Rubin for her generous support of this publication.

Due to space constraints, credit information for cited material can be found at the back of the book.

TCG books are exclusively distributed to the book trade by Consortium Book Sales and Distribution.

Library of Congress Control Numbers:
2024014639 (print) / 2024014640 (ebook)
ISBN 978-1-55936-966-4 (paperback) / ISBN 978-1-55936-929-9 (ebook)
A catalog record for this book is available from the Library of Congress.

Book design and composition by Lisa Govan
Cover design by Mark Melnick
Cover photograph by Jefferson Hayman, *A Wondrous Gray*

First Edition, March 2025

FOR ADAM, OF COURSE

CONTENTS

FOREWORD

By Heidi Schreck

I met a wide-eyed, baby Jordan Harrison in 2003 when I was hired to replace a more famous actor who had to drop out of his first New York reading. I'd moved to the city days earlier and was ecstatic to be getting my big break. The theater world is tiny and chatty and everyone I knew was buzzing about this dazzling wunderkind out of Paula Vogel's program at Brown who wrote formally daring, super-weird plays. Being asked to read his *Museum Play* for a real live audience at Playwrights Horizons felt like a miracle, a sign my new life would be filled with artistic wonders, and also that I would become a famous actor in no time. (Not true. I didn't get paid to act for another four years.) The real miracle, of course, turned out to be Jordan, a visionary artist in a cute red-orange hoodie who would become one of my playwright heroes, a beloved collaborator, and my lifelong friend.

The Museum Play is a haunting, wickedly funny meditation on memory and desire, and encountering it for the first time I remember being stunned by its incandescent theatricality.

Trapped in Jordan's claustrophobic hall of wonders, I found myself grappling with questions about nature, time, and our human need to catalog and control our messy, mortal lives, sometimes to the point of extinction. Revisiting it now, I can see that this early work contains so many of the marvels that make something undeniably a "Jordan Harrison play": Poetry grounded in fierce human need; wondrous, invented worlds that allow us to return to our own reality with fresh eyes; an infectious sense of play, even in the face of tragedy; and passionate, brainy stories filled with inventors, artists, visionaries, and tricksters who, like Jordan, know that playacting can sometimes be a matter of life and death.

The four plays in this remarkable collection, *Doris to Darlene*, *Amazons and Their Men*, *Maple and Vine*, and *The Amateurs*, are overflowing with these delights. They are also suffused with empathetic curiosity about the world and a tender humanism, a quality that has only grown more and more luminous in Jordan's writing over the years. I've had the pleasure of seeing or performing in all these works, often multiple times, and I am honored to be sharing them with you.

The audacious dark comedy *Amazons and Their Men* is particularly dear to me because I was lucky enough to perform in it twice (at the old Ohio Theater), and also because it dives headfirst into thorny questions about art and ethics and still manages to be riotously entertaining. Loosely inspired by the life of the brilliant filmmaker and Nazi propagandist Leni Riefenstahl ("The Frau"), the play riffs on her failed attempt to direct and star in a film of Heinrich Von Kleist's *Penthesilea* about the mythical battlefield face-off between Achilles and the Queen of the Amazons. The Frau is determined to transcend her role as a state patsy and create a love story for the ages that can't be co-opted by fascists.

In *Amazons*, the Frau has invented her own wondrous world, her film, over which she believes she has total control.

We get the pleasure of being on her set, watching her odd and wonderful creation, which is over-the-top and, at least early on, unabashedly joyous, filled with the ebullience of grown-ups playing make-believe. The Frau casts herself as the love-struck Penthesilea and, to save money, recruits her Achilles from the Jewish ghetto and hires a Romani telegram deliverer to play Patroclus. (She also pays him in chocolate biscuits.) Meanwhile, her sister, a long-suffering extra in all of her films, is conscripted to play all the nameless Amazons killed in the background (my part!). Named simply "The Extra," she dies hilariously on film, over and over, by eating a poison grape, by taking an arrow intended for her sister, etc. A disposable human, as far as the film is concerned.

The Extra's series of fake deaths mirror the horrific atrocities being enacted outside the Frau's set, and the looming threat of war that keeps interrupting her shoot. The Frau believes the art she creates justifies itself by being "beautiful" and might also be a force of good, but only if she can protect it (and herself) from the brutality outside her window. She doesn't care that her efforts to cut what she sees as "ugly" out of her frame resemble the methods of her former employers. She too is willing to sacrifice human lives at the altar of her vision, a decision that makes her as morally reprehensible as her enemies.

And yet . . . The Frau is one of Jordan's most captivating creations. Yes, she is vain and self-obsessed, but so are most of us to some degree, and it's hard not to laugh uncomfortably at our own flaws when we see them embodied by a witty, over-the-top diva. In the end, the play is too complicated to entirely dismiss the Frau's efforts to create an alternate reality. On the one hand, she commits the unforgivable moral failure of blocking out the atrocities around her. The Frau reflects back to us, her comfortable audience, the fact that our beautiful lives have been built on the suffering of others, and that like the Frau we would rather live in delusion than stay awake to that truth. The play also finds something touching, even courageous, in her pursuit of a singular vision. When the Frau is asked why she has to imagine another world, she replies with a question: "Where else will we go when this one ends?"

Years after playing The Extra, this line still haunts me (the truth is I could still recite all of this beautiful play from memory). Those of us lucky enough to perform in a Jordan Harrison play know the delights of traversing the poetry of his language, the rewards that come from paying close attention to every carefully chosen comma. One sweltering evening at the old Ohio Theater, I remember Brian Sgambati, playing Achilles, asked my character: "Do you have . . . someone?" There is a pause written after the line, and I recall being overwhelmed by a subterranean river of grief that was lurking in the silence Jordan had placed there. That silence, I realized, held so many of The Extra's secrets. The fact that she had once loved a woman and now her heart was broken was contained there, and so was the reality that she had made the soul-crushing decision to hide her to keep herself alive. (I remember also that my left thumb moved unconsciously to touch my ring finger in that pause, and I panicked when I realized that I had left my wedding ring on. Backstage after the scene, I ripped it from my finger, and I have never seen it since.) This moment taught me a secret about Jordan's language: Beneath his gorgeous, carefully wrought sentences lurks a raging and chaotic life force that is always threatening to burst forth.

This agonizing tension between the tranquil surface and the violent depths, between illusion and reality, shows up everywhere in Jordan's plays. In his scathing, stylish comedy *Maple and Vine* Katha and her husband, Ryu, stressed out by their high-pressure jobs and grieving after a miscarriage, make the delightfully extreme choice to resolve this tension by running away to join a 1950s reenactor community called the "Society of Dynamic Obsolescence" (the SDO). They are convinced that by moving to a nostalgic fantasy of 1955 America, their lives will become "simpler" and more meaningful. As Dean, an SDO recruiter, explains to Katha:

"In the '50s it's different. In the '50s you have to *go* places. You have to *talk* to people. You pick up the phone to make a call and there's an operator on the other end and you say, 'Good morning.' Or, say, you want to find something out, you go down to the library and Miss Wilkes looks it up in the Dewey Decimals. There's a separate store for meat, and fish, and fruit, and a gent behind each counter who knows your name. A man brings the milk every morning."

The SDO turns out to be more than just friendly librarians and *Leave It to Beaver* porn, though. The cult is fanatically invested in "authenticity," which means that Katha and Ryu, who is Japanese-American, are soon grappling with the misogyny and overt racism that lurks under the smile of a nice 1950s gent, and Dean is forced to fuck his boyfriend in the bushes, while his wife, Ellen (adopting the persona of an amped-up Donna Reed), pretends not to notice.

In the hands of a less interesting writer, this is when Katha and Ryu would attempt to flee; instead, they double down and discover a kind of twisted pleasure, and a new, bracing sense of identity in this fucked-up fantasy. As Ellen points out to Katha, repression can be a galvanizing force, it offers the possibility of self-discovery, of "rich subtext" and the possibility of forging a new self. "Someone you can really grow into." By moving to a place where he can only see his partner under cover of night, Dean gets both the erotic thrill of sneaking around and (perversely) a renewed sense of the outsider identity he lost when the world became more accepting of gays. All of the characters in *Maple and Vine* are overwhelmed by what they perceive to be the existential freedom of contemporary life. They long for boundaries, they long for restrictions and restraints that will give clarity to their lives, even if that comes at a huge cost.

A fierce yearning for self-definition, a desire to understand the contours of the self, permeates all of Jordan's plays, and it manifests in art, invention, discovery, make-believe and a buoyant sense of play. Jordan's unabashed love of performance imbues his work with joy, and it is also intrinsic to his characters' acts of self-creation. Jordan's plays show us that we are all pretending all the time, playing house, making ourselves up as we go along.

This desire to understand the self plays against the backdrop of history in Jordan's rollicking, fourteenth-century fatalistic comedy *The Amateurs*. This moving, mind-expanding piece follows a troupe of actors who go from town to town performing a Noah's Ark mystery play during the Black Death. Jordan has said he was fascinated by what he describes as "the first flicker of humanism" that comes from a spark lit by Noah's Wife in this (real) morality play. Unlike most biblical characters who enacted God's divine plan without question, Noah's Wife decides—bafflingly and fascinatingly—that she would prefer not to join her husband on the ark.

Jordan has said in interviews that this tiny expression of human agency, remarkable for the time, fascinated him and made him wonder what it meant that this moment arose in the midst of a devastating plague: "I felt interested in that in the same way that I'm interested in looking at a Giotto fresco and seeing this thaw from a world in which only God matters to a world in which human beings had choices," he has said. "What was it about experiencing the Black Death that made humans more interested in humans?"

For the characters in *The Amateurs*, death is everywhere. They don't think of their play as Art—it's a means of survival, financial and otherwise. It also becomes, for some of the characters, a defiant act, a way to assert agency in the face of unmitigated horror. *The Amateurs* traffics both in heightened comedy and bleak reality, but unlike the Frau with her beautiful illusions, these characters are living in a reality that is so powerful it refuses to be denied. Written a few years before the Covid pandemic, there is now an uncanny immediacy to watching these performers wonder where they can safely assemble an audience. How long can they continue to make theater in a plague? And when it's their one means of survival, how can they stop? (The play was still being performed in Washington, DC, in the first week of the pandemic, and audiences gasped when two characters kissed near the end of the play. The simple act of affection came to hold all the collective dread of the moment.)

In its pursuit of answers to how art can navigate a plague, *The Amateurs* jumps ahead seven centuries. I will not spoil it for you, but like the actress playing Noah's Wife, Jordan himself stretches against—and exhilaratingly breaks through—the confines of his script. (I will also note proudly that I made a small contribution to this section as a writer in exchange for a new winter hat from Jordan.) When Jordan deposits us back in the fourteenth century, the characters seem to become more dimensional before our eyes, as if by magic. In the act of enduring a crisis, the humans have rendered themselves more human.

This interest in self-creation also manifests, perhaps most joyously (and tragically), in the erotic, heartrending paean to the witchy power of art in *Doris to Darlene, a Cautionary Valentine*. This is one of the earliest plays in this collection and feels in some ways like the most innocent. It has at its center a Young Man (baby Jordan?), a brilliant, insecure teenager in the midst of discovering both the profound pleasures of art and the power of his flowering sexuality as a young gay man. His desires on both fronts are ignited by his high-school music teacher, Mr. Campani, a once-aspiring opera singer, who introduces the Young Man to the sublime experience of listening to Wagner's *Ring Cycle* (spoiler: Its genius makes both of them throw up) and also offers this small-town boy his first real glimpse that there is a future for "people like him."

And because we are in a Jordan Harrison play, this story of self-becoming becomes wondrously expansive and fully magical, carrying us through time to the 1960s and taking us into the world of another teenager, a girl named Doris, who is on the verge of transforming into Darlene, a wildly famous girl-group singer. Doris is in love with her music producer Vic Watts, who is also besotted with Wagner. The song he creates for Doris contains the DNA of "Liebestod" from *Tristan and Isolde* in its hook. Darlene's celestial voice singing "Shoppa loppa shoop shoop. He's sure the boy for me . . ." to that snippet of Wagner will make her a star and also one day bring solace to the Young Man, who listens to it obsessively on his headphones. Meanwhile, another young man, King Ludwig of Bavaria, has fallen in love with the real Wagner, and it is this love that inspires him to commission *The Ring Cycle* and also eventually to drown himself. Liebestod, "Love and death," transcends time and the boundaries of the human psyche to unite all of these characters in their sacred humanness. As Mr. Campani explains to his students, only one of whom is listening:

> "The soprano has paced herself like a long-distance runner and, after four hours, she can finally spend the rest of her huge voice. 'Do I alone hear this melody?' she sings.
>
> Tristan lies dead at her feet, but she looks out into the audience and sees him resurrected. 'Do I alone hear this melody?' The onlookers don't hear anything, and they pity her. But Wagner allows us to share in her madness. His orchestra plays the music in her head.
>
> We all know what it's like to have a song in our head no one else can hear. To walk around all day humming a commercial jingle. To look at someone and hear a hundred violins."

This intertwining of our dreams and our messy reality, our divinity and our mortality, is to me the sacred force that animates all of Jordan's plays. Within their beautiful, jewel-like structures lurks death, and also a tempestuous, fulsome life force. They remind us that we are alive and also that we will die, and also that since those are our given circumstances, we should do our best to make the kind of music only we can make.

—HS
October 2024

HEIDI SCHRECK is a writer and performer. Her play *What the Constitution Means to Me* played an extended and sold-out run on Broadway, and it was produced throughout the country. A filmed version of the play premiered on Amazon Prime. Heidi performed in the world premiere production of *Amazons and Their Men*.

MAPLE AND VINE

Maple and Vine had its world premiere at the 35th Annual Humana Festival of New American Plays, produced by Actors Theatre of Lousiville (Marc Masterson, Artistic Director; Jennifer Bielstein, Managing Director) in Louisville, Kentucky, on March 4, 2011. It was directed by Anne Kauffman. The scenic design was by Brian Sidney Bembridge, the costume design was by Connie Furr Solomon, the lighting design was by Jeff Nellis, the sound design was by Benjamin Marcum; the stage manager was Melissa Rae Miller, the dramaturg was Amy Wegener, and the assistant director was Rachel Paul. The cast was:

KATHA	Kate Turnbull
RYU	Peter Kim
DEAN	Paul Niebanck
ELLEN, JENNA	Jeanine Serralles
ROGER, OMAR	Jesse Pennington

Maple and Vine had its New York premiere at Playwrights Horizons (Tim Sanford, Artistic Director; Leslie Marcus, Managing Director) on December 7, 2011. It was directed by Anne Kauffman. The scenic design was by Alexander Dodge, the costume design was by Ilona Somogyi, the lighting design was by

David Weiner, the original music and sound design were by Bray Poor; and the production stage manager was William H. Lang. The cast was:

KATHA	Marin Ireland
RYU	Peter Kim
DEAN	Trent Dawson
ELLEN, JENNA	Jeanine Serralles
ROGER, OMAR	Pedro Pascal

Maple and Vine was commissioned by Actors Theatre of Louisville and Berkeley Repertory Theatre (Tony Taccone, Artistic Director; Susan Medak, Managing Director). It was originally developed by The Civilians (Steve Cosson, Founding Artistic Director), and written with support from Guggenheim and Hodder Fellowships. It also received developmental support from Playwrights Horizons, the Perry-Mansfield Performing Arts School & Camp New Works Festival, and the Kesselring Fellowship through the Orchard Project and the National Arts Club.

CHARACTERS

KATHA, mid-to-late thirties.

RYU, mid-to-late thirties.

DEAN, late thirties.

ELLEN, late thirties, also plays JENNA.

ROGER, mid-to-late thirties, also plays OMAR.

TIME

2011.

PART ONE

1

In the darkness, we hear:
Sounds of a rainforest.

The rainforest stops abruptly, and we hear:
Sounds of an ocean.

The ocean stops abruptly, and we hear:
Sounds of a babbling brook.

And back to the rainforest.

RYU: Make up your mind.
KATHA: I've been awake for two hours.
RYU: Oh baby.
KATHA: I've been counting the seconds between the jungle insects.
There's a pattern. *(Talking along with the sounds)* Chirp-chirp.
(Pause) Chirp-chirp. Then it gets longer. You don't care.

RYU: I know what you're going to say, but what if you took a pill.

KATHA: I don't want to be zonked out all of tomorrow.

(Pause. She listens to Ryu breathing. We hear a woman's strident voice from the street below.)

WOMAN IN THE STREET: Simon. I know you're in there.

KATHA: Oh no.

WOMAN: Simon buzz me in.

    Why are you DOING THIS TO ME?

KATHA: She's back.

RYU: Who?

KATHA: She usually comes around two.

WOMAN: Why are you DOING THIS TO ME?

(Ryu presses a button on the alarm clock and blue glowing numbers read 2:03.)

RYU: She's right on time.

KATHA:
    It isn't funny.
    This is, like, the farthest
    I'll ever get from being
    at work. This is it.
    I should be having a
    dream, / I should be
    somewhere else, but
    instead I'm just—here.

WOMAN *(Overlapping at " / ")*:
    I came all this way, I took
    THREE TRAINS so
    I don't see how you can be
    DOING THIS TO ME!

RYU: Jesus.

    No one deserves this Simon.

KATHA: No, Simon. No one
deserves this.

(Katha continues in a clenched, terrible way—stoked by the voice outside.)

I lie here all night thinking about the whole day in front of me I write imaginary emails I make imaginary trips to the copy room so when I actually LIVE IT it's like I'm doing it all over again like like Sisyphus or like Hell, I think it's probably very much what Hell would be like, this kind of cold like repetition with no chance of—	Simon, if I have to stand out here in the cold any longer I think I'm really going to LOSE IT. RYU: Baby please— You're shaking.

WOMAN: Simon!
RYU: Who's Simon?
KATHA: Who knows.
RYU: Is he the one with the pug?
KATHA: It's not like I've ever seen our neighbors.
WOMAN: SIMON!
KATHA: And yet I feel like I know him.
RYU: Baby how about a pill.
KATHA: You're always trying to medicate me.
RYU: I'm always trying to help you. It's been six months.
KATHA: It takes as long as it takes.
RYU: Of course.

KATHA *(A beat)*: What if this is *me* now.

RYU: No.

KATHA: Hold me a while?

RYU: Sure. I can do that.

(He holds her. It helps, a little.)

2

Dean speaks out to us. He wears an immaculate 1950s suit and well-shined wing tips. He takes off his hat, politely, before speaking. Revealing slick, aggressively parted hair.

Ellen stands farther off, almost out of the light. She wears a smart, feminine suit, with hat and gloves.

DEAN: First of all, welcome. Welcome to the SDO.
I bet you're all feeling pretty anxious.
"Am I going to use the right words."
"Am I going to walk the right way."
I mean, gosh, you've just taken a pretty huge step, right?

The first thing to remember is that all of us were newcomers at one point.

The other thing to remember—and this one really helped me—the other thing to remember is that the 1950s *weren't in black and white*. It sounds silly, but it's easy to think like that. All we've seen are the photographs. Old TV shows. But people in the '50s had yellow shirts and red sneakers just like you and me. So the main thing to remember is that you can live in color. You don't have to go around trying to act like someone in an old photo. I mean anyway you can't, because they're a photo, and you're . . . you.

That's what this place is for. So you can feel like you again.

I'm sure you all have a lot of questions.
  "What do I wear?" "How do I talk?"
  "How do I explain this to the kids?"

Ellen and I will help you answer all of these perfectly normal questions.

Everyone, this is my lovely wife, Ellen.
ELLEN: Hello everyone.
DEAN: Isn't she something?

3

Katha and Ryu's apartment, the next morning. Katha sits slumped in pajamas, staring at her laptop computer. Maybe she's still in bed. A bowl of cereal sits beside her, untouched. She looks happy in a tranquilized sort of way. Ryu is fully dressed. He's also looking at a laptop, but more actively—typing, sipping his coffee.

We hear period-sounding voices from Katha's computer:

MALE VOICE: Don't you like it?
FEMALE VOICE: Like it? *(Soaring music plays)* It's more exquisite than any dress I could ever have imagined.
MALE VOICE: Puff sleeves.
FEMALE VOICE: The puffiest in the world. You are a man of impeccable taste, Matthew.

KATHA: So beautiful . . .

MALE VOICE: Well, you don't / want to get your dress dirty.

RYU: What?

KATHA *(Still watching the video, rapt)*: Just, the way Matthew doesn't ever say "I love you" but you just *know*?

RYU: Who's Matthew?

KATHA: Oh, sorry. It's *Anne of Green Gables*.

RYU: Didn't you already watch that?

KATHA: There are twenty-six installments. *(Sheepish)* It's my childhood. Don't begrudge me my opiates.

RYU: I never begrudge your opiates.

(He walks out of the room.)

KATHA: It's a nostalgia thing. But I'm not sure whether it's nostalgia for the 1880s or the 1980s. My mother and I watched it all together on TV.

(Ryu comes back in, brushing his teeth.)

It always seemed like a nice life. Go to the one-room schoolhouse. Do arithmetic on your slate. Dip some girl's pigtails in the inkwell.

(Ryu disappears into the bathroom to spit.)

It seemed like a nice life.

RYU *(Off)*: I was on StreetEasy? There are some really affordable places in Nyack.

KATHA: Nyack?

(He comes back in.)

RYU: It'd be quieter, we'd have space. It's just the commute.

(She hits pause. The music stops.)

KATHA: Space for what.

RYU: You know, space.

KATHA *(Thin ice)*: Space for kids?

RYU: Space for whatever.

KATHA: Let's—not have this conversation now.

RYU: Why not?

KATHA: I'm getting ready for work.

RYU: You don't look like you're getting ready. You look like you're at a slumber party.

KATHA: I'm eating breakfast.

(She grabs her cereal bowl. She starts the video again. Soaring music from the computer. Ryu shakes his head. He starts to put on his coat.)

RYU: Well, see you tonight.

KATHA *(Not looking up)*: Okay.
    I'm home pretty late.

(Ryu's hand on the doorknob.)

What's your day like?

(Ryu starts to cry.)

Oh. Oh no. *(She hits pause)* What'd I say?

RYU *(Through tears)*: It's just—it's like every day. I'll get *through* it. And then I come home, and you're— There isn't any—

KATHA: Here. Come here.

RYU: I'm the one who's supposed to be there for you.

KATHA: There aren't any rules.

4

Dean speaks directly to us:

DEAN: It wasn't that the modern world was too fast, or too noisy. In a way, it was too *quiet*. Let me explain. In the twenty-first century, everything's pretty easy, right? You have your drive-thru espresso. Your drive-thru pharmacy. Or why go to the store when you can get it online? You hardly have to interact with anyone—except for all those people you've never even met who enter your life through your computer, pulling you every which way.

In the '50s it's different. In the '50s you have to *go* places. You have to *talk* to people. You pick up the phone to make a call and there's an operator on the other end and you say, "Good morning." Or say you want to find something out, you go down to the library and Miss Wilkes looks it up in the Dewey Decimals. There's a separate store for meat, and fish, and fruit, and a gent behind each counter who knows your name. A man brings the milk every morning.

In the modern world, I used to make it through half the day without talking to a single soul. I used to have it so easy. And now, looking back—I realize how lonely I was.

5

At the office, late that morning. Katha stares at her phone, catatonic. Omar and Jenna watch her from a distance.

OMAR: Pssst.

JENNA: What's going on?

OMAR: Haven't you noticed?

JENNA *(Nodding)*: She should really rethink the sweater.

OMAR: No, I mean—she hasn't moved in like ten minutes.

JENNA: Why not?

OMAR: 'Cause she's depressed I guess.

JENNA: What about?

OMAR: Nothing.

JENNA: How do you know it's nothing?

OMAR: Her husband's a doctor.

JENNA: What kind?

OMAR: Plastic surgeon.

(Katha appears to be giving herself a private little pep talk. Maybe she gives herself a light slap on each cheek.)

JENNA: Ohmygod.

OMAR: What's she doing?

JENNA: Ohmygod.

(Katha picks up the receiver.)

OMAR: Every day she comes in later.

JENNA: I know, isn't it great?

OMAR: No, I mean: What if they let her go.

JENNA: Let her go. I'll take her job.

OMAR *(Loving it)*: Don't be terrible! Besides, you wouldn't get it.

JENNA: Why not?

OMAR: You're too nice.

JENNA: I know, I'm nice right?

OMAR: You're *too* nice.

    In that job you have to be able to tell people / No.

KATHA *(Overlapping with Omar's "No")*: No! I will not hold!

(She has been put on hold. She hangs up, starts to dial again.)

13

JENNA: And I suppose you can tell people No?
OMAR *(Arch)*: Maybe.

(Omar starts to leave.)

JENNA: Fancy salad place for lunch?
OMAR: Always.

(And he's gone, headed toward Katha's office.)

KATHA *(Brightly)*: Yes, you just put me on hold? Do not do that again.
> . . .
> Marcus please.
> . . .
> Katha at Random House.
> . . .
> Well I'm pretty sure he's at his desk for *me* because he left me three messages about the labradoodle book.
> . . .
> An early *lunch*, what a delight. You'd think the man putting together the most urgent coffee-table book of our times wouldn't have time to—
> . . .
> No. I'll be here.

(Katha hangs up. She stares at her phone.)

I'll be here.

(Katha sucks her thumb unconsciously. Omar comes sidling up to the doorway.)

OMAR: Katha? Knock knock.

KATHA: Who's there?

OMAR: Omar.

KATHA: Omar who.

OMAR *(Concerned)*: You know, *Omar*.

Oh, I get it—we're doing a thing, a knock-knock thing.

(Short pause.)

KATHA: You know for a homosexual you're not very funny.

OMAR: Well, you're my boss, so.

KATHA: So.

OMAR: So we don't really have that relationship? *(A beat)* Are you ready?

KATHA: Ready . . .

OMAR: You have the Department Head meeting in ten minutes.

(For a moment, Katha seems to forget how to breathe.)

Unless you want me to tell them you're busy sucking your thumb.

(He exits.)

KATHA: "Unless you want me to tell them . . ."

That's good. Maybe he is funny.

You're talking out loud.

(She stares at her phone. Inhales and exhales. She picks up the receiver and dials just two numbers.)

Yes. Put me through to Human Resources.

6

Ellen speaks directly to us. Dean stands farther off now.

ELLEN: In the beginning, most people try a little too hard with the lingo.

It's easy to get carried away. There are lots of fun terms: "Don't be a square." "Back-seat bingo."

But you don't want to use them all in one sentence.

DEAN: "Hey cat, don't be a square, how 'bout we jump in my hot rod and play a little back-seat bingo?"

ELLEN: I'm not that kind of girl!

DEAN: Oh yes you are.

(They have a laugh at this.)

ELLEN *(To us again)*: That was a lot of fun. But you see the problem. You can end up sounding like you're a person at a theme party, not a person. The most colorful slang from the '50s comes from the Beats and the Hotrodders, so nice ordinary people will want to use those words sparingly.

DEAN: What people don't realize is that a lot of the most common '50s sayings are still in use in 2011, so they'll come naturally to you.

"Cool it." "Make out." "Have a blast."

"Word from the bird."

Just kidding. I was just making sure you were paying attention.

ELLEN: Oh Dean.

Sometimes you just razz my berries.

7

Early that afternoon. Katha and Ryu in Madison Square Park, with hot dogs. Katha isn't eating hers. Ryu still has his scrubs on.

KATHA: Happy? I don't know.
RYU: I mean the last time you really—felt like yourself.
KATHA: I guess when we rented bikes in Amsterdam? And we got falafel?

(Ryu's phone beeps. It's a work text.)

That was almost two years ago.
RYU *(Reading the text)*: What about Cape Cod—was that after? When we pulled the bikes over . . .
KATHA: And we had oysters from that stand.
RYU: That was good.

(Beat.)

KATHA: So the secret is bikes.
RYU: Or food.

(He takes a bite of his hot dog, trying to be jaunty.)

KATHA: Great, Ryu.
     Then we're all set, we'll just get some . . . *bikes* / and and
RYU: Baby.
KATHA: and some hot dogs and some Cherry fucking / *Garcia*
RYU: Baby okay / okay
KATHA: and it'll be like it never happened!
RYU: Of course it happened. It was terrible. But that doesn't mean we have to give up.

17

KATHA: Oh right, "Snap out of it, Katha—it's been six whole months, get over it. / Chin up, kiddo."

RYU: I didn't say that. I would never / say that.

KATHA: "Six months, time to pop out another one!"

RYU: Now you're just / being crazy—

KATHA: Maybe I don't want to love something for all that time again just to have it, to have it / stolen away!

RYU: Settle down.

KATHA: We saw him, Ryu! We saw him! *(Quieter now, spent)* He was real.

RYU: Of course he was.

He was mine too.

KATHA: I'm sorry—shit.

You must get / tired of this routine.

RYU: Don't be sorry.

KATHA: I love you.

RYU: I love you.

KATHA: I want us to be happy.

RYU: I think . . . people aren't happy. People have *never* been happy. The whole idea is a tyranny. Slaves building the pyramids . . . *Serfs.* They didn't have enough time to ask, "Am I happy?" This is not even a hundred-year-old idea: "Am I happy."

KATHA: Maybe that's what happy *is.*

RYU: What.

KATHA: Not having enough time to wonder if you're happy.

(Ryu's phone beeps again.)

RYU: No, that's just busy.

(He looks at it.)

I should, I'm sorry—

18

(He stands up, brushes crumbs off his pants.)

We'll keep talking tonight.

KATHA: You just got here.

RYU: You think it stops?

KATHA: I know

RYU: Bags of blood, and bags of *fat* . . .

KATHA *("Tasty")*: Mmm

RYU: . . . and fifteen year olds who want boobs.
     I have to go back. You do too.

KATHA: No I don't. I quit.

(Ryu takes her in—she is strangely cavalier.)

RYU: You quit?

KATHA: I quit. Finito Mussolini.

RYU: When?

KATHA: This morning.

RYU: Why didn't you say that before?

KATHA: I didn't feel like talking about it.

(Pause. Ryu is deeply weirded out.
  His phone rings now.)

RYU: Jesus. *(The phone rings)* I'm going to cancel my proce-
     dures. I mean you're clearly— *(The phone rings)* Are you
     sure you're not—

KATHA: I'm not a flight risk. Go. *(The phone rings)*

RYU: I'll be right back. *(Answering)* Hello?

(Ryu runs off. Katha doesn't know what to do with herself. She
takes a first bite of her hot dog.

Dean enters in his '50s garb. He is lost, squinting at street
names. There is something unmistakably, gorgeously out of place
about him.)

DEAN: Excuse me.

KATHA (*Giving him the signal for "I just have to swallow this"*): Mmph.

DEAN: Oh, sorry.

(*He offers her the handkerchief out of his breast pocket in one smooth gesture.*)

KATHA: No, it's fine. Sorry.

DEAN: Not at all. Do you know where 200 Fifth Avenue is?

KATHA: Oh yeah, it's confusing. The entrance is on 25th. That's right by where I work. Worked.

DEAN: Well, lucky I ran into you.

(*He tips his hat, starting to go.*)

Thank you.

KATHA: Job interview?

DEAN: What? No. Why do you ask?

KATHA: Just, the suit and everything. It's just pretty put together.

DEAN: Thank you. I have the same one in navy and dark brown.

KATHA: This whole thing you have going— (*Making a circling gesture with her hands, as if circumscribing his outfit*) —it's like something out of the '50s.

DEAN: Yes.

KATHA: Is that what they're doing downtown now? Let me guess, there's nothing shocking left so the only shocking thing is to be straightlaced. We've come full circle.

(*He just looks at her.*)

Or is it less. Self-conscious.

DEAN: I'm not part of a fashion movement. If that's what you're suggesting.

KATHA: Oh I don't mean to make it sound—

DEAN: That's all right. We're used to people being suspicious.

KATHA: "Suspicious"?

DEAN: Of the way we do things. Especially people who are content with the way the world is nowadays.

KATHA: "Content."

What's that like?

(He seems to really see her for the first time.)

DEAN: What I mean is, we're used to explaining ourselves to people.

KATHA: Who's we?

DEAN: May I sit down?

8

Dean speaks directly to us:

DEAN: I'm called back, now and then, on business. Spreading the word.

And it's not just my job to tell the rest of the world about us. I have to decide what to tell *us* about *them*. I have more access to the news, and if it's gossip about so-and-so is dating so-and-so, of course I don't tell you—but when a plane crashes into the World Trade Center I tell you, when the war in Iraq starts I tell you.

Because I have more access to the outside world, it can be a struggle for me. I have a cell phone, for emergencies. I keep it in a drawer in my house. I keep the drawer locked.

Just knowing it's there can be hard. It can be a distraction. That's why people today can't think straight, because there are so many distractions. They are not quiet in their mind. If you're here, you probably know that already.

It may be hard at first. I won't lie to you. When you first come to the SDO, you're used to a different kind of freedom. In the Society of Dynamic Obsolescence, there are very specific boundaries. By which I mean, if you're a gardener, you garden—you won't get invited into the house of the man you're working for. If you are a homemaker, you make your home. That's what you do. You don't start an Ultimate Frisbee team, you don't go backpacking in Thailand. Your husband and kids are going to be home soon and dinner has to be on the table. You are not free. But in another way, you're more free.

We may seem behind bars to them, but to us, they are behind the bars.

9

Katha and Ryu returning to their apartment, early that evening.

RYU: I thought you were like college friends. I never imagined you'd befriended this—strange, clean man who speaks in complete sentences.

KATHA: Didn't you like him?

RYU: I didn't like that he was trying to sell us something.

KATHA: He wasn't *selling* something. He was explaining his way of life. How long has it been since we met someone who seemed so . . .

RYU: Don't say happy.

KATHA: He can't be much older than us. He was us a few years ago.

RYU: So he said.

KATHA: And now there he is with his briefcase and his little hat, he's got it all figured out. But it's silly, right?

RYU: It's not just silly. It's a cult.

KATHA: It's not a cult. They have nonprofit status.

RYU: I'm not sure I even get it. It's like Civil War reenactors?

KATHA: Except for you live there.

RYU: Crazy.

KATHA: But I think the intriguing part is when you hear 1950s you think it's going to be all *Stepford Wives*. You think identical houses, identical cars, a kid on each lawn all bouncing their balls in unison. But it's not that. It's not just suburbs. There's a whole universe in there.

RYU: Did you just call it "intriguing"?

KATHA: You can be anything there. Beat poets. Secret Communists. They need dissenters too, you heard him. We wouldn't have to be June Cleaver and . . . her husband, help me

RYU: Ward

KATHA: Ward Cleaver.

RYU: You said "We."

KATHA: What?

RYU: "We" wouldn't have to be June—

KATHA: Oh, I mean "we" like "one." One wouldn't have to be June Cleaver.

RYU: Huh.

Are you hungry? I'm starving.

KATHA: Again?

RYU: How about this. How about we order in, we get a bottle of wine, get out some actual *plates*. And then maybe later we can . . .

KATHA: I told you, it's icky when you plan it.

RYU: It's been two months.

KATHA: Six weeks.

RYU: Got it. No sex.

KATHA: No *planning*.

RYU: Oh, fine, so I'll just come and take you in the night some-time, is that what you'd prefer?

(Pause. A feeling like maybe it is. Ryu takes out his cell.)

Sushi or Middle Eastern?

KATHA: I don't know. Was there sushi in the '50s?

RYU: Doubtful.

KATHA: They probably didn't even have takeout. It'd be, "Honey, fix me my dinner."

RYU: Now it's starting to sound good.

KATHA *(A deterrent)*: Remember I'd be the one doing the cooking.

RYU: You have your moments. You make a good grilled cheese.

(She makes an ironic "I'm the champion of the world" gesture.)

So sushi? Say yes, 'cause I'm dialing.

KATHA *(Almost to herself)*: I used to make a good red sauce.

RYU: Dragon Roll?

KATHA: I wonder if we could.

RYU: What.

KATHA: Do it, I wonder if we could live there.

RYU: You're being serious?

(He looks at her. She looks at him. He lowers the phone.)

KATHA: They do trial periods. Just six months, to see.

RYU: Six months?

KATHA: Although he said most people don't feel settled for about a year.

RYU: You're not in your right mind. You're just reaching for anything that's different.

KATHA: Dean said you might have that reaction.

RYU: Dean said—

(He contains his sudden anger.)

I want to make sure I understand. A man you just met in the *park* is part of this cult, the Society of Dynamic—what was it?

KATHA: "Dynamic Obsolescence." The SDO for short.

RYU: And all the members of this cult—

KATHA: Why don't we find another word besides "cult"—

RYU: And all the members of this non-cult devote themselves to re-creating a rigorously detailed 1950s America.

KATHA: 1955. It's always 1955.

RYU: And you are really entertaining the idea that we would leave our jobs—

KATHA: Done—

RYU: Leave our jobs and move to this gated community that just cropped up right in the middle of a landlocked Midwestern state, where we don't know anyone and we have no contact with the outside world, and we, what, we live off the land and drink ice-cream sodas and pretend there's no internet?

(Short pause.)

KATHA: It sounds better when you say it out loud, doesn't it.

10

Ellen speaks directly to us. She smokes, wonderfully. This time Dean is standing farther off, just out of the light.

ELLEN: Here are some things you've never heard of:
Hummus.
Baba ghanoush.
Falafel.
Focaccia.
Ciabatta.
Whole-grain bread.

(She raises her eyebrows significantly: "Yes, not even whole-grain bread.")

Portobello mushrooms.
Shiitake mushrooms.
Chipotle peppers.
Chipotle anything.
Jamaican jerk.
Miso.
Sushi.
That one is hard for me.
But I do without.
You'll do without too.
Gruyère.
Manchego.
Parmigiano-Reggiano—the parmesan in a can is all right.
No kalamata olives
No pine nuts
No pesto

No *lattes.*
That's hard for a lot of people.

What you get
Is salt.
You get pepper.
Mayonnaise. Mustard.
You get dried oregano.
Bay leaves.
Paprika, if you want a little kick.
Sanka.
It's a relief, the limitations. You'll find that it's a relief.

It may be hard to maintain a vegetarian lifestyle. Some people have tried. You're always welcome to try, if it coincides with the rest of your dossier. For instance, it might coincide with the dossier of a beatnik English professor—but if you're taking on the identity of an oil man or an ad executive, it would be pretty disruptive not to have steak and a martini for lunch. Disrupting means you're not period-appropriate.

One question we get a lot is health concerns.
   "Do I *have* to smoke?"
   "Do I *have* to drink?"
   "Do I *have* to eat hot fudge sundaes."

Of course, we can't ask for more commitment than you're willing to give. But we think you will get much more out of the experience with total commitment, total authenticity.

What's a little hypertension if you're happy.

11

Split scene: Ellen is rummaging through Katha's closet; Ryu is in the living room with Dean.

ELLEN: Just once a year. During recruiting season.
KATHA: It must be hard, coming back.
ELLEN: Not at all.
KATHA: You don't get, I don't know, *tempted?* "Ooh, HBO." "Ooh, internet."
ELLEN: Mostly I'm just reminded how hard it was. When I see all the really desperate cases.

(This hangs in the air.)

KATHA: Well? What's the prognosis?
ELLEN: You can keep the ones with cotton, wool, or silk. But throw out the poly-blends.
KATHA: Throw out?
ELLEN: Or storage. But most people decide to stay after the trial period. It doesn't really matter, as long as you keep them out of the SDO. The same goes for Lycra, Ultrasuede—most of it wasn't in homes until the '70s. No digital timepieces, of course. And absolutely no Velcro *anything.*
KATHA: Isn't that always the rule?
ELLEN: Oh, you're a funny one.
KATHA: I don't know . . .
ELLEN *(Cheerful in a slightly metallic way)*: No, it's good to know what your skills are.

(Ellen disappears into the deep recesses of the closet.)

(Off) Oh dear. Most of these will have to go.

KATHA: I thought this was just a consultation?

(Dean and Ryu. Dean makes notes on a clipboard.)

DEAN: Of course there are certain things about your situation
that will impact your dossier.

RYU: My situation.

DEAN: Yours and Katha's.

RYU: Katha's and mine.

DEAN: Oh dear, I'm not making myself clear. When we have
a mixed-race couple, that tends to suggest certain details
about their dossier. *(Glances down at his clipboard)* You'd be
living in the North, I imagine?

RYU: North of what?

DEAN: The Mason-Dixon.

(Beat.)

RYU: There's a Mason-Dixon Line in the gated community?

DEAN: We have everything in microcosm, yes. So there are
areas with the spirit of the South and areas that have more
the feeling of the North. The Midwest. The West is still
under construction, so that won't be an option for another
year or two.

RYU: Well, then—I guess we would probably live in the North,
yes.

DEAN *(Looking at the clipboard)*: How do you feel about boxes?

RYU: Boxes?

(Back to Ellen and Katha. Ellen is holding up a frock on a hanger.)

ELLEN: This one will work nicely.

KATHA: That was my mother's.

ELLEN: And this one.

(Pause.)

KATHA: That's it?

ELLEN: And the solid-color sweaters. I'm afraid you have a very synthetic closet.

KATHA: What am I supposed to wear?

ELLEN: I sew all my own clothes now. I'll teach you. It's simple if you use patterns, and fun. You'll want to change your hair, of course. And you'll probably want to try the support undergarments before you get to the SDO. You can find a lot of them online. There's a whole different architecture to the undergarments. It really helps with period posture and bearing.

KATHA: Is it the same for everyone?

I mean, I'm sure the beatnik chicks aren't wearing girdles, right?

ELLEN: Beatnik chicks.

KATHA: I just don't know if the whole housewife thing is the way I want to go.

(Pause.)

ELLEN: Sure, smoking reefer and reading Ginsberg is fun for a day.

But you seem like you'd want something more complicated. Some repression, some rich subtext. Someone you can really grow into.

KATHA: Repression . . .

ELLEN: In the '50s, people keep things to themselves. They hold their heads high. *(An enticement)* People have a lot of secrets.

(Beat.)

I know, you think a housewife is just someone in a pretty dress. But a housewife makes things *work*. If there's a silence, she fills it. If there's a wound, she dresses it. You're a tall girl, Kathy—

KATHA: Oh, it's "Katha."

ELLEN *(Cheerful)*: I know what I said.

You're a tall girl. If you didn't slouch so much *(Corrects Katha's posture)* you could really command a room.

(Katha looks at herself in a mirror.)

KATHA: And that's . . . allowed, in 1955?

(Ellen checks to make sure they're alone.)

ELLEN: It's different for girls. It's a different kind of power. It's not about shaking a big stick. We aren't trying to be men. What we do is more indirect.

But in the end, we get what we want.

(They share a smile. Back to Ryu and Dean.)

DEAN: The nice thing is you can do a trial period. So if it turns out it isn't a fit, you're free to leave at any time.

RYU: Why does that always have an ominous ring to it?

DEAN: Maybe because you're a distrustful person.

RYU: Excuse me?

DEAN *(Warm, frank)*: How can you be any other way in a big city? Identity fraud, online profiles . . . All of your information is just—out there. That's one of the things people love about the SDO. There's less information. A kind of privacy long since extinct. A more innocent world to raise the kids in.

You do want children, don't you?

31

(Beat.)

RYU: We tried, once. And Katha . . . lost it at twenty weeks, so

DEAN: I'm sorry.

RYU: So, I want to try again. But Katha—isn't so sure.

DEAN: Not yet.

(Pause. They lock eyes.)

For many women, that becomes very important after moving to the SDO.

(Ryu stands up.)

RYU: I should see how Katha's doing.

DEAN: Listen, Ryu. Just listen for a second. I want to ask you something. Have you ever gone hiking for the day in the clean air and come back feeling refreshed?

RYU: Sure.

DEAN: You stand up straighter, right? You think more clearly. Everything's better when you come back, at least until that feeling wears off. So then: Why do you ever come back?

(Katha comes in wearing one of the dresses that passed muster. Her hair is up in a kerchief that Ellen gave her. She does a little twirl.)

KATHA *(To Ryu)*: Well? What do you think?

ELLEN: I love it.

RYU *(To Katha)*: Can we talk alone please?

DEAN: Absolutely, what a great idea. Take your time.

(Dean and Ellen stand a ways off, but don't exit. They watch Ryu and Katha during the following:)

KATHA: I know what you're going to say.

RYU: What am I going to say.

KATHA: That this is all crazy,

That it'll never work,

That they're a couple of irony-free androids and what if everyone there is like them.

RYU *(Impressed and a little bewildered)*: That *is* what I was going to say.

(They glance at Dean and Ellen. Ellen waves.)

KATHA: They're not going to be our best friends.

They're not going to be coming over for Tupperware parties every day.

It's still going to be You and Me, without all the things that make it impossible for us to be You and Me here.

DEAN: How are you folks doing over there?

KATHA: Fine, just another minute!

RYU *(Sotto voce)*: He called us a Mixed-Race Couple.

KATHA: We *are* a mixed-race couple.

RYU: But he said it with capital letters.

(She gives him a "you're being paranoid" look.)

You know how much I'd be making there? Four figures.

KATHA: Money goes further there. It's adjusted for inflation. Deflation.

RYU: I went to medical school, Katha.

KATHA: You're the one who's always talking about the hours. The emptiness. The injecting goo into trophy wives who think you're their best friend. Give it six months. Think of it like a vacation. A vacation from your life. And if you miss all that, I'm sure they'll be dying to have you back.

(Beat.)

Do you love your job?

RYU: No.

KATHA: Do you love your life?

RYU: No.

KATHA: Do you love me?

RYU: Yes.

12

DEAN: The more people who come to the community, the more accuracy we're capable of. So it's not just good because "Hey, the more the merrier"—it's good because everyone who joins us contributes to the authenticity.

Our city planners are a good example. You see, fifty years ago, the roads were narrower and the sidewalks were wider. Did you know that? And our city planners make sure that is accurately represented. A lot of times they'll work together with the landscape architects. So we have city parks that are spotless for the nice neighborhoods. Fountains and every- thing, really nice. And we have parks with graffiti for the neighborhoods that maybe aren't as nice. The kind where homosexuals and communists might meet at night. There might be candy wrappers on the grass. The trees might have the names of lovers carved in them. The graffiti was a lot tamer back then, of course. We have a pamphlet for that.

Some of the technology has been hard to track down. Typewriter ribbon, mimeographs. Our engineers had to learn how to replicate them. Now they can do it so it's just like new. I mean just like old.

(Ellen laughs wholesomely.)

This is all to say, you might want to think about how *you* can contribute. And if you can't think of something, you might consider joining your local Authenticity Committee. Ellen can tell you about that, she's the Vice President.

ELLEN: Six years running.

DEAN: My wife, a woman of influence.

13

Back at the office. Omar sits at Katha's desk now. Katha stands behind him, training him. They both look at the computer screen.

KATHA: I usually dump the Unsoliciteds in this folder.

OMAR: "Siberia." Cute.

KATHA: That way they aren't haunting me before I have time to deal with them. Usually I give myself an hour on Friday morning and just burn through them.

There's this one guy, Mr. Firestone? He must be in his eighties at least. He sends us all his war stories, and I mean war stories like *war*. Korea. Really, um, representational. And he always calls, asking for the hard copy back. We don't do that. He knows we don't do that. He's just looking for a way to get me on the phone—I mean you.

OMAR: Um, Katha, I wanted to thank you . . .

KATHA: Thank me?

OMAR: I don't want this to be weird, but you really made my career, by leaving I mean.

KATHA: Well, you can have it.

OMAR: I know I can.

KATHA: No, I mean, I don't want anything to do with it.

OMAR: You really burned out.

KATHA: I don't know if that's the word I'd—
Fine, I "burned out."

OMAR: Do you have any advice for me?

KATHA: Advice . . .

OMAR: I mean, to not burn out like you?

KATHA: Um. Take breaks. Try to punch out at five. I don't know.
With you I sense a . . . *(As though she's saying "ruthlessness")* stability I didn't have, so.

(Omar smiles at this.)

OMAR *(Suddenly confidential)*: Is it true you're joining a cult?

(Short pause.)

That's what they're saying.

KATHA: Who.

OMAR: Everyone.

KATHA: If it's easier for you to believe, then yes, it's a cult.

OMAR: What do you mean easier to believe?

KATHA: If it means you don't have to wonder which of us is crazy: Me, for leaving? Or you, for working a sixty-hour week just so you can pay for an apartment the size of a matchbox, while you spend the rest of what you make buying drinks to numb yourself while you complain to your husband which makes him hate you and makes you hate yourself even more because you're supposed to be this woman, this powerful woman because that's what you're supposed to BE, except for you don't feel powerful, you feel like someone who doesn't SLEEP or DREAM or do anything but just get THROUGH it.

OMAR: Wow.

KATHA: I'm sorry, that was—not really about you, was it.
Good luck. With everything, Omar. Really.

OMAR: What is this place you're going, anyway?

(Short pause.)

KATHA: You know how you'll go hiking for the day in the clean air and come back feeling refreshed? You feel better, you think clearer. So then . . . why do you ever come back?

OMAR: I don't really go hiking, so.

(Short pause. The phone beeps. Jenna's voice comes through the speaker.)

JENNA: Fancy salads?

OMAR *(Pressing a button on the phone, leaning toward it)*: Totally.

JENNA: Is she still there?

(He looks at Katha, sheepish.)

OMAR: Yeah, we're just finishing up in here.

(The phone beeps a farewell sound.)

Sorry. You were saying?

KATHA: No. That was all.

14

Ellen speaks out. Dean stands farther off.

ELLEN: We take our job very seriously on the Authenticity Committee. It's not just clothes and mimeograph machines—it's about everyone's *emotional* experience. And the question we have to answer again and again is how far do you take it, in the name of authenticity.

For instance, we have a Japanese-American fellow moving in right now. And it's interesting, what the research tells us, what we have by 1955 is already a kind of *counter-prejudice* . . . People have started to feel shame and remorse that American citizens were interned, during the war. So prejudice might not look like "Get out of my neighborhood." It might look more like "Here, I baked you some cookies, neighbor." Of course, it isn't always cookies. *(Beat)* It can be complicated to navigate, but authenticity is very important to us.

(Dean comes forward to join Ellen, sensing her losing her footing. His arm around her shoulder.)

DEAN: The SDO is . . . *built* on the idea of giving up one kind of freedom for another kind of freedom. Ellen and I had to give things up. *(Beat)*
   But there's something about facing obstacles—it has a way of binding families together, husbands and wives. You will not believe the rewards that come from authenticity.

15

Katha is holding flashcards, testing Ryu.

RYU: Eisenhower.
KATHA: Easy. Vice President?
RYU: Nixon.
KATHA: First Lady.

RYU: Mamie.

KATHA: Soviet president.

RYU: Khrushchev. These are too easy.

(She flips past a few cards.)

KATHA: Best-selling car.

RYU: Chevy?

KATHA: Buick.

When was the Evacuation Claims Act?

RYU: 1948.

KATHA: *What* was the Evacuation Claims Act?

RYU: Truman agreed to compensate Japanese-Americans for their forced evacuation during the war.

KATHA: And?

RYU: And?

KATHA: How did it turn out?

RYU: Not . . . well.

KATHA *(Reading)*: "Thirty-eight million dollars were set aside for the more than one hundred thousand Japanese-Americans who had been moved to internment camps. But this turned out not to be nearly enough compensation to replace the decimated farms and blacklisted businesses, not to mention the emotional cost of internment." This is good stuff, this will really help you create your character.

RYU: My character.

KATHA: Well, not your "character," per se, but remember they said it's good to add details, period details, to feel emotion-ally— Like maybe you have a little sister, Reiko . . . *(Ryu's eyes widen at this)* . . . and you had to watch her grow up in the camps. Maybe you have a lot of pent-up anger, righteous pent-up anger.

RYU: You sound almost excited.

KATHA: I don't know, it might be a way to feel more connected.

RYU: Connected?

(Short pause.)

KATHA: I just / mean

RYU: Connected?

KATHA: how you never talk much about your heritage, it's just never been a big thing for / you so

RYU: Oh what, because I'm not, what, doing *ikebana*? You think I'm self-hating or something? "Heritage." I'm from California, Katha, / Long Beach, California—

KATHA: Fine. Fine. Forget it. You win. Katha is un-PC. Bad Katha.

(Pause.)

RYU: Kath. What will it be like when it's just the two of us?

KATHA: You mean—

RYU: When we're alone. Will we be us, or '50s-us?

KATHA: I think the idea is, there's no difference, if we do it right.

RYU: But will they know, if we slip?

KATHA: Like will they have our house bugged?

RYU: It's a serious question.

KATHA: In fifth grade, my favorite teacher was Mrs. Hatzlett. She taught music. I loved her class. But one time, just to show my friends I was cool, I called her Mrs. Fatslett. And soon the whole school was calling her Mrs. Fatslett.

RYU: I know this is going somewhere.

KATHA: What I'm saying is, I don't think anyone remembered that I was the one who said it first, and I don't think Mrs. Hatzlett could have *known* it was me, but—she knew. She could tell something was different because of the way I was, around her. So what I'm saying is, I think they'll know like *that*. If we're breaking the rules.

(Pause.)

RYU: But what about, for instance, in bed.

KATHA: Oh.

RYU: Do we have to be period . . .

KATHA: *Oh*

RYU: . . . appropriate? I mean, do we have to not do things we might normally do?

KATHA: Like?

RYU: Like most of what we do!

I was reading, oral sex was illegal in thirty-six states.

KATHA: That doesn't mean people didn't do it.

RYU *(Conspiratorial)*: True.

KATHA: As long as we can make sure it's accompanied afterward by period-accurate feelings of shame and confusion . . .

RYU: So it's only bad if we feel good about it?

KATHA: Yes. I think that's right.

RYU: But we're doing this to be happy in the first place . . .

KATHA: Right.

RYU: I'm so confused.

KATHA: I love you.

RYU: I love you too.

Let's have shame-free oral sex, while we can.

KATHA: What if we had a Safe Word.

RYU: A Safe Word. Like S&M?

KATHA: Like, absolute emergency, one of us needs to acknowledge the twenty-first century—absolutely *has* to talk about sushi or hybrid cars—

RYU: Or oral sex.

KATHA: But only for emergencies.

It would have to be a word no one would ever say back then.

(Pause.)

RYU: "Facebook."

KATHA: Wasn't that a word?

It just meant something else.

RYU: "Twitter."

KATHA: Also a word.

RYU: This is hard.

(Pause.)

KATHA: "AirPod."

RYU: "Xbox."

(She makes a face.)

"Kim Kardashian."

KATHA: Something with some dignity.

(Short pause.)

RYU: "Hybrid car."

KATHA: Too clunky.

(Short pause.)

"Portobello."

RYU: Too whimsical.

KATHA: "Latte."

RYU: Too lame.

KATHA: "Hillary Rodham Clinton."

(Pause.)

RYU: "Hillary Rodham Clinton."

KATHA: It has *heft*, right?

RYU: You wouldn't say that by accident.

KATHA: It's modern, it's blunt—I already kind of miss it.

RYU: You sure you want to do this.

KATHA: Yes.

   Are you sure?

RYU *("You promise?")*: Six months.

   (She nods.)

   Goodbye Hillary.

KATHA: Goodbye Hillary.

RYU: Hello Ike.

   (Short pause.)

KATHA: "I like Ike."

   I like Ike . . .

   (He joins in. It grows into a joyful, impulsive dance.)

BOTH: I like Ike!

   I like Ike!

   I like Ike!

   I like Ike!

   (Blackout.)

16

Dean speaks out. Ellen looks on from a distance.

DEAN: A lot of people ask me, Dean, isn't it hard pretending all the time? And what I tell them is I tell them about a TV show called *The Adventures of Ozzie and Harriet.* Most of you have probably heard about it, even if you haven't seen it. Nowadays you have TV shows about people who solve crimes using ESP, and people who solve crimes with math, and people who solve crimes with talking cars. But back then people just wanted to see a family, like their own family but a bit nicer, like their own family but a bit more attractive.

(Lights rise on a modest but attractive 1950s living room.)

And what was so special about this TV family the Nelsons is that they weren't actors, not really. They were themselves. They used their own names. Ozzie, Harriet, David, and Ricky. They got up every morning and drove to the studio a few minutes away, and they ate their breakfast in a dining room modeled after their own dining room, but a little bit cleaner.

(Katha enters, wearing a housedress and a short new period haircut. She goes by Kathy now. She pulls the curtains open and looks out into the sunny morning.)

And they acted out their own problems and obstacles, only those problems were a little smaller, a little simpler, so you could be sure to solve them in a single episode. And a curious thing: The longer they pretended, the less they could tell what was pretend and what was real.

(The doorbell rings.)

KATHY: Who could that be?
DEAN: So it's kind of funny to me when people get so suspicious of pretending. I mean, don't you think people pretend every day, without knowing it?

We all imagine the life we'd like to have, and it takes a little pretend to get it.

(Kathy opens the door.

There are two beautiful bottles of fresh milk resting on the welcome mat.)

END OF PART ONE

PART TWO

1

Sounds of a factory—a nice, clean, civilized factory. Roger is showing Ryu around. They wear dungarees, work shirts, and suspenders. (Roger is played by the same actor who played Omar. Much more stoic now.)

ROGER: This floor is all Boxers. Lots of fellas start out here. The Packers are one floor down, and below that you've got Secretarial.

RYU: Specialized.

ROGER: There you go.

(Roger picks up an unmade cardboard box. While he's talking, he assembles it with effortless quickness and grace.)

First thing is to make sure you do the narrow flaps first, before the wide flaps. Then you want to add a dot of glue to each corner. Dot, dot, dot, dot. No more than a dot or it turns into a mess. *Now* it's time for the wide flaps. Then you got your tape, make sure it's nice and wet.

(He brushes the tape with a brush, wetting the glue.)

Then it goes snip, and down the chute.

(Roger pushes the completed box down a chute.)

RYU: Got it.
ROGER: Why don't you do one for me.

(Ryu starts to make a box. He folds the narrow flaps first.)

Good . . .
RYU: So. Is this . . . fulfilling?
ROGER: What?
RYU: Here at the factory—is it gratifying?
ROGER: I'm not sure I know what you mean. The work isn't too hard. You get thirty minutes for lunch. The owner is nice.
RYU: Yeah?
ROGER: He says hello when you pass him in the hall. Every June there's a picnic at his place. His wife makes potato salad and there's a three-legged race. Madge and I won last year.
RYU *(Sincere)*: That sounds . . . good.
ROGER: You came from the big city, right?
RYU: That's right.
ROGER: What'd you do back there?
RYU *(Not looking at Roger)*: Taxi driver.
ROGER: Must meet some crazies doing that.
RYU: It was all right.
ROGER: You folks find a place to stay?
RYU: Yeah, over on Maple and Vine?

ROGER: Over by the high school, right?

RYU: It's two blocks away. Little yellow ranch house.

ROGER: Oh yeah, that used to be the Gibson place.

RYU: Oh. Where'd they go?

(The slightest pause.)

ROGER: Moved somewhere bigger, I imagine. Very ambitious guy, Donner Gibson. He had a mulatto wife, she was so light you might not even know it. Probably fooled some people. *(Ryu blinks)* Gibson was at the steel mill, last I heard. They like to move people up over there. Here too. You won't be a Boxer for long if you've got the drive. And nobody doubts you little guys have the drive, right? Not anymore.

(Uncomfortable beat.)

I mean after the war.

RYU: Oh, right.

ROGER: *Kamikaze.* Those little guys had drive, you gotta hand it to them.

RYU *(Playing along, hoping this will end)*: Oh, yeah, you better watch out.

ROGER: There you go. So, I'm gonna leave you to it. If it takes you more than thirty seconds a box, you're probably too slow. And you'll keep getting faster. Just give me a holler if you need anything.

RYU: Okay, thanks.

(Ryu finishes the box. He lifts it up. A feeling of small satisfaction.)

2

Kathy has been setting out hors d'oeuvres. She wears a cocktail dress. Something smooth is playing on the hi-fi. Ryu comes in, wiping sweat off his brow.

RYU: Hi.

KATHY: How was your first day?

RYU: Well it's not exactly rocket science, but—I started out okay and I got better. Thirty seconds a box. It's more physical than you'd think.

KATHY: I can see that.

RYU: You fall behind and forget about it.

KATHY: Better wash up. The Messners will be here any minute.

RYU: Shit, I forgot.

KATHY: You'll be fine, it's only cocktails. Just put on a clean shirt. And a spritz of that cologne I got you.

(The doorbell rings.)

Oh dear, that's them. Hurry—oh wait, do these look okay?

RYU *(Smirking)*: You cooked?

KATHY: I cook every night, remember?

(She winks at him.)

RYU: Oh, yeah.

KATHY: Try one.

RYU: What are they?

(He pops one in his mouth.)

KATHY: Pigs in a blanket.

RYU *(With a mouthful)*: Sauce is good.

KATHY *(Proud)*: It's ketchup and mayo.

(Ding-dong. The doorbell again. Kathy goes to the door, Ryu heads off.)

Coming!

(She opens the door. Dean and Ellen are standing there. Ellen holds a wrapped present.)

DEAN: Hello, hello!

KATHY: Ellen, Dean. Won't you come in? Oh—

ELLEN *(Handing her the gift)*: It's just a little something for the house.

KATHY: You shouldn't have.

(Ellen looks around. She might be inspecting things for authenticity but disguises it as the curiosity of a houseguest.)

ELLEN: Looks like you're all moved in . . .

KATHY: We're nearly there, yes. *(Comically miming a pain in her back)* Oof.

DEAN: "Oof"?

KATHY: All those boxes. But the neighbors have been wonderful. Heavy lifting. Bringing *pies*.

DEAN: Well what d'you expect? They're your neighbors.

KATHY: We just never had such—visible neighbors! *(Almost to herself)* Audible maybe.

ELLEN *(Still inspecting)*: It's a charming house. I've always thought it was charming from the street but this is even nicer.

KATHY: Please, won't you sit down.

What can I get you all to drink?

ELLEN: Dubonnet, please.

DEAN: Yes, I'll have a Dubonnet too. With ice.

ELLEN *(Nodding)*: Ice.

KATHY: Two Dubonnets.

(Just as Kathy heads off to make the drinks, something strikes the outside of the window.)

ELLEN: What was that?

DEAN: I think it was . . . something hitting the outside of the house.

(Something hits the window again. It's a pebble.)

ELLEN: Oh how strange.

DEAN: I better go see what it is.

KATHY *(Reentering with drinks)*: Did that come from outside?

DEAN: Probably just some neighborhood urchins.

ELLEN: Be careful, darling.

DEAN: Don't be silly.

(Dean goes out the door.)

ELLEN: Oh how strange.

*(Maybe it doesn't sound like Ellen thinks it's all that strange.
Light shifts to outside the house. Roger is there, in the shadows, pebble in hand.)*

DEAN: How dare you.

ROGER: How dare I?

DEAN: Ellen is in there, we're with friends—this is very embarrassing.

ROGER: You made your excuses.

DEAN: How did you know I'd be here?

ROGER: You always check in with the newbies the first week.
    And he said Maple and Vine.
DEAN: You did your homework.
ROGER: You wanted to see me too.
DEAN: What are you talking about.
ROGER: That's why you placed him on my floor.
DEAN: Lots of fellas start out in Boxing, especially / when
    they're—
ROGER: Or else Packing, or the steel mill, or anywhere! But no,
    he's right there with me, on my watch. Like some kind of
    message.
DEAN: I told you to leave me alone, remember?
ROGER: Guess I forgot.

*(He pulls Dean into a kiss. They kiss forcefully, angrily. Roger
starts to touch Dean.)*

    Say it.
DEAN: Say what.
ROGER: You know what. Say it.
DEAN *(Barely audible)*: I want you to fuck me.
ROGER: What was that?
DEAN: I want you to fuck me.
ROGER: What are we going to do about that?

(Short pause.)

DEAN: The park at midnight.
    Ellen sleeps like a log.
ROGER: I remember.

(Beat.)

    God I miss fucking you.

DEAN: I'm not like you.
    I don't need this.
ROGER: Could have fooled me.
DEAN: Get the hell out of here.

(Back inside the house. Kathy has just opened the present.)

ELLEN: It's a tea cozy.
KATHY: Oh, how wonderful. We don't have one!
ELLEN: It's supposed to be a frog.
KATHY: I think I see it.
ELLEN: It's, what's the word, abstract.

(Ryu enters.)

RYU: Hello, Ellen.

(Ellen bows slightly.)

ELLEN: Hello.

(Ryu locks eyes with Kathy.)

KATHY: Look what Ellen brought us.
ELLEN: I have a friend who knits them, she's very talented. You'll
    meet her soon.

(Dean reenters. Ryu shakes his hand.)

RYU: Mr. Messner.
DEAN: Please, Ryu. Call me Dean.
ELLEN: Is everything all right?
DEAN: Of course. Fellow lost his way, he was looking for Elm.
    So I told him he had his trees mixed up.

(Dean laughs at his own joke.)

ELLEN: You should have invited him in.

DEAN: Oh, no. He didn't look like a very sociable fellow, I'm afraid. Not one of ours.

KATHY: I should say not, throwing rocks at people's windows. Hasn't he heard of a knocker?

(We hear a buzzer from off.)

Oh, those are my crab puffs.

(She goes. A short but heavy silence.)

ELLEN *(To Dean)*: They loved the cozy.

RYU: We did, we loved it.

KATHY *(From off)*: We did!

ELLEN: Tell me, Ryu— Did everyone make you feel at home at the factory?

RYU: Very much. The Floor Manager was nice. Fellow named Roger.

ELLEN *(This might be directed toward Dean, lightly)*: How nice.

RYU: He seemed sort of . . . preoccupied with my heritage?

ELLEN: Some people are still adjusting. To think, just a few years ago we were putting you people behind fences, and now you're working right there alongside us. Isn't it grand. *America.*

(Kathy returns with the crab puffs just in time to hear this. Ryu and Kathy share a wide-eyed look—This is happening.)

KATHY: I'm a little nervous how these turned out, this is a brand-new recipe for me.

DEAN: It smells delicious.

KATHY: I know crab is a trifle *exotic*, but you put cream cheese in anything and it's bound to turn out well.

DEAN: Mmm.

ELLEN: Well, aren't these nice and simple.

(Ellen deposits the rest of hers in a napkin.)

RYU: These are *really good*, honey.

(Short pause. Ellen sees that Dean is unusually quiet, she'll have to keep the conversation going.)

ELLEN: You should come with me to the Authenticity Committee sometime, Kathy.

KATHY *(Noncommittal)*: That would be nice.

ELLEN: Monday, Wednesday, and Friday in the school gymnasium. We'd love to have you.

*(Dean and Ryu chew solemnly.
Ellen discreetly corrects Kathy's posture.)*

Remember . . .

(There is a kind of cut—lights down and up again quickly. Everyone is playing charades now. They're all a bit tipsy. Ellen takes the game very seriously, her true colors showing. It's Kathy's turn, she mimes a movie camera.)

Movie!
Four words.
Fourth word.
Four syllables.

(Kathy acts bored. She mimes looking at a watch. She taps her foot.)

RYU: Um.
"Waiting."
"Boredom?"

(*Kathy acts even more emphatically bored.*)

"Impatient."
ELLEN (*Chastening*): Four. Syllables.

(*Kathy makes a gesture for clearing the first attempt away, starting over. She starts to wrap her arms around herself, rather embarrassed, as if to suggest a couple making out.*)

DEAN: *From Here to Eternity!*
KATHY: YES!

(*Ellen and Ryu look at Dean, incredulous.*)

DEAN: I love that movie.

(*Another cut, lights abruptly down and up. The two couples are now slow dancing to a waltz on the hi-fi. Ryu is struggling. Still, it's fun.*)

It helps to count at first.
DEAN AND ELLEN: One-two-three, one-two-three.
RYU: One-two-three, one-two-three.
DEAN: With the emphasis on the *one*-two-three.
RYU: *One*-two-three, *one*-two-three.
KATHY: That's it.
DEAN (*Speaking in waltz rhythm*): And then, when you're comfortable with that . . .

(*He gives Ellen a twirl.*)

ELLEN: Ta-da.

(Another cut, lights down and up. Everyone in different positions, a bit drunker now. Ryu is pouring himself another drink. Ellen is telling one of her favorite stories.)

So I said to the girl seated next to me, I said, Lorna, there's nothing I hate more than a *soggy cake*. And what does the hostess come in with, right that very moment?

KATHY: A soggy cake!

DEAN: Right!

ELLEN *(Mimicking the hostess entering proudly)*: "*Baba au rhum.*" This enormous rum-soaked thing. I was so embarrassed.

DEAN: So she ate every bite on her plate.

KATHY: Oh that's so funny. Isn't that funny, Ryu?

RYU: Does anyone need a refresher?

DEAN: You know what I'd love? A vodka rocks.

RYU: Grey Goose okay?

DEAN: Grey Goose, what's that?

RYU: Vodka, my friend.

ELLEN: No, he means: *What's that.*

RYU: Oh you mean—

KATHY *(Suddenly sober)*: We're so sorry.

DEAN: That's all right, it happens to everyone.

KATHY: I'll pour it out.

DEAN: Gin will be fine, Ryu.

ELLEN: Smirnoff. That's a kind of vodka we like.
     They've been making it such a long time.

(Another cut. Dean and Ellen are gone now. Kathy and Ryu are splayed on the couch.)

KATHY: Well that wasn't so bad, was it?

RYU: I don't know about Ellen.
KATHY: I think she's just . . . shy.

(They lock eyes for a moment. Then, overlapping:)

KATHY AND RYU: "Four Syllables!"
KATHY: Oh dear. Well, I think we're off the hook for a while. I better get to work on this.
RYU: Let me help you.
KATHY: Nonsense. That's my job.

(She starts to clear the plates. Ryu lying on his back on the couch.)

RYU *(Content)*: I'm beat.
KATHY: You had a long day.

(She continues to clear. Ryu sits up suddenly.)

RYU: Kath.
KATHY: Mm?
RYU: "Hillary Rodham Clinton."

(Short pause.)

KATHY *(Sotto voce)*: Already?
RYU: I'm sorry.
KATHY: What is it?
RYU: I saw something tonight.
KATHY: You saw something?
RYU: It was Dean.
         Outside.

3

Split scene. At the factory, Ryu assembles a box while Roger times him.

ROGER: Ready,
    Set,
    Go.

(*At the same time, Kathy stands in the kitchen, squinting at an open cookbook.*)

KATHY: "Celery is often underrated, yet it can be the secret star of any dish. First, cut the stalks lengthwise. Then cut cross-wise to dice. Try to make the dice as small and uniform as possible, both because it is aesthetically more pleasing and because the small pieces will cook more uniformly."

(*Kathy starts to dice an onion, just as Ryu finishes the box.*)

ROGER: Twenty-two seconds.
    You sure you haven't made boxes before?
RYU: No. But I used to work with my hands.
ROGER: Thought you said you were a taxi driver.

(*Short pause.*)

RYU: Oh, I mean back before.
ROGER (*Nodding solemnly*): Back in the old country . . .
RYU: I did *ikebana*. You know what that is?
ROGER: Something with knives.
RYU: Flowers. Flower arranging. It's not so different really—the planes of the petals, the sort of minimalist thing.
ROGER: I gotta say, your English is—wow.

RYU (*A touch ironic*): Thank you. I work hard.

ROGER: Make a better life for the missus. I get it.

   Hey, tell me something about her.

RYU: Well, she's um, pretty as a picture.

ROGER (*Playful*): Yeah, but can she cook.

RYU: She's getting there.

(Light shifts to Kathy, who has returned to the cookbook.)

KATHY: "Strain liquid through a fine mesh strainer into another large stockpot." *(Looking around)* Fine mesh strainer . . .

(And back to the factory.)

ROGER: Kathy, right?

RYU: Yeah.

ROGER: She must be something else.

   I mean, if you'd do all this for her.

(This hangs in the air. How much does Roger know about them?)

RYU: When we lived in the city, sometimes it was like I never saw her. Even when I was with her I never saw her. But here, it's like . . .

ROGER: You see her.

RYU: But you know how it is, you've got a wife.

(Roger just smiles.)

Was it . . . her idea, to come here?

ROGER (*Lightly rueful, not answering the question*): It's always someone's idea, right?

RYU: Women can be pretty persuasive.

(Maybe Roger gets rather close to Ryu here.)

ROGER: Little friendly advice, Ryu. *(He pronounces it "Rye-You")* I've seen guys come here, they're used to letting their wives wear the pants. Guys who don't learn how to wear the pants, they don't fit in too well.

RYU: Did you ever . . .

ROGER: What.

RYU: Not fit in? *(Quickly retreating)* I'm sorry.

ROGER *(Coded)*: Sometimes, when people come here, it means making sacrifices. Socially speaking.

RYU *(Coded)*: And does that work out . . . for people?

ROGER: I'll let you know when I find out.

(Roger exits. The phone rings in Kathy's space. The factory light fades.)

KATHY: Hello?

> . . .

Ellen, hello!

> . . .

No, no. Just wrestling with *mirepoix*.

> . . .

Oh. Well, you're kind to think of me. I just hope I have something to wear. Do you think gloves are too much?

> . . .

To the wrist. Of course.

(Kathy laughs, scandalized by something Ellen says.)

Opera length! In the afternoon?

RYU *(Off)*: Honey?

(Ryu comes in.)

KATHY: No, no, thank *you*. To tell you the truth, it was getting a little quiet around here.

. . .

Perfect. Two o'clock. Bye now.

(She hangs up.)

That was Ellen. I'm going to the committee with her tomorrow.

RYU: She finally wore you down, huh.

KATHY: I don't know, it might be fun. How was work?

RYU: I'm down to twenty-two seconds.

KATHY: That's wonderful.

RYU: Closing in on the record.

KATHY: How are things with the boss?

RYU: Now I'm an ikebana master. In addition to banzai and karate.

He said he'd never seen a foreigner learn so fast.

(Kathy shakes her head, bemused.)

Is it bad it feels a little good?

KATHY: What.

RYU: Low expectations.

KATHY: I'll forgive you if you forgive me. My main accomplishment today was learning the difference between chop and dice.

RYU: And?

KATHY: Dice means I only cut off a small piece of my finger.

RYU: What did you make?

KATHY: Chicken stock.

(Beat.)

It was amazing, Ryu. It took *seven hours.*

I had to chop, I had to dice, I boiled the water.

I skimmed, I strained. Things changed shape. Chemistry.

When it was done—there was something there that wasn't there before.

RYU: So we're having chicken stock for dinner.

KATHY: I made something. With my hands. I know it sounds small.

RYU: It doesn't.

(Beat.)

KATHY: I think I might be a little happy.

4

Kathy is having a dream. Jenna and Omar sit in her living room. Suburban quiet now, in place of the din of the first sleeping scene.

KATHY: Kathy slept through the night now. There were crickets outside her window for lulling her to sleep.

Kathy had dreams every night now, but every night she dreamed about the world they'd left behind.

JENNA: Fancy salad place?

OMAR: Always.

JENNA: I can never make up my mind. So many dressings.

OMAR: I know, right?

JENNA: I think I'll get the chipotle-balsamic.

OMAR *("It's your funeral")*: Indulge.

JENNA *(Crestfallen)*: I thought it was low-fat.

OMAR: Not like the ginger-miso. You get the chipotle-balsamic, you might as well be having a whole focaccia.

JENNA: The focaccia's lower-cal than the ciabatta, right?

OMAR: Not like the parmesan flatbread. So. I was eye-flirting with this guy at the gym—he was, *Oh*.

JENNA: "Oh." What's "oh"?

(He raises an eyebrow.)

I mean I know what "oh" is but I want *details*.
OMAR: Let's just say he's not having the ciabatta.

(Dean enters.)

DEAN: Excuse me.
OMAR: Here he is now.
DEAN: Do you know where 200 Fifth Avenue is?
OMAR: You just found it, Mister.
DEAN: Oh. Thank you.

(Omar and Dean start to neck.)

JENNA *(Faux-annoyed)*: You guys, we're right here.
KATHY: You're—in the wrong place.

(Omar and Dean still necking, deeply. Shirts are coming off.)

JENNA: Tell me about it. Like get a room, right?
KATHY: No, I mean— Everyone's in the wrong place.
JENNA: Kind of hot though. Least somebody's getting some.

(Omar starts to pull Dean away. Jenna follows them.)

You guys, where are you going?
RYU *(From off)*: Kathy?
OMAR: To get a room.

(Ryu enters.)

KATHY: Everyone's wrong.

RYU: Kathy?

KATHY: Everyone's—

(He touches her. Kathy wakes with a start in the living room. Ryu is standing next to her, his hand on her shoulder. The others are gone.)

Wrong.

RYU: Shhh, you're okay. You were sleepwalking again.

KATHY: Where are we?

RYU: Home.

KATHY: I mean—when?

RYU: 1955.

(Beat.)

Come back to bed.

KATHY: I'm going to sit up a little while.

RYU: You sure?

KATHY: Until things settle.

(Beat.)

Do you ever . . . forget?

RYU: Sometimes, when I first wake up.
But then there's the wallpaper.

(She takes in the dark living room.)

And you in your nightie.

(He tugs at the hem of her nightie.)

KATHY: My head is spinning.

RYU: I have an idea.
KATHY: Warm milk?

(He lowers to his knees.)

RYU: Close your eyes.
KATHY *(She does)*: We're awake, right?
RYU: Just relax.

(He starts to lift up her slip.)

KATHY: Baby, I don't think / we should—
RYU: What are you afraid of? The neighbors aren't watching.
KATHY: What if they are?
RYU: Close your eyes.

(His head disappears under her slip.)

5

Ellen speaks directly out. She is seated, addressing an unseen circle of people.

ELLEN: Well, ladies. I wanted to talk today about a bit of a touchy subject. Contraception. As you know, we've been letting people determine their own boundaries. But it seems to me that the disruptions have become . . . rather disruptive. For instance, when I go to the drugstore, I'm just a bit surprised to see a long line of ladies getting their prescriptions filled for birth control. I'm surprised to see Catholic families, prominent Catholic families, with only a single child. And very recently a girlfriend of mine was bragging that her husband was positively cheerful in his attitude toward wearing a condom. Cheerful!

What's to be done. Well, there's the usual letters to the editor. But I think we should consider drafting a bill. The birth-control pill wasn't in homes until 1960—as long as it remains available, women will continue to disrupt. The ability to bear children is a power and a privilege, and those of us who aren't too busy running a community must embrace that privilege, yes? Without the birth-control pill, it would be much easier to accurately portray a woman's role at the center of the family, financially dependent on her husband and rooted to the home.

Speaking of which, I want to officially welcome our newest homemaker on the committee, Kathy Nakata.

(Kathy enters, in a smart coat and gloves to the wrist.)

KATHY: Thank you. *(To the entire group)* Thank you so much for having me.
ELLEN: Kathy and her husband have been with us a couple of months now. Right now it's just the two of them.

6

Kathy is reading a hardcover copy of Peyton Place *while something simmers on the stove. Ryu comes in the door, lunch box in hand.*

RYU: Honey, I'm home.
KATHY: Hi.
RYU: Something smells good.
KATHY: Chicken à la King.
RYU: My favorite.

(He plants a quick kiss on her.)

KATHY: Should be just a few more minutes.
RYU *(Referring to the book)*: How is that, anyway?
KATHY: Well it isn't Tolstoy. But I think she has a real narrative
   gift. Everyone on the block is reading it.
RYU: I know—even the boys at the factory are reading it.
KATHY: I bet they're flipping forward to the cheeky parts.
RYU: You think anyone's town is really that bad?
KATHY: I'm sure.

*(In another part of the stage, light on Dean and Roger lying in a
park somewhere. Post coitus.)*

DEAN: Fuck.
ROGER: Yeah. You can say that again.

(Beat.)

Change of pace, fucking when it's light outside. When
everyone's just sitting down to supper.

*(In another part of the stage, light on Ellen at the dinner table,
alone. A casserole sits in front of her, growing cold. Light remains
on her during the rest of the scene.)*

DEAN: You sure this is safe?
ROGER: Sure. Never seen anyone on this side of the pond.

(Dean starts to put his clothes on.)

Same time next week?
DEAN: Too soon.
ROGER: Too soon?

DEAN: It has to get to the point where I'm so full of . . .

ROGER: Cum?

DEAN *(Irritated at his coarseness)*: *Wanting.* So full of wanting that it . . . overcomes the guilt.

ROGER: Yeah, you're pretty good at the whole guilt thing. Me, I like to think, after a long week of work, I deserve a little present.

(Roger watches as Dean puts his pants on.)

Just a little longer. Please.

DEAN: It's nearly supper.

ROGER: Let her wait an hour. I waited all week.

(He pulls Dean back down by his belt loops. They kiss, more tenderly now. Focus shifts back to Kathy and Ryu.)

KATHY: I was at the committee today.

RYU: Again?

KATHY: There was a vote.

They voted to outlaw the Pill.

RYU: They can do that?

(A slight nod from Kathy.)

There are other options, right?

KATHY: Or, I was thinking. Or. We could not worry about it.

RYU: Oh Kathy, do you mean it?

KATHY: Now that we're here. *(The hint of a contract in this)* I can imagine having a baby . . . here.

(Pause.)

It's four months now.

RYU: I know.

KATHY: We have to decide sooner or later.

(Back to Roger and Dean, lying down.)

ROGER: Sometimes I wish we didn't have to hide. You know? Sometimes I wonder if there's a place like that. A place where it'd be you and me sitting down to dinner in one of those houses.

DEAN: You know, Roger. I'm not sure you understand.
    We don't know each other.

ROGER: What?

DEAN: You and I—we don't *talk* to each other.
    We got what we needed from each other, so.

(He extends his hand for a handshake. It's a punch in the gut to Roger.)

ROGER: I wish you wouldn't—
    (Sotto voce) I mean it's just the two of us here.

DEAN: I'll see you around.

ROGER: No you won't. You never see me, really.

DEAN: What's going on?

ROGER: I've been thinking for once.

DEAN *(Putting on his hat)*: It was a mistake to stay. I've confused you.

ROGER: This is really enough for you? You don't ever think what if it was you and me in one of those houses?

DEAN: I have a house.

ROGER: Jason. I love you.

(Dean stops in his tracks.)

DEAN: Don't—EVER—call me that.

(Back to Kathy and Ryu.)

RYU: If we decide to stay . . . what do we tell it?

KATHY: ?

RYU: I mean would the baby know the things we know? *(Sotto voce)* He could grow up thinking there isn't anywhere else.

KATHY: Maybe that's a gift.

RYU *(Hotter)*: We had a choice, to come here, but he—

KATHY: Or she.

RYU: Don't you wonder what it'd be like for our *child*—growing up here?

> I just don't want it to be . . . hard.
> "Hillary Rodham Clinton."

KATHY: No. You can do this.

(Ryu shakes his head. Kathy starts to exit toward the kitchen.)

RYU: Like Reiko.

(This stops her.)

> I was almost out of high school when we went to the camp, but Reiko was only . . .

(He doesn't seem to remember.)

KATHY: Seven.

RYU: Seven.

KATHY *("How terrible")*: God.

RYU: She was all right at the camp. She made friends so fast. It was when it was over, when we moved back home—I'll never forget watching my little sister learn she was different. The way the kids looked at her at school. The Evacuation Claims Act couldn't fix that. I don't want our little girl to go through that.

KATHY: It'll be different for her. The world is changing, one step at a time.

(Little beat.)

RYU: Is it?

KATHY: But it's 1955, not 1945. / That's what I mean.

RYU: And never 1956 or '57 / or Civil *Rights*—

KATHY: We're right smack dab in the middle of things changing—and we're the ones who get to help people change their minds!

RYU: That's fine for us—but what I'm saying is maybe our *child* deserves to know there are sixty years of history / that she's—

KATHY: Will you please try not to disrupt—

RYU: We have to TALK about this!

(He has grabbed her by the arm. He releases her.)

I'm sorry.

KATHY *(Not looking at him yet)*: No. That was good.

RYU: What?

KATHY: You took charge. Remember you can do that. You're the husband.

(Back to Ellen. She stands up, hearing someone at the door.)

ELLEN: Dean? Is that you?

(Dean comes in.)

DEAN: Darling, I'm so sorry. I lost track of time.

(He kisses her on the cheek.)

ELLEN *(Lightly)*: That's not like you.

(He starts to take off his coat and hat.
Back to Kathy and Ryu.)

KATHY: It'll still be us, every day. You have to remember that. We'll keep talking about what she has to know. I'm sure there's a pamphlet—
RYU: No. We have to decide for us. The minute we stop being us . . .
KATHY: What?
RYU: I don't know.

(Back to Dean and Ellen.
Dean goes to the dining table.)

DEAN: You must have been cooking for hours.
ELLEN: Oh, that's all right. I'll put the casserole back in the oven. It'll warm right up.
DEAN: It looks delicious.
ELLEN: Oh, don't sit down. There's mud on your pants.
DEAN: Well look at that. It must've been that walk in the park.

(Short pause.)

ELLEN: Go put on a fresh pair, and I'll toss those right in the wash.

(He starts to go.)

DEAN: Ellen?
ELLEN: Yes?
DEAN: I'm a lucky man.

7

At the factory. Roger and Ryu with lunch boxes.

RYU: Bologna and cheese.
ROGER: Turkey lettuce tomato.
RYU: Wanna trade?
ROGER: No deal.
RYU: I don't blame you.
ROGER: I mean, what *is* bologna anyway?
RYU: It's Italian. *(Playful)* Very continental.

(*Roger leans over slowly and takes a bite of Ryu's sandwich, looking at him the whole time.*)

Oh, hey, what are you, um—what do you think?
ROGER *(Still looking at him, intense)*: Salty.

(Short pause.)

RYU: I better get back to work.
ROGER: Hey, we got ten minutes. Stick around. I was just playing.
RYU: Sure, okay.
ROGER: You're a good worker, Ryu. I like having you around.
RYU: Thanks.
ROGER: How's Kathy liking the committee?
RYU: Too much.
ROGER: Buncha hens.
RYU: Everything else is good though. More than good.
ROGER: You wearing the pants?
RYU: I'm wearing the pants.

ROGER: That makes one of us.

(Pause.)

RYU: If you ever want to talk about it . . .
ROGER: Thanks.
RYU: Listen, Roger—
　　Kathy and I are thinking of starting a family.
ROGER: Congrats, sport! It's about time.
RYU: Yeah, and I was wondering, maybe, I was wondering, if it
　　might be time for me to have a raise.

(Short pause.)

ROGER *(With some difficulty)*: I'm sorry, sport
RYU: Oh
ROGER: You're one of the best on the floor, but standard raise is
　　after half a year. You've barely been here, what is it?
RYU: Five months. Stuckey was only here three when he got his.
ROGER: Sorry.

(Roger starts to go.)

RYU: Were you at my house, a few months ago?

(Roger stops.)

ROGER: Was I at your house?
RYU: I thought I saw you, out my window.
ROGER: Why would I be at your house?
RYU: I guess it must have been someone else. Whoever it was,
　　it seems like a fella could get in a heap of trouble if some-
　　one saw him.

(Pause.)

ROGER: Let me tell you about a heap of trouble, Ryu.

See, I know you're really a nice guy. And I know you wouldn't want to do something to mess up your prospects here. Because I've been giving you the good word. I've seen lots of people come through here and nobody does well without the good word from the floor manager, especially the non-whites. And if you think that it can't get worse for you than making a thousand boxes a day, then you better take a look at those poor suckers laying tar on the roads or putting spikes in the railroad tracks. Is all I'm saying. Because I think you and the wife could do really well here, despite your being a little "different" and all, as long as you have the good word. So why don't you keep your head down and do your work and eat your fucking bologna. See you later.

(He leaves abruptly.)

8

Kathy at the front door.

KATHY *(Calling off)*: Good night, Judy! I haven't forgotten about your cake pan! I'll bring it to the committee tomorrow.

(Kathy comes in and turns on a lamp. She sits on the arm of the sofa. She touches her stomach, her coat still on.
  Ryu comes in suddenly, startling her.)

How was work?

RYU: Work was shit.

KATHY: Language.

RYU: You think I give a fuck?

(Beat.)

Why don't you have your apron on?

KATHY: I'm sorry, I was—

RYU: Great, that's just great— Work is shit and no dinner in the oven.

KATHY: My appointment was running late.

RYU: You're always at that fucking committee.

KATHY: It wasn't the committee.

RYU: Well it sure seems like you're always there. I'm hungry.

KATHY: There are two TV dinners in the freezer. I thought we could heat them up and watch *Lucy*.

(Beat.)

RYU: What kind?

KATHY *(Hopefully)*: Salisbury steak.

(Something relaxes in Ryu.)

RYU: Hey. I'm sorry I was sore.

KATHY: What happened today?

RYU: I didn't get the raise

KATHY: Oh Ryu

RYU: And then Roger got angry.

KATHY: He got angry?

RYU: When he said no—I told him what I saw.

KATHY: You mean . . .

RYU: I thought that might change his mind.

KATHY: You mean blackmail?

RYU: I don't know, I didn't think that far. I just thought maybe then he couldn't treat me like a second-class citizen. I'm faster than everyone on that floor, Roger included.

(They're tipping into Douglas Sirk melodrama, but it feels real to them:)

KATHY: You'll show him. Some day you'll be running that factory.

RYU: Damn right. Damn right I will.

KATHY: I'm glad you said it. Now he knows who he's dealing with.

(Pause.
  He takes her and kisses her. Suddenly heated.
  They separate for a moment, surprised by this new fire.)

RYU: Even when this place is messed up? It makes me feel closer to you.

(They kiss.)

KATHY: I should— I have something to tell you.

RYU *(Still kissing her)*: Let me guess. Those ladies passed another bill.

KATHY: I told you, / it wasn't—

RYU: Oh right.

KATHY: I went to see Dr. Anderson.

RYU: —

KATHY: I'm pregnant.

RYU: Oh my god.

KATHY: You're not upset, are you?

RYU: Upset? Are you kidding?
     I'm thrilled!

(He picks her up and whirls her around.)

I'm fucking ecstatic!

KATHY (*Amused*): Language!

RYU: Why would I be upset?

KATHY: I just thought, if you still weren't sure, about staying . . .

RYU: Oh.

KATHY (*Not endorsing this*): . . . then I imagine there are alternatives.

RYU: Alternatives.

(*Beat.*)

KATHY: "Hillary Rodham—"

RYU: No. We're going to have a baby, and we're going to love it.

(*He takes her hand.*)

What other choice is there?

KATHY: The ladies at the committee will be so excited. They were rooting for us. I think they really like me there. They were saying I could be a vice president some day.

RYU: My wife, a woman of influence.

(*They kiss.*)

9

Kathy, seated, speaks out. Ellen sits to her left.

KATHY: Thank you. I wanted to speak today about tolerance. Since Ryu and I first moved here, so many of you have welcomed us with open arms. And while I admit that the hospitality feels wonderful, I worry that it may be jeopardizing the authenticity of our experience—and your own. One of the first things we learn about the SDO is that families are brought together by the struggle against a common obstacle. And yet, in the effort to be neighborly, these obstacles are sometimes neglected.

(She looks to Ellen for support, finding her footing.)

Many of you have asked me what it's like to have an Oriental as a husband. And I told you that Ryu is just like you. But that isn't altogether true, is it. He isn't like you. He came from another country, a country where suicide is noble and gardens are made of rocks, not grass. A country that, in the very recent past, was at war with your own. I'm not like you either, if I would have him as my husband.

Yes, it's the North. Yes, it's 1955. There's a kind of kindness born out of guilt, about the camps. But that's not the same as tolerance, is it.

(With difficulty:)

We're not talking about flaming crosses on our lawn, that would be extreme. But here are some ideas. You might stare at me in the supermarket line. You might tell Ryu how much you like Chinese food. Your teenage boys could bang trash can lids outside our house, late at night. These are just a few ideas.

I know, it's hard. For all of us. It's hard to find the—

We're all doing our best here, and I know that we'll be able to find even more ways to give each other an authentic experience. Thank you.

ELLEN *(Proud)*: Thank you, Kathy.
Questions for Kathy Nakata.

10

Kathy is asleep in bed with Ryu, dreaming.

Ellen and Roger sit at the foot of the bed. At least, it looks like Ellen and Roger. They wear '50s clothing, but they act more like Jenna and Omar.

KATHY: Kathy still dreamed about the world she left behind.
ELLEN *(To Roger)*: So I tried the Master Cleanse?
ROGER: That's the one Beyoncé did.
ELLEN: Gwyneth too.
KATHY: But tonight was different somehow . . .

    (Kathy sits up in bed. She is visibly pregnant now.)

ELLEN: I only lasted four days.
ROGER: It gets boring right?
ELLEN: Totally. Lemon juice and cayenne, it's just like . . .
ROGER: *Bo*ring!
ELLEN: *Bo*ring!
ROGER: Oh hi, Katha.
KATHY: "Katha."
ELLEN: Can we do anything for you?
KATHY: I—forget what I came in here for.
ELLEN: White-Out, maybe?
ROGER: Or a fax sheet?
ELLEN: Maybe if you go and come back, you'll remember.
KATHY: Maybe.

    (Kathy starts to lie down again.)

ROGER *(Back to Ellen)*: Okay whatever. So what's going on with
    you. Any new suitors?

ELLEN: Well there's Ben. And there's Jerry.

ROGER: What?

ELLEN: Oh I was joking, like, "Ben & Jerry's"?

ROGER: Oh. Ha.

ELLEN: Like Saturday nights at home with a pint?

KATHY: Ryu?

ROGER: Look on the bright side. You could have an Oriental for a husband.

ELLEN *(Delighted by the scandal)*: She's *right* over *there*.

KATHY: Ryu.

(Roger and Ellen start to exit.)

ELLEN: I feel bad. Maybe I should bake her some cookies.

ROGER: You never bake *me* anything.

KATHY: Ryu!

(Ryu turns on a lamp and she wakes up. The others are gone now.)

RYU: Are you okay?

KATHY: I was having a dream.

RYU: A nightmare?

KATHY: Not exactly. It was about now.

RYU: —

KATHY: I mean, the place we live now. Sort of. As opposed to where we used to live. I mean it was *about* there, but it looked like here.

RYU *(Almost asleep, humoring her)*: Wow.

KATHY: Do you ever dream that way?

RYU: What way, honey.

KATHY: About here? I mean maybe it's like moving to a foreign country. For a while, you only dream in your own language. Your sleep takes you back home. So that's the sign of real fluency—when you start dreaming in the new language.

RYU: It's four in the morning.

KATHY: Sorry. I was just / thinking.

(Sound of a brick crashing through a window.)

Oh my god.

(Ryu gets out of bed.)

What was that?

(Ryu goes into another room and returns with a brick in his hand.)

RYU: There's a note.

(He unwraps the paper from the brick.)

KATHY: What does it say?

RYU *(Baffled)*: It's just one word.

(Kathy reads it too.)

KATHY: What does it mean?

11

Dean speaks out, with Ellen looking on.

DEAN: Thank you all for coming. It has come to our attention that a vandal, or possibly a coordinated team of vandals, has chosen to attack the public spaces of our community.

ELLEN: And private—

DEAN: And in some cases, the private spaces too.

(Light rises on Roger, elsewhere. He shakes a spray-paint can and starts spraying a word onto a wall. We can make out the letter "G.")

This person, or persons, is using a word designed to undermine our beloved town— And when I say undermine, I mean not only our morals and our civic beauty, but our authenticity.

(Roger has now spray-painted the letters, "G," "O," and "O.")

This is, above all, an attack against our hard-won authenticity. So, to the vandal, or vandals, I say, simply:

(We can make out the entire spray-painted word now: "GOOGLE.")

If this isn't the community for you, we ask you to leave peacefully at once, or face the consequences.

12

Dean and Ellen arriving home.

ELLEN: I still don't understand, why would they paint our house and none of the others on the block?
DEAN: We're public figures, Ellen.
ELLEN: The windows of your car. The door to your office.
DEAN: Plainly we were targeted because of our position in the community.

ELLEN: You mean you. *You* were targeted.

DEAN: What are you suggesting?

ELLEN: Could it be someone you know.

　　　Could it be—

DEAN: It could not.

(Pause.)

(Grasping at straws) What if it was the Communists?

ELLEN: Don't be ridiculous. This isn't about Communists.

DEAN: No, but could it be helpful if it was?

(She looks at him.)

The whole community is rattled. We name a few names. Possible suspects . . .

ELLEN: Names like who?

(A cell phone rings. They freeze.)

It must be an emergency.

(It rings again—a terrible, unmistakably modern ring.

Dean takes keys out of his pocket. He goes to a drawer. It rings again.

Dean has opened the drawer. It rings again. He answers.)

DEAN: Hello?

(Light on Roger, elsewhere. Maybe he's in a phone booth.)

ROGER: I have to talk to you. I mean really talk.

(Dean tries to sound as neutral as possible.)

DEAN: We're talking.

(He moves a little farther from Ellen.)

ROGER: Didn't you get my messages?
DEAN: Is that what you call them?
ROGER: "Google." Our Safe Word.

(Short pause.)

Why didn't I hear from you?

(Pause.)

Is she there?
DEAN: Of course.
ROGER: I have to talk, like ourselves. I can't be this person any-
more. I feel ugly. All the time. It isn't worth it. I want to be
with you. And I don't just mean fucking.
ELLEN: Who is it? /
DEAN: Headquarters.
ROGER *(Overlapping at "/")*: For a while it worked. I'm not say-
ing it didn't.
    But I wake up next to her and for the first second I'm
awake I think I'm with you—and then it all comes back
to me, and there's still a whole day of being someone else
ahead of me.
DEAN: It's not someone else. It's you.
ROGER: If it's not someone else, why am I different in my dreams?

*(Pause. Ellen has moved to Dean. Touching his shoulder support-
ively, possessively.)*

Jason, don't hang up. Jason? I'm sick for you. I was scared that if I didn't play along . . . But it's worse being here and not seeing you. Or seeing you on the street and you look like you don't even know me. That used to be hard for you too.

(Short pause.)

What if we just walked away?

(Short pause.)

It would be so easy. We could just keep walking till there's highways and Best Buys and Toyotas. I'll go without you if I have to.

DEAN: No you won't.

ROGER: Watch me.

(Roger hangs up. His light goes out.
Pause.
Dean flips the phone shut. He puts it in his pocket, not the drawer.)

DEAN: That was Headquarters. I have to go right away.

ELLEN: Where?

DEAN: To the city. It's an emergency.

ELLEN: What kind of emergency?

DEAN: You know I can't tell you, darling.

ELLEN: Will the community need to know?

DEAN: That's what we'll have to decide.

ELLEN: How long will you be gone this time?

DEAN: As long as it takes.

ELLEN: A day? Two days?

DEAN: As long as it takes.

ELLEN: Why don't I come with you?

DEAN: The community is unsettled. They need you.

ELLEN: They're not so unsettled, *we're* unsettled!

(Beat.)

I think I should go with you.

DEAN: You know you don't make sense out there, darling. I love that about you.

(He touches her face.)

You're my best girl.

ELLEN: I wasn't always.

(He kisses her on the cheek.)

DEAN: I better be off.

ELLEN: Why don't I make you a sandwich?

DEAN: That's all right.

ELLEN: Dean. You forgot your hat.

(She holds the hat out to him. The stakes seem curiously high. He goes to take the hat. He kisses her suddenly, deeply—it's meant to assuage her, but it feels like the gesture fails.)

DEAN: Well then. *(He goes to the door)*
I'll bring you something back. Some new fabric, maybe.

ELLEN *(A sudden outburst)*: Please don't leave me.

DEAN: I'll see you soon.

(And he's gone.)

13

Kathy, even more pregnant now, speaks to the seated circle.

KATHY: I don't have any answers. I'm sorry. All I know is that the Authenticity Committee has never been more necessary than it is now. Something has happened that may have changed our world forever. That word. There is simply no way to respond to it authentically. But I wonder: Why is it such an act of violence, when every one of us has it in our heads every day?

(She scans the circle for signs of unrest.)

It's impossible to forget the things we know about the world outside. It's possible, I suppose, that when you try to forget something, it can get louder and louder until all you can do is say it out loud. If that's what happened to the vandal, could it happen to you or me? How can we help each other not be . . . destroyed by the things we remember? I just think we need to ask the big questions.

(Pause.)

I'm sorry, I know Ellen should really be leading us through this . . . complicated time. I'm sure she's going to be here soon. I know she would never willfully miss a meeting.

14

Kathy is visiting Ellen, who looks a wreck. Maybe she wears a robe and slippers.

ELLEN: Five days.

KATHY: Have you called the police?

ELLEN: It's outside their jurisdiction.

KATHY: What do you mean?

ELLEN: I mean it's . . . outside.

KATHY: I see.

ELLEN: He's sometimes called away like this—but never this long.

KATHY: They must really need him there.

(Pause.)

Forgive me, but has it always been . . . happy between you two?

ELLEN: What do you mean?

KATHY: Forgive me if I'm being personal— It's just, an attractive man like that, going off on the road . . .

ELLEN: You mean did he ever stray.

KATHY: Yes, thank you.

I don't mean to pry.

ELLEN: Oh, Kathy, that's exactly what you mean to do.

KATHY: I'm sorry?

ELLEN: When you first moved here, we wondered if you'd mix with the community. "I don't want to be a *housewife*." But you've really involved yourself, Kathy. You're so *involved*. You'd think you were after my job.

KATHY: I don't think I deserve that, Ellen.

ELLEN: Oh?

KATHY: You've been locked up in this house all week, no one's seen hide nor hair of you, the girls at the Authenticity Committee are saying, "Off with her head," but I stand up for you, Ellen, I say Ellen is under a lot of stress, Ellen needs our love and support right now.

ELLEN: They said, "Off with her head"?

KATHY: Well, there was a little more decorum than that.

91

ELLEN: Look at you. You really think you can take over. And what exactly qualifies you to run a community? Is it your crab puff recipe? Or is it your miraculous fertility?

KATHY: You think I'm awfully naive, don't you. But I know some things you don't.

ELLEN: All you know is how to keep that Jap husband of yours on a short leash.

KATHY: *Ellen.*

ELLEN: Or don't you even know that much? Maybe that's why you're always making eyes at my husband.

KATHY: Dean IS A HOMOSEXUAL!

(Short pause.)

He and Roger. Ryu saw them together. Dean is a fucking homosexual.

(Pause. Ellen laughs to herself.)

ELLEN: Don't you think I know that?

KATHY: What?

ELLEN: Dean and Roger have always been together.

Long before we came here, they were together.

KATHY *(Sotto voce)*: Are we talking about?—

ELLEN *(Not sotto voce)*: The real world, yes.

KATHY: Are you saying—what are you saying?

ELLEN: Jason and I first met in college . . .

KATHY: Jason?

ELLEN: Dean's real name.

We were class of '95 at Sarah Lawrence. We were roommates the last two years. After graduation, we moved to New York together. That's when he met Roger. His first boyfriend. Roger moved in it seemed like overnight. Whenever they fought, Jason would come and talk to me. And I would listen.

KATHY: You were in love with him.

(Short pause.)

ELLEN: I was in love with him.
>I'm still in love with him, God help me. It's such a stupid old story, isn't it.

KATHY: It's not stupid.

ELLEN: Jason and Roger got jobs at start-ups. I got my master's at NYU. We went to bars at night. Everything you're supposed to. But it was too easy.

KATHY: Too easy?

ELLEN: That's what Jason said. When we were trying to figure out what was wrong with us.

KATHY: So it was Jason's idea?

ELLEN: You'd press a few buttons and a tub of Häagen-Dazs would come ten minutes later. DVDs. We put the trash at the end of the hall and someone made it disappear. I took a whole class online. I got an A. There was no one watching over you, no one telling you how to live. We could do anything we wanted . . . so we didn't want anything. Or we didn't know what we wanted. I'm not making sense.

KATHY: No, I think I—

ELLEN: And then one day Jason met a man from a place where it was different. A man with a hat and a briefcase. Jason asked me to come with him. To be with him. He made it fun. He got down on one knee, he gave me a ring. We were laughing. Me and my gay husband. But the longer we were here, the less it was like pretend. I cooked, I cleaned, he supported me, he called me "darling"—and once in a while, he would even—

KATHY: You don't have to tell me.

ELLEN: I don't see why not. He would fuck me, Kathy. Once in a while. *Quid pro quo.* But I never got pregnant, I couldn't get pregnant—like the universe knew it was pretend or something. But whenever I worried that it was all pretend, I'd look down at my ring and that was real. Even the feeling of not having a baby when everyone was supposed to be having them—that was real too, that was mine. That was something more than I had in the other world. Do you understand?

KATHY: Yes.

(Ellen looks at her ring, touching it.)

ELLEN: It was real for Dean too.

KATHY: Of course it was.

(Pause. Ellen shakes her head.)

ELLEN: The two of them, that was different. When they were together, it was like there wasn't anyone else in the world. But something went wrong. I never knew what, exactly. In the end they were always bickering, cheating on each other. Maybe they figured instead of cheating on each other, they could cheat *with* each other. Or if they had to hide, then it would make things more—

(A sudden break) I'm tired of seeing it from his perspective.

KATHY: Of course.

ELLEN: Dean carried out his homosexuality in a perfectly authentic way, with the right shame and secrecy. Of course I saw the clues—he'd say he couldn't sleep, he'd go out for night walks . . . And I'd suspect, the way a '50s wife would suspect. And I'd be grateful that I was the one he came home to. And it was harder than our old life, and it was better.

(Pause.)

KATHY: But, if you already knew about Dean, then why are you . . .

ELLEN: Such a fucking mess?

KATHY *("I wasn't going to say it")*: Well.

ELLEN: Because I know he isn't coming back this time. He had to choose, and he didn't choose me.

(With sudden difficulty) What am I going to do?

KATHY: I'm going to speak firmly for a moment, Ellen.

You have to bury your husband. You have to fit this into your Dossier.

ELLEN: —

KATHY: The key will be to make everything as true as possible.

ELLEN: How?

KATHY: Maybe we say that Dean and Roger *were* homosexuals, yes.

They both had wonderful wives, but their deepest desires were eating at them from the inside.

ELLEN: But Dean, no one will believe that he would / just leave his—

KATHY *(Placating)*: We'll say that Dean rejected that part of himself. He cut things off with Roger, he prayed, he . . . killed the darkness in himself. But Roger couldn't accept it. That's why he started terrorizing the community.

Finally he asked Dean to meet him in a park one night. And, when Dean rejected him again . . . Roger shot him.

ELLEN: And himself. He killed himself too.

KATHY: Good.

(Beat.)

The official story will be a little different, of course: We'll call it a mugging, maybe . . . a tragic mugging. Dean couldn't sleep, he was out for one of his night walks, maybe he ran into a vagrant.

(Short pause.)

We'll buy you a widow's dress. We'll have a beautiful funeral. Dean was so important to this community.

ELLEN: And I'm supposed to just . . . be that forever? The widow everyone's sorry for?

KATHY: Or you could leave.

(They lock eyes.)

But think how rich it will be. How complicated. When you pass by, people will whisper, why was Dean in that particular park, so far from his house? Some people might even whisper that he ran off to be a homosexual in that other world. People will whisper. What could be more authentic than that?

But everyone will be so moved by how you handle it. With your head held high and proud through all the gossip.

ELLEN: Yes.

KATHY: And when you're ready, you'll come back to the committee.

(Short pause.)

ELLEN: What about his responsibilities? Dean did more in that job than anyone knows.

KATHY: Just leave that to me.

ELLEN: You're being so nice to me. Why do you even want me to stay?

KATHY: Because you're my neighbor.

(Beat.)

You've been so helpful to me, Ellen. I'm so happy I can help you now.

15

Ryu speaks out. Kathy stands farther off, enormously pregnant now.

RYU: First of all, welcome. Welcome to the SDO.
I'm sure you all have a lot of questions.
"What do I wear?"
"How do I talk?"
"How do I explain this to the kids?"
Kathy and I will help you answer all of these perfectly normal questions.

KATHY: The most important thing to remember is that all of us were newcomers at one point. I mean gosh, we're *still* newcomers. Ryu and I have only been here, what

RYU: Fourteen months.

KATHY: Fourteen months. And Ryu's already the manager at the box factory. I'm so proud.

RYU: Honey . . .

KATHY: Now I'm embarrassing him, but I think it's important to know how life in 1955 can really focus you.
In the modern world, people are always talking about their problems. Always asking, "How can I be happier?" Maybe if I had a different diet, maybe if I had a different therapist. A different childhood. In the '50s, you have to keep it together. You aren't just living for yourself. You have a responsibility to make life wonderful for your husband and your child—and your community. *(Suddenly more personal)* It's amazing how . . . healing that responsibility can be.

(Ryu comes forward to join Kathy.)

RYU: We're not saying life is better in the 1950s. Or simpler.

KATHY: God no.

RYU: We're not saying people are happier. What we're saying is they're more *present*.

KATHY: Thank you, yes.

RYU: We are not in pursuit of the past.
We are in pursuit of the present.

(The baby kicks inside Kathy.)

KATHY: Oh.

RYU: What is it?

KATHY *(Hand to her belly)*: The present.

16

Kathy is asleep next to Ryu, dreaming.

Dean and Ellen in the living room, still dressed in '50s clothing.

KATHY: Kathy hardly ever dreamed of that other world anymore. Most nights she dreamed a row of houses just like the ones at Maple and Vine.

DEAN: It was a lovely day, wasn't it.

ELLEN: It was. One of the loveliest I can remember.

DEAN: I'm a little hungry. Are you hungry, darling?

ELLEN: Yes, a bit. I suppose I should get dinner on the table.

KATHY: But tonight her dream was different.
In this dream, everything was a little bit easier.

ELLEN: Were you thinking of something in particular?

DEAN: Oh anything, really. Whatever you can whip up.

KATHY: In this world, there was a button to call for everything.

(There is a knock at the door. Ellen opens the door and there is an entire Thanksgiving dinner sitting on the welcome mat.)

DEAN: That looks wonderful, honey.

ELLEN: Thank you.

KATHY: There was a button for bringing the milk, and a button for crab puffs, and a button for soggy cake, God knows why.

(Dean examines the turkey.)

DEAN: It smells delicious.

ELLEN: It does, doesn't it.

(There is another knock at the door.)

Who could that be now?

KATHY: There was even a button for bringing the things you most desire, so you didn't have to go looking for them in the night.

(Ellen opens the door and Roger is there. He looks at Dean.)

DEAN: Well, what are you waiting for? Come on in.

ELLEN: Are you hungry, Roger?

ROGER *(Looking at Dean)*: Always.

KATHY: All of these buttons were part of a brand-new machine. And the genius of this machine was that it brought things to people, instead of bringing people to things.

ELLEN: I'll put a record on. It's so much nicer to eat with music.

DEAN: Something slow and pretty.

(Ellen doesn't lift a finger, but light rises on the hi-fi. A beautiful piece of night music starts to play.)

ROGER: What is that? Brahms?

ELLEN *(There is no album cover)*: I'm not sure, the album cover just says "Classical for Lovers."

KATHY: This worked with information too—so there was no more need to go to a library to learn the answer to something. Now you only had to wonder for a few moments.

DEAN: It's Chopin. The "Raindrop Prelude."

ROGER: Ah yes.

ELLEN: You could almost dance to it.

KATHY: And before long, there was no more need to go anywhere.

(Roger stands. He holds out his hand to Dean.)

ROGER: Well?

DEAN: I have two left feet.

ROGER *(Gentle)*: I know.

KATHY: There was no longer anyone watching over you. No one to tell you what you could or couldn't do.

(Dean takes Roger's hand. They start to slow dance to the music, very simply and beautifully.)

The new machinery worked so smoothly that people never sensed how it was changing them.

(Ellen watches them dancing while she eats. Content. The dream doesn't get scarier exactly, so much as it gets more hypnotically tranquil, more enveloping.)

These warm and well-fed people didn't realize that they were dying inside.

(Ryu stirs in bed.)

RYU: Kath.

KATHY: It was so easy to get what they wanted that they no longer wanted anything.

(Dean and Roger come apart. The dream starts to fade away.)

RYU: Kathy.

KATHY: It was so long since they'd had to go anywhere or talk to anyone, that they forgot who they even were.

They thought they knew, but somehow, slowly, they'd forgotten.

RYU: Kathy.

(Ryu touches her and she wakes up. The music goes out.)

KATHY: What?

(The others are gone now.)

RYU: It's okay. You were talking in your sleep.

KATHY: What was I saying?

RYU: I couldn't make it out. But you sounded scared.

KATHY: I was having a dream.

RYU: A nightmare?

KATHY: Yes.

RYU: Well you're okay now.

(We hear the soft crying of a baby in a crib next to the bed. Ryu picks up the baby.)

Shhh. Shhh.

(He hands Kathy the baby.)

We're here at Maple and Vine, and your daughter is almost sleeping through the night.

(He holds Kathy as she rocks the baby.)

It was all a bad dream.

KATHY: Yes. Yes it was, wasn't it.

END OF PLAY

AMAZONS AND THEIR MEN

PRODUCTION HISTORY

Amazons and Their Men had a workshop production as part of Summerworks 2007, presented by Clubbed Thumb (Arne Jokela, Meg MacCary, Maria Striar, Cofounders). It was directed by Ken Rus Schmoll. The scenic design was by Sue Rees, the costume design was by Kirche Leigh Zeile, the lighting design was by Garin Marschall, the sound design was by Leah Gelpe, the original music was by Matt Carlson; the production stage manager was Jeff Meyers. The cast was:

THE FRAU	Rebecca Wisocky
THE EXTRA	Heidi Schreck
THE MAN	Brian Sgambati
THE BOY	Satya Bhabha

Amazons and Their Men subsequently had its world premiere at Clubbed Thumb on January 5, 2008 with the same cast and creative team, except the role of The Boy was played by Giro Perez.

Amazons and Their Men was written with the support of Jerome and McKnight Fellowships from the Playwrights' Center (P. Carl, Producing Artistic Director) in Minneapolis, Minnesota, and a New Works Grant from the Rhode Island Foundation. It was further developed in PlayLabs 2006 at the Playwrights' Center, the Hibernatus Interruptus Festival at Geva Theatre (Mark Cuddy, Artistic Director; John Quinlivan, Managing Director).

CHARACTERS

THE FRAU, thirty-five to forty-five.
On camera, she plays Penthesilea, queen of the Amazons.
THE EXTRA, thirties.
On camera, she plays several different nameless Amazons.
THE MAN, thirty-five to forty.
On camera, he plays Achilles.
THE BOY, twenty.
On camera, he plays Patroclus,
and, later, The Goddess of Love.

HISTORICAL NOTE

This much is true: In 1939, the German film director Leni Riefenstahl (*Triumph of the Will, Olympia*) began work on a film version of *Penthesilea*, in which she was to play the starring role. When Germany invaded Poland, filming was abandoned and Riefenstahl's screenplay was lost. All that survives are production notes in which she delineates the thirty-four key scenes of the film. While I was inspired by these facts, this is not a historical play: Riefenstahl isn't named; even the war isn't named. Historical details are meant to sneak through, as if by accident, at the end of a take.

This play takes place **On Camera** and **Off Camera**.

In the **On Camera** scenes, we should feel the narcotic pull of a camera's view, although there is never a camera onstage. An important question is, of course: How much of the action do we actually see? It seems to me that some kind of physical shorthand is desirable. (It is probably unnecessary to panto-mime drawing an arrow in a bow, but the actors might follow the path of the arrow with their eyes.) Above all, the staging of the On Camera scenes should help us to "film" the scenes in our heads, complete with pans, zooms, and jump cuts. On Camera scenes begin with titles, like so:

THE GREEKS DECIDE TO OFFER THE AMAZONS AN ALLIANCE. PENTHESILEA REFUSES.

These titles—many of which are taken from the scene head-ings of Leni Riefenstahl's film treatment—are projected at the beginning of the scene.

Off Camera scenes feel like a return to earth; a return to logic; a return to chairs and inside voices. But, aside from a couple noted exceptions, the characters still wear the classical costumes from the Frau's film.

"Nazi cinema exploited the limitations of human imagination, seeking to obliterate first-person consciousness and to replace it with a universal third person."

—ERIC RENTSCHLER, *THE MINISTRY OF ILLUSION*

"In Penthesilea I found my own individuality as in no other character."

—LENI RIEFENSTAHL,
"WHY AM I FILMING PENTHESILEA"

"She doesn't want to live off camera . . . What point is there existing."

—WARREN BEATTY, REGARDING MADONNA,
TRUTH OR DARE

PROLOGUE.

THE FRAU *(Voice only)*: Interior. Night.

(Light on Penthesilea, blonde and beautiful.)

THE FRAU AS PENTHESILEA: The camera first sees her reflected in a lion's eye.

(Light on Achilles, in chains.)

THE MAN AS ACHILLES: What kind of woman keeps lions for pets?

PENTHESILEA: A woman who loves fresh kill.

ACHILLES: What is your will with me, woman?

    If you wanted me for meat, we wouldn't be having this conversation.

PENTHESILEA: But instead of answering him, she waves her hand . . .

(Light on the Extra, who fans them with a palm frond.)

THE EXTRA: . . . And a hundred golden ladies summon a desert breeze.

ACHILLES: An army of women!

PENTHESILEA: In Amazonia, the male is a rare flower indeed.
Now, brave warrior, relax. Cool your brow in the court of Penthesilea.

ACHILLES: Why have you put me in chains?

PENTHESILEA: She doesn't need to answer—
Her close-up says everything.

THE EXTRA: The music plays. The focus softens.
Penthesilea falls in love with Achilles.

PENTHESILEA *(Smoldering)*: Let me be food for your ravenous dogs.
Let me be breakfast.
Let me be dust.

THE EXTRA: Achilles falls in love with Penthesilea.

ACHILLES *(Smoldering)*: Let me trail like a corpse behind your flashing-hooved horses.
Let me be baggage.
Let me be ballast.

(The Extra fans them as they kiss.)

THE EXTRA: The camera loves them.
The camera doesn't see anyone else.
(Speaking of herself) So she is hired to play Anyone Else.
The Extra. Anyone Else is her specialty.

PENTHESILEA: Your lips are dry. Some grapes, my pet?

ACHILLES: Achilles belongs to no woman.

PENTHESILEA: Some grapes for my new lion!

(The Extra goes and returns instantly, her face obscured by a plate of grapes.)

THE EXTRA: An Extra has to be nondescript. An Extra has a whole arsenal of nondescription at her disposal. Sometimes you'd catch her elbow in the corner of the frame, over the star's shoulder. She became a good listener.

THE FRAU: Cut! *(Breaking out of her Penthesilea character)* Who said you could talk to the camera?

THE EXTRA: I'm sorry.

THE FRAU: This is *my* story.

(She rips off her blonde wig and looks out toward the audience, where the cameras would be.)

I said CUT!

SCENE 1   Off Camera

Lights out on all but the Extra.

THE EXTRA *(Out)*: It is my story too. Only she doesn't know it
   yet.
      When the camera goes off, the star becomes smaller.
   Mortal. Everyone knows this. But few people know that
   when the Extra puts down her spear and steps off the soundstage and back into her life, she grows larger. She has a
   story too.

(Beat.)

The first person the Frau cast was herself.

(Light on the Frau.)

THE FRAU: Who else to play the Amazon queen?

THE EXTRA *(Out)*: Right away, a problem.

THE FRAU: Penthesilea was a blonde . . .

THE EXTRA: But the Frau was not.

THE FRAU *(Eyeing the wig)*: It would be necessary to practice.

THE EXTRA: The next person she cast was Achilles.

But while he too was blonde . . .

(Light rises on the Man.)

THE MAN: She hired a dark-eyed man from the ghetto to play him.

THE EXTRA: . . . So that no one on screen would be blonder than she.

THE MAN: And also because he came cheap. And because of his strong back. And because of the constellation of moles leading the eye down his strong back.

THE FRAU *(Salacious)*: You are *very* talented.

THE MAN: That is what I am told.

THE FRAU *(Approaching)*: They say you have no formal training, but you have instincts.

THE MAN *(Taking a step back from her)*: Everyone has instincts.

THE FRAU: You don't act like you want this job.

THE MAN: How do I act?

THE FRAU: Like I *owe* you the job.

THE MAN: What exactly is the job?

THE FRAU: The man who is my match.

Do you think you're up to it?

THE MAN: How will you pay me?

Everyone in the ghetto says: She has lost favor with the Minister of Propaganda. She is no longer playing with state money.

THE FRAU: I made the state's films with the state's money. Now I am making my own film. A love story inside a war story.

THE MAN: What will you pay me?

THE FRAU: I will pay you in fame.

(He scoffs.)

I am offering you a steady job.
   (Regarding the star he wears) It may be good for you to keep busy.

(Light shifts. Everything accelerating now.)

THE EXTRA: Two months later, in the darkest age of the last century, she started filming her adaptation of *Penthesilea*.

(During the following, the Frau goes and puts on the blonde wig.)

On a soundstage outside the great city, the Frau learned how to ride bareback, she learned to land a punch,
THE FRAU AS PENTHESILEA: She learned how to be blonde.
THE EXTRA: All for nothing. Of the thirty-four scenes in her screenplay, none were completed. What you will see are mere scraps of image. Here. Watch. See what you can snatch from the cutting room floor.
THE FRAU *(Out)*: Roll film!

SCENE 2   On Camera

THE GREEKS DECIDE TO OFFER THE AMAZONS AN
ALLIANCE. PENTHESILEA REFUSES.

THE FRAU: The camera swoops over dunes and choked little
     rivers.
THE EXTRA: Settling on the Amazon army, a row of tiny specks
     in the desert.
THE FRAU: Tracking closer
THE EXTRA: And the armor.
THE FRAU: Closer
THE EXTRA: The jewel on an elephant's brow.
THE FRAU: Sound in
THE EXTRA: Tambourines!
THE FRAU: A feminine noise, strange to this war.
     Close-up
THE MAN AS ACHILLES: Achilles turns his proud head toward the
     music.

THE FRAU: Closer-up

ACHILLES: Women of Amazonia! I offer you an alliance. Together we can defeat Troy!

THE FRAU: Cut to

THE EXTRA AS AMAZON 1: An Amazon takes aim with her slingshot—there will be no alliance!

THE FRAU: The camera, panning

AMAZON 1: The stone in flight

THE FRAU: Jump cut

ACHILLES: Achilles ducks

AMAZON 1: Too late!

ACHILLES: His helmet falls

THE FRAU, ACHILLES AND AMAZON 1: Crash!

AMAZON 1: To the ground.

ACHILLES: His head suddenly naked

THE FRAU: Extreme close-up

ACHILLES: He
   is
   beautiful.

AMAZON 1: The Amazon queen makes her way through the crowd.

THE FRAU AS PENTHESILEA *(Breathless)*: Who knew he'd be beautiful?

AMAZON 1: Her faithful army doesn't see the first symptoms of love on her face.

PENTHESILEA: Only the camera does.

ACHILLES: Achilles picks up his helmet, looking her in the eye the whole time.

PENTHESILEA *(Faux-innocent)*: Did you drop something?

ACHILLES: He is proud

PENTHESILEA: Even in his humiliation

ACHILLES: He is *terribly* proud of himself.

THE FRAU: CUT!

(The Frau breaks character.)

Couldn't you make him a bit more beautiful? A bit more *proud*?

THE MAN: I'm trying.

THE FRAU: Like a lion, here, watch. *(She puffs out her chest)* See my—

(End of fragment.)

SCENE 3　　　　　　　　　　　　　On Camera

PENTHESILEA SPARES ACHILLES' LIFE IN BATTLE.

THE FRAU: Exterior. Day.

THE MAN AS ACHILLES: Achilles

THE FRAU AS PENTHESILEA: And Penthesilea.

ACHILLES AND PENTHESILEA: Spear to spear.

ACHILLES: You're new here.

PENTHESILEA: Here is new to me.

ACHILLES: You came to fight?

PENTHESILEA: I came to be queen of you.

　　　　We need to replenish our numbers.

　　　　Your manparts are useful to us.

THE EXTRA: Penthesilea appraises him like a piece of meat.

PENTHESILEA: In your country, are they all made like you?

THE EXTRA: The camera appraises him like a piece of statuary.

ACHILLES: Are they all made like *you*, in your country?

THE EXTRA: Something passes between them

ACHILLES AND PENTHESILEA: In soft focus
THE EXTRA: But the Amazons only see their queen
PENTHESILEA *(Romantic)*: Defenseless
ACHILLES *(Self-important)*: With her mortal enemy.

(The Extra enters the scene as Amazon 2.)

THE EXTRA AS AMAZON 2 *(Drawing her bow)*: My queen, your
mortal enemy!
PENTHESILEA: The Amazon who takes aim at Achilles is felled
by an arrow.
AMAZON 2 *(Hand flying to her throat)*: Blood?
PENTHESILEA: Penthesilea rushes to comfort the dying woman.
AMAZON 2: From my own queen's quick quiver?

(A bit of a pietà.)

PENTHESILEA: *Shh*, my dear. My heroic dear. *Shh, shh.*
  The pain won't last. The veins will spend their contents.
  It's this hole in your throat that's the trouble.
  How could you have known he was *my* prize.
  You couldn't have known where your loyalties would get
  you. Your own blood is carrying you to the beds of all the
  empresses that ever lived. And your left breast is waiting
  for you there, marvelous, on a rose red cushion. The tip of
  my arrowhead has made you complete. *Shh, shh, shh.*
AMAZON 2: And the faithful Amazon dies in her arms . . .
  (Wheezingly) with a wheeze.
PENTHESILEA *(Dropping the Amazon's head)*: Fetch me a shovel.
THE EXTRA *(Still on the ground, dead)*: The soundtrack wells up,
  in place of tears in her eyes.
PENTHESILEA: Has anyone seen Achilles?
THE EXTRA: The camera dollies in close, so close that we can
  see the perspiration on her brow.

PENTHESILEA: Has anyone seen Achilles?

THE EXTRA: . . . As if we needed further evidence of her wicked little crush.

THE FRAU: And . . . Cut.

Good.

(Pleased with herself) Very good, everyone.

Very—

(End of fragment.)

SCENE 4 — Off Camera

THE EXTRA: Between takes, the Frau retreated to her office, where the journalists came to ask: Where had the film come from?

THE FRAU *(Poised, as if in an interview)*: Penthesilea, the woman warrior. When I was at university, I looked for her everywhere in the ancient texts. In her first appearance, the epic *Aethiopis*, she is granted just two sentences:

THE EXTRA: 1. "The Amazon queen arrives to aid the Trojans in war."

2. "Achilles kills Penthesilea and the Trojans bury her."

THE FRAU: Her first appearance and already she is forgotten.

Then I discovered the play by Heinrich von Kleist, who revises both statements:

1. Penthesilea enters the war to aid no one but herself.

2. She kills Achilles and dirties her face with his blood.

Now here was a woman to be interested in.

SCENE 5 On Camera

**ACHILLES' CHARIOT CRASHES. THE AMAZONS BLOCK
HIS WAY.**

*Achilles holds the reins, taut, with nothing attached to them. Or per-
haps they lead off into the wings? Stagey.*

THE MAN AS ACHILLES: Fly you, my steady steeds, fly! I must
escape her before I lose myself. I must escape myself.

THE FRAU: The camera lurching, hoof-high.

ACHILLES: She makes my heart stop. She makes my heart race.
She has that effect. She has that affect.

THE FRAU: The camera, breakneck.

ACHILLES: She makes my tongue stop. She makes my tongue
race, faster than my mind can think of words. But not faster
than my chariot!

THE FRAU: At this speed, the camera can't tell the blue backdrop
from the great desert sky.

ACHILLES: My men taken captive, yet I run! But wouldn't it be more cowardly to stay and kneel at her feet and call her Queen?

(The Extra, playing Amazon 3, steps forward and cuts his reins.)

THE EXTRA AS AMAZON 3: You're not going anywhere.
ACHILLES: And why not?
AMAZON 3: Because she has claimed you for her prize.
ACHILLES: I will fly on foot if I have to!
AMAZON 3 *(Shouting after him, as he runs)*: Your heart will not escape!
THE FRAU: Cut!

(Pause.)

Maybe if you were less corny?
THE EXTRA: I'm sorry.
THE FRAU *(Out)*: Again.

ACHILLES' CHARIOT CRASHES. THE AMAZONS BLOCK HIS WAY.

(Just as before:)

ACHILLES: My men taken captive, yet I run! But wouldn't it be more cowardly to stay and kneel at her feet and call her Queen?
THE EXTRA AS AMAZON 3: You're not going anywhere.
ACHILLES: And why not?
AMAZON 3: Because she has claimed you for her prize.
ACHILLES: I will fly on foot if I have to!
AMAZON 3 *(Shouting after him)*: Your heart will not esca—!
     (Breaking character, as the Extra now) I'm sorry.

THE FRAU: Yes.

(Off Camera now:)

THE EXTRA *(Out, as if to the crew)*: I'm sorry.
THE MAN: It's not her, it's the line.
THE FRAU: What?
THE EXTRA: He's sorry.
THE FRAU: WHAT?
THE EXTRA *(Cueing the Man)*: He's *very* sorry.
THE MAN: I'm sorry.

(The Boy enters.)

THE BOY: Telegram, ma'am?

> *(They all spin toward him. In plain clothes, he seems like a visitor from another planet.)*

THE FRAU: Ten minutes, everyone.
THE BOY: It is from the Ministry of Culture.
THE FRAU: This should be sobering.

> *(As she opens the telegram, we see the Minister of Propaganda in a pool of light. He speaks out.)*

THE MAN AS THE MINISTER OF PROPAGANDA: Dear Fräulein—
THE FRAU: The Minister was always a flatterer.
THE MINISTER: Some are saying: You'd do better to leave ancient history and portray our own country's great story, still being written. *Stop.*
THE FRAU: The Minister was always a Modernist.
THE MINISTER: Others are saying: You'd do better not to shelter Jews and homosexuals in the embrace of your fiction. *Stop.*

(This knocks the wind out of her. The Minister tips his hat.)

To your health, Fräulein.
     (As his light winks out) Stop.
THE FRAU: Three sentences. The Minister was always cheap.
     Boy!

(The Boy takes out a pencil, paper.)

THE BOY: Ready, ma'am.
THE FRAU *(Dictating; not heated, but quick and sharp)*: My dear
     sir *Stop*. There is no place for your war on my set *Stop*. My
     camera interested in a noble war *Stop*. My camera bored
     with your pomp and your circumstance *Stop*. My actors too
     busy to fill your work camps *Stop*. My actors too beauti-
     ful to fill your work camps *Stop*. No interest whatsoever
     in your grim telegrams *Stop*. I feed your telegrams to the
     horses for lunch *Stop*. I feed your telegrams to the ladies
     who lunch *Stop*. This wire already extravagant *Stop*. Stop
     sending *Stop*. Stop calling *Stop*. Stop *Stop*.
     (To the Boy) That is all.
THE EXTRA: She knows the Ministry will not be pleased . . .
THE BOY *(Lingering)*: Good evening then, ma'am.
THE EXTRA: . . . But this is to be her masterpiece, and she won't
     have their fingerprints on it.
THE FRAU: What, you expect some kind of tip?
THE BOY: No, ma'am.
THE FRAU *(Brightly, to the Extra)*: Take him to the pantry. Give
     him a chocolate biscuit.
THE EXTRA: How old are you?
THE BOY: Twenty, ma'am.
THE FRAU *(Brightly)*: No one is too old for a chocolate biscuit!
THE BOY: Good night, ma'am.

(He exits.)

THE EXTRA: He wanted *money.*

THE FRAU: There isn't any to spare.

THE EXTRA *(Under her breath)*: Maybe if you wrote shorter telegrams . . .

THE FRAU: We are already over budget for the month.
Equipment Rental. Horses. *Actors.*
Tomorrow we shoot the first Patroclus scene and there is no Patroclus!

THE EXTRA: We could sell the crystal, if it comes to that.

THE FRAU: Do you think *you* could play a boy?

THE EXTRA: I played Hamlet in drama school.

THE FRAU: You do have a certain mannish way about you.

THE EXTRA: I played Don Juan, in trousers. The audience stood at the end!

THE FRAU: The stage is one thing, but the camera isn't nearly so forgiving. Beautiful Patroclus, who Achilles loves like . . . a brother.

(The Frau looks at the Extra, scrutinizing.
The Extra offers her face for observation—she blinks, prettily.)

We'll give it a try.

THE EXTRA: Thank you.

THE FRAU: This time, you'll have close-ups.

SCENE 6   On Camera

**BACK AT THE CAMP, ACHILLES IS WELCOMED BY
PATROCLUS.**

THE FRAU: The camera circles the Greek campfire, shifting
from light to desert dark.

THE MAN AS ACHILLES: Achilles cannot disguise the stars in his
eyes.

THE EXTRA AS PATROCLUS: His companion, Patroclus, wraps
him in a blanket. Trying not to lose him to whatever force
has possessed him.

THE FRAU: But the camera tells us he has already lost the battle:

PATROCLUS: Out of focus, he barely makes it into the frame.

THE FRAU: Instead, Achilles fills the screen:

ACHILLES: She is Aphrodite clad in Ares! She is a sheep in wolf's
clothing!

She is both sexes she is neithersex she is nethersex
She is made of wolves and stars!

PATROCLUS: You want her.

ACHILLES: No.

PATROCLUS: You want to belong to her.

ACHILLES: No. She is a beast, she is a snake!

PATROCLUS: She makes you speak in metaphor.
That can't be good.

ACHILLES: Only because she is less than human—
The human words fall off her like arrows off well-made armor.

PATROCLUS: Then . . . we still belong to each other?

ACHILLES: Always.

PATROCLUS: But when he looks into Achilles' eyes, he sees *her* there

THE FRAU AS PENTHESILEA: Stretching like a tigress

ACHILLES: Deep in those two dark mirrors.

THE FRAU: (A very clever double exposure technique, which I invented.)

(Patroclus is stung.)

PATROCLUS: She's in you already.

ACHILLES: Patroclus, no.

PATROCLUS: She wants to blind you to anything else, to anyone else!

THE FRAU: Cut cut CUT!

(Off Camera now:)

THE MAN *(To the Extra, under his breath)*: She scares me.

THE FRAU: This isn't working.

THE EXTRA *(Under her breath)*: Shhh. She can help you.

THE FRAU: You're not pretty enough.
We're going to need a real boy.

(The Frau stalks off.)

THE MAN: Why is she so terrible to you?
THE EXTRA: She's my sister.

(Pause.)

THE MAN: The Frau is your *sister*?
THE EXTRA: I've been in twenty-seven of her films. I get to die in each one. Sometimes I die more than once in one film. It's my specialty.
THE MAN: Your specialty?
THE EXTRA: I've died by arrow, I've died by leprosy, gangrene, torn to pieces by angry mob, angry dogs, typhoon, starvation, walked the plank, thrown to sharks, mountain lion, mountain goat, mountain climbing accident. Guillotine. (I played a furious head without a body—did you know your head can live for thirty seconds without your body?) And the sword-and-sandal pictures: I died by locust swarm, asp to the breast, wrath of God. Cannonball, catapult, crucifixion. I'll never have my name above the title but I'm the best there is at dying.
THE MAN: You have a talent for dying.
THE EXTRA: For dying *inconspicuously*, yes.
THE MAN: That isn't a talent I aspire to.

(Short pause.)

THE EXTRA: She will keep you safe, I promise. She has already spoken to Them on your behalf.
THE MAN: Them . . .
THE EXTRA: The men who make decisions. The men who have no trouble falling asleep at night.
THE MAN: What if you're wrong?

THE EXTRA: She is very useful to Them. She makes their images. She can keep you safe.

THE MAN: Nowhere is safe.

THE EXTRA: Here, in her fantasy, it is safe. *(Beat)* I know this all must seem . . . melodramatic at times. She is not a writer. She is not an acting teacher. But when you see it all up on the screen, you won't believe it. You won't *believe* it. It happens to me every time. Her genius is in what she keeps and what she throws to the cutting room floor. Nothing will end up in the frame that she doesn't want there. Not even Them.

But you must be useful to her, in turn.

THE MAN: And how can I be useful?

THE EXTRA: Be beautiful.

THE MAN: Is that all?

THE EXTRA: And act well. But more important, be beautiful.

SCENE 7   Off Camera

THE EXTRA: The Frau sinks into her favorite armchair, smoking
    one of her rare cigars.

THE FRAU: Thinking
    and
    thinking
    and
    thinking.

THE EXTRA *(Entering the scene)*: The Extra swallows her pride.

THE FRAU *(As if she's saying "nemesis")*: Sister.

THE EXTRA: Sister, I have an idea.

THE FRAU: Speak.

THE EXTRA: What about the messenger boy?
    The one who brings the telegrams?

THE FRAU: You mean

THE EXTRA: He might play your Patroclus.
    He will be cheap. And he is not unattractive.

THE FRAU: Perhaps, if I hire him, the telegrams will stop coming?

THE EXTRA: Those big, dark eyes!

When he arrives on the set with your messages, the cameramen whisper:

(Like a secret password) "Did you bring a little something for me?"

THE FRAU: How imprudent of them.

THE EXTRA: What do you mean?

THE FRAU: There are others, outside the arts, who are not as tolerant as you and me.

THE EXTRA *(Out)*: She takes a big puff on her cigar, and those words seem to hang,

like the smoke,

in the air.

THE FRAU: Anything outside of God's design we can choose to abide or . . . not to abide.

THE EXTRA: What if God's design is not immediately apparent to us? Is there anything in the world that isn't God's design?

THE FRAU *("I seem to have touched a nerve")*: You are very theological tonight.

THE EXTRA: Sometimes, I think you talk like Them. I don't like it.

THE FRAU: You think I talk like—

THE EXTRA: Your former patrons.

THE FRAU: *Employers.*

THE EXTRA: I see you: Using the same camera angles you used to film the rallies. The special lens you built for seeing an entire army assembled. Only it is a different army this time.

THE FRAU: I invented those techniques. Why shouldn't I use them?

THE EXTRA: They are good for filming bodies, not people.

THE FRAU: What are you saying?

THE EXTRA: I am saying: I think you are making something that will please Them.

(Pause.)

I am not trying to draw blood. I only want / you to see—
THE FRAU: Why are you here, if you find my film so distasteful?
THE EXTRA: Because I think you are an artist, and some days even a great one. But—
THE FRAU: But—
THE EXTRA: With that, there comes a responsibility—
THE FRAU: "Responsibility"! Art is not responsible.
THE EXTRA: Why is that?
THE FRAU: Because, in art, beauty comes before justice.
THE EXTRA: I hear they are often the same thing, beauty and justice.
THE FRAU: In art?

(She blows a ring of smoke.)

I'm afraid they are almost never.

(A knock from outside.)

Enter.

(The Boy comes in.)

THE BOY: Telegram, ma'am.
THE FRAU *(Looking to the Extra)*: I see.
THE BOY: It is the Ministry.

(Continuous into:)

As the Frau reads the telegram:

THE EXTRA: She hadn't always dreaded the arrival of the Minister's telegrams.
    But no one knew exactly what had passed between them.
    In interviews, she would say, simply:
THE FRAU: Who can live in the past?
THE EXTRA: But if the journalists were patient, and they brought her a box of chocolate biscuits, they were sometimes rewarded.
THE FRAU: Years ago, when I was Fräulein not Frau,
    I stood in the doorway of an important party.
    The Minister of Propaganda was there.

(Light rises on the Minister of Propaganda, played by the Man. A German accent would be good.)

THE MAN AS THE MINISTER OF PROPAGANDA: . . . In a smart tuxedo.

THE FRAU: This champagne is repellent, don't you think?

THE MINISTER OF PROPAGANDA: Do not pretend to be a sophisticate.

You are more alive than all these people.

I have seen your films.

THE FRAU: Ah, my little alpine adventures.

THE MINISTER OF PROPAGANDA: Every frame vibrates with energy.

You must direct a film of our upcoming rally.

THE FRAU: Your rallies are not for me.

I'm an actress at heart—I want nice parts to play.

THE MINISTER OF PROPAGANDA: What sort of parts interest you?

THE EXTRA: . . . He says, ambiguously.

But she does not seem to notice:

THE FRAU: I have always wanted to play Penthesilea.

From Kleist's great drama.

THE MINISTER OF PROPAGANDA: Why Penthesilea?

THE FRAU: She is beautiful but fierce. She is headstrong.

She is a warrior but she puts love above everything else.

(Short pause.)

THE MINISTER OF PROPAGANDA: You have just described yourself, Fräulein.

THE FRAU *(Visibly pleased but trying to hide it)*: Perhaps.

THE MINISTER OF PROPAGANDA: With one exception:

I would wager you never put love above anything.

THE FRAU: I do the work that must be done.

I can think of no other way to live my life.

THE MINISTER OF PROPAGANDA: Then we are the same, you and me.

THE FRAU: We are *not* the same.

THE EXTRA: . . . She says, tossing back the champagne.

THE FRAU: I am an artist.

THE MINISTER OF PROPAGANDA: Look how you pick a fight.

THE EXTRA: He says, sliding his hand down her back.

THE MINISTER OF PROPAGANDA: Look how you pick a fight.
You *are* an Amazon.

THE FRAU: *Sie sind nicht Achilles,*

THE EXTRA: . . . She says.
(Translating) "You are no Achilles."

(The Frau steps out of the scene.)

THE FRAU *(Poised again)*: From then on, our relationship was civil at best.

THE EXTRA: . . . She would say in the interviews, many years later. After the war, it was necessary that they be adversaries.

THE FRAU: Often, it was much less than civil.

THE EXTRA: But the journalists sensed she was leaving some of the story on the cutting room floor:

(The Frau is pulled back into the scene.)

THE FRAU *(As before)*: We are *not* the same. I am an artist.

THE EXTRA: Perhaps she'd accepted his hand on her back.

THE MINISTER OF PROPAGANDA *(As before)*: Look how you pick a fight.
You *are* an Amazon.

THE FRAU: An Amazon with no army to command . . .

THE MINISTER OF PROPAGANDA: I will ask one more time, Fräulein. Make a film of the upcoming rally: You will have a queen's budget. You will have an army of underlings to command. When it is finished, you will have all the fame you need to make *Penthesilea*.

THE EXTRA: Perhaps she took another flute of champagne.

THE FRAU: The preparation, the editing: We are talking about years of my life.

THE MINISTER OF PROPAGANDA: Your Amazon queen will wait.

THE FRAU: You think?

I suspect she is impatient, like me.

THE EXTRA: Perhaps she took his arm and accepted his introductions to important people.

THE MINISTER OF PROPAGANDA: Actress, dancer, mountaineer—and now, the Ministry's chief directrix!

THE EXTRA: Perhaps she said her goodbyes and walked home, the painful shoes dangling from her right hand.

Although it was late, she lay awake, thinking of the men she'd charmed and the new alliance she'd made.

Outside her window, the boots of soldiers went:

THE FRAU: Left-right, left-right

THE EXTRA: Over the stones of the Pariser Platz.

The Frau lay awake all night.

Haunted by the Minister saying . . .

THE MINISTER OF PROPAGANDA: "We are the same, you and me."

THE EXTRA: . . . She started to dream up the film that would prove him wrong.

SCENE 9   On Camera

**BACK AT THE CAMP, ACHILLES IS WELCOMED BY
PATROCLUS.**

*Repeated scene. With the Boy as Patroclus now. Much more chemistry
with Achilles this time—and less camp.*

THE MAN AS ACHILLES: She is Aphrodite clad in Ares! She is a
    sheep in wolf's clothing!
        She is both sexes she is neithersex she is nethersex
        She is made of wolves and stars!
THE BOY AS PATROCLUS *(Simply, sadly)*: You want her.
ACHILLES: No.
PATROCLUS: You want to belong to her.
ACHILLES: No. She is a beast, she is a snake!
PATROCLUS: She makes you speak in metaphor.
        That can't be good.
ACHILLES: Only because she is less than human—

The human words fall off her like arrows off well-made armor.

PATROCLUS: Then . . . we still belong to each other?

ACHILLES: Always.

THE FRAU: And again, the camera peers into Achilles' eyes

ACHILLES: But this time it sees only

THE BOY: Him, poised like a panther

THE MAN: Reflected in those two dark mirrors.

(The Frau is stung.)

THE FRAU: Cut Cut CUT! We have another problem.

THE MAN: What now.

THE FRAU: He's *too* beautiful.

THE BOY: I'm sorry.

THE FRAU *(Shouting off)*: Makeup!

THE MAN *(To the Boy)*: Don't be sorry.

THE FRAU *(Shouting off)*: Get him out of that eyeliner! He's not the Queen of Sheba!

THE MAN *(To the Boy)*: You're doing very well.

THE FRAU: Give him a scar or something. Muddy his face.

THE BOY *(To the Man)*: Thank you.

THE FRAU *(Out)*: I thought I said c—

(End of fragment.)

THE EXTRA: The next day

THE MAN *(To the Boy)*: Hello.

THE EXTRA: The Man eats his lunch at the edge of the grounds

THE MAN: I said Hello.

THE EXTRA: And the Boy brings the telegrams

THE BOY: Hello.

THE EXTRA: The messenger bag dusting his right thigh.

THE MAN *(Like a secret password)*: Did you bring a little something for me?

THE BOY: Sorry.

THE MAN: You're asked that a lot.

THE BOY: Yes.

THE MAN: You are even darker than me. Are you Jewish?

THE BOY: My parents came from Romania.

THE MAN: Gypsies!

THE BOY: That is a word for us.

THE MAN: You don't wear an earring.

THE BOY: And I won't tell you the future.

THE MAN: But you know it?

THE BOY: Yes.

THE MAN: Do you read her messages?

(Pause.)

THE BOY: Every day.

THE MAN: And they tell you about the future?

THE BOY: They tell me about the Frau.

THE MAN: And . . .

THE BOY: There is a place for her in the future, if she wants it.

THE MAN: Is there a place for us, in the future?

THE BOY: It doesn't take special powers to see what will happen to us.

THE MAN: We're safe here. As long as we're working.

THE BOY: You think so?

THE MAN: She told me.

THE BOY: You're trusting.

THE MAN: You're beautiful.

(The Man kisses him. Impulsively, but the kiss lasts.)

THE BOY: I don't do this.

THE MAN: Now you do.

THE BOY: Someone will see.

THE MAN: Then we'll tell them we're rehearsing.

(They kiss again.)

SCENE 11   Off Camera

THE EXTRA: Later that day

THE BOY *(To the Frau)*: Telegram, ma'am.

THE EXTRA: In the Frau's chamber

THE FRAU: You are still delivering messages?

THE BOY: I need the money. You pay me with chocolate biscuits.

THE FRAU: You are late.

THE BOY: I'm sorry.

THE FRAU: The telegrams never come after noon.

THE BOY: I was held up. There are many messages today.

THE FRAU: Every day, the real world chatters on.

How am I supposed to imagine another world?

THE BOY: Why do you have to imagine another world?

THE FRAU: Where else will we go when this one ends?

(The Extra takes the telegram from the Boy.)

THE EXTRA *(Taking the telegram)*: It's from Mummy.

144

THE FRAU: Mummy

THE EXTRA: It's Mummy.

THE FRAU *(Shaken)*: It's been so long.

THE EXTRA *(Out)*: They have not spoken since Mummy bought her hot chocolate on the Strassengammerplatzenplatz

THE FRAU: And she told me Papa wouldn't stand for my play-acting any longer

THE EXTRA: And she gave her a choice:

THE FRAU: To be with my family or become a star.

THE EXTRA: The rest is history.

(The Frau stares at the envelope.)

THE FRAU: I'm afraid.

THE EXTRA: Read it.

THE FRAU: What if Papa were sick, how could I continue my work?

THE EXTRA: Read it.

THE FRAU: And yet I must continue.

THE EXTRA: Read it!

THE FRAU: I think I will read it.

(We see Mummy in a pool of light as the Frau reads. She is played by the Man. [Nothing too broad please—perhaps Mummy is a sort of late Jeanne Moreau type: husky voice, black lace veil.])

THE MAN AS MUMMY:

My little

my little

my little treasure *Stop*.

I know we haven't talked for thirteen years since I bought you hot chocolate on the Strassengammerplatzenplatz, and you told me you would choose your playacting over your loving family, but I hear from your sister that you're in the mountains in the great blue Tyrol and I thought you should come home because there is going to be a war here too there's no need to make one up! Your father is dying with a great big tumor in his knee and gallstones and kidney stones and all kinds of round strange stones inside him *Stop.* How did they get in there I wonder *Stop.* I know you will make the right choice this time *Stop.* You'd better *Stop.* Your loving Mummy *Stop.*

(Pause.)

THE FRAU: This is a very expensive telegram.
MUMMY: I sold my wedding ring to buy it.

(As her light winks out.)

Stop.

(The Frau crumples the telegram in her fist.)

THE EXTRA *(To the Boy)*: I should want to tap out a reply.
THE BOY: Yes of course, ma'am.
THE EXTRA *(To the Frau)*: Shall I give them your regards?
THE FRAU: "The right choice this time."
　　　She thinks I had a choice!
THE EXTRA: There is always a choice.
THE FRAU: . . . Says the woman in charge of nothing and no one.

(Beat. Referring to the telegram again.)

　　　Rather unfair of her to bring up ancient history.
THE EXTRA: History is for bringing up.
THE FRAU: Must you always be an insurgent?
THE EXTRA: Must you always be a dictator?

BOTH: Yes.

(*Pause.*)

THE EXTRA (*Tenderly, taking a different tack*): You were his favorite. You would give up the chance to see him again?

THE FRAU: I can see him in my memory, clear as a newsreel. I would prefer the memory to . . . maudlin fumblings.

THE EXTRA: Yes, it won't be edited to perfection. Yes, there will be wasted words. Bad takes. We will hold Papa's hand and watch the light leave his eyes.

THE FRAU: We will not.

(*Short pause.*)

THE EXTRA: What should I write to them?

THE FRAU: Tell them my work is all-consuming.

Tell them I am unable to leave the set.

THE EXTRA: Then I'll tell them the truth.

ACHILLES GOES TO THE AMAZON CAMP IN PURSUIT OF PENTHESILEA.

THE EXTRA: The German mountains do their best to impersonate the Trojan desert:

THE MAN AS ACHILLES: Achilles travels on foot, under the night sky.

THE FRAU: (My blue-velvet opera cape, stretched wide.)

ACHILLES: The sand still burning from the heat of the day.
      At the mouth of a great cave . . .

THE FRAU: (Aluminum foil over chicken wire.)

ACHILLES: Achilles spots a raging campfire.

THE FRAU: (Shreds of yellow silk blown by a fan.)

ACHILLES: While the Amazons sleep, a lone figure leans over the fire, as if deciphering the next day's battle plans in the jumping flame.

PENTHESILEA *(Spinning around)*: Who goes there?

ACHILLES: The son of a goddess.

The servant of your beauty.

PENTHESILEA: Why have you come?

THE EXTRA: (But something isn't quite right.)

ACHILLES: Why does a man visit a woman alone?

PENTHESILEA: To challenge her to a duel?

THE EXTRA: (The shadow cast by the "fire" is too steady.)

ACHILLES: Do you value yourself so little?

PENTHESILEA: On the contrary:

When men are taken with me, they are often struck speechless. The very agility of your tongue betrays a campaign of flattery.

THE EXTRA: (The rocks of the "cave" too shiny.)

PENTHESILEA: I challenge you to a contest of spears!

ACHILLES: I would not want to tear that beautiful breast.

THE EXTRA: (The "moon" proclaims itself too loudly.)

THE FRAU: Cut!

THE MAN: What?

(Off Camera now:)

THE FRAU: Ten minutes.

(The Man leaves.)

I must have been mad. We need location shots! We need Africa! We need sand and rock and fire! I've been making an airless thing, a dead thing.

THE EXTRA: There are nine cameramen. There are a hundred blonde horsewomen. How do you propose we get to Africa?

THE FRAU *(Small, almost bashful)*: Planes?

THE EXTRA: Will you ask the Ministry for planes? When we are at the brink of war?

THE FRAU: If we use the Ministry's planes, it will be a Ministry film.

THE EXTRA: What will that mean?

THE FRAU: They will place their symbol on the Greek helmets.

They will want marches for the soundtrack.

They will try to make it a film about war, not a film about love.

(Short pause.)

THE EXTRA: You are making a film about love?

SCENE 13   On Camera

COMBAT SCENES BETWEEN THE THREE ARMIES.

THE EXTRA: The next day, she shoots everything in close-up:

THE FRAU: Closer. I can still see our weak Northern sun. Closer!

THE MAN AS ACHILLES: The sweat on their backs.

THE FRAU: Tighter

THE EXTRA AS AMAZON 4: The bright sand, like jewels, in their hair.

THE FRAU: Jump cut

ACHILLES: The whip at the horse's back—

THE FRAU: Jump cut

ACHILLES: The wheels of his chariot—

THE FRAU: Jump cut

AMAZON 4 *(Wielding a spear)*: An Amazon spear between the spokes.

THE FRAU:	ACHILLES:
And the camera	And the chariot
crashes toward the ground.	crashes toward the ground.

AMAZON 4: Earth / under

ACHILLES: Under wheel /over

AMAZON 4: Over foot / under

ACHILLES: Under hoof.

THE FRAU: Crushed under the horse, a nameless Amazon hisses:

AMAZON 4: Have you forgotten the Queen's challenge? Would the world's greatest hero run from the contest of spears?

THE FRAU: Instead of her face, the camera focuses on the cracked earth behind her.

THE EXTRA: Suddenly, a cameraman's foot dirties the edge of the frame.

THE FRAU: Cut!

(End of fragment.)

SCENE 14 Off Camera

The Man with the Boy, who has a telegram.

THE BOY: Do we dare?

THE MAN: I've always wanted to see you tell the future.

(The Boy opens it. The Man looking over his shoulder.)

THE BOY *(Reading the telegram with much pomp)*: "My Esteemed Friend,"

THE MAN: Ooh, "Friend"?

THE BOY *(Faux-formality)*: May I continue?

THE MAN: Please.

THE BOY: "My Esteemed Friend,

I will submit your request to the Minister of Defense *Stop*. Two planes to fly six actors and a skeleton crew of four to Cairo *Stop*. You would retain control, as requested, but I will approve final cut personally *Stop*. Confident your always fine work will meet our standards *Stop*. To your health, Fräulein. *Stop*."

(*Pause. The Boy looks up from the telegram.*)

Do you think they're fucking?
THE MAN: Don't be disgusting.
THE BOY: "My Esteemed Friend . . ."
THE MAN: "My Friend" means fucking.
  "Esteemed Friend" means "I *hope* we'll fuck."
THE BOY: Well, My Friend . . .

(*The Man grins. Quick kiss.*)

It looks like you're going to Africa.
THE MAN: You mean *we're* going to Africa.
THE BOY: She won't take me.
THE MAN: She knows there wouldn't be a film without you.
THE BOY: I hope you're right.
THE MAN: Cairo, just think! We can sit in the sun. We can smoke hashish. When the film is done, we'll go off to the desert . . . find some well-appointed cave and wait for the planes to leave. We don't ever have to come back to this country and its future.

(*They kiss.*
  During the following, from another part of the stage, the Frau slowly turns her head to see them.)

THE EXTRA: Three stories up, through the leaves of the elm tree,
  Behind the closed blinds of her apartment,
  The Frau watches them.

SCENE 15   On Camera

**ACHILLES TELLS PATROCLUS THAT HE WILL DUEL
WITH THE AMAZON QUEEN.**

THE FRAU: *Wide* lens, to amplify the distance between them.

THE BOY AS PATROCLUS: What if you fall to her spear?

THE MAN AS ACHILLES: I am more than a match for her.

PATROCLUS: That is not what I fear—

THE FRAU: The camera circling Achilles

PATROCLUS: I'm afraid you will allow her to win.

ACHILLES: She is my destiny.

THE FRAU: Circling his heroic torso, till it finds the face of
    Patroclus:

PATROCLUS: Spangled with tears.

ACHILLES: Dry your eyes, boy.
    Everything on this black earth must come to an end.

PATROCLUS: Not this. We are meant to be constellations!
    We are meant to hang together in the sky!

THE FRAU: The camera comes to rest on both men.

(The following at a low whisper, out of character, while they continue to physically act the scene. The Frau doesn't notice and continues filming.)

THE BOY *(Whisper)*: Soon we will do this for real.

THE MAN *(Whisper)*: What do you mean?

THE FRAU: The image sharpens
   The focus deepens
   The composition settles.

THE BOY *(Whisper)*: You know what I mean.

THE MAN *(Whisper)*: I will talk to her.

THE FRAU: The two men stand at either edge of the frame, like the fine white columns of the Acropolis.

THE MAN *(Whisper)*: I will persuade her.

THE FRAU: Most cunningly, focus shifts from their bodies to the desert beyond

THE BOY *(Whisper)*: How will you persuade her?

THE FRAU: And the open desert becomes the uncrossable distance between two souls.

THE MAN *(Whisper)*: Don't be stupid.

THE BOY *(Whisper)*: Don't be a whore.

THE FRAU: CUT!
   (Off camera now)
   You are, what, chatting?

THE MAN: No.

THE FRAU: Your lips were moving.

THE BOY: I'm sorry.

THE FRAU: There are no lines!

THE MAN: We were improvising.

THE FRAU: All I need in this scene is your bodies.
   Your bodies will tell the story.
   Your bodies and the camera.

SCENE 16 On Camera

PENTHESILEA FALLS TO ACHILLES IN BATTLE. SHE IS UNAWARE OF WHAT IS HAPPENING AROUND HER.

THE FRAU: POV shot, ground level.

THE MAN AS ACHILLES: The boots of the advancing Greeks are upon her.

THE FRAU: Although she is unconscious, the camera still sees with her eyes: A thousand men against the desert sky.

THE EXTRA: (The same wide lens that filmed the armies at the rally.)

THE FRAU: Just when her fate seems certain, the hero speaks:

ACHILLES: He leaves this place a shadow, whoever lays a hand upon my Queen!

THE FRAU: Cut to an Amazon in the front lines, whispering:

THE EXTRA AS AMAZON 5: Can it be, love hast turned him against his own people?

ACHILLES: I will take this splendid woman back to Athens with me. The rest of you may stay and fight for Helen, who pales in comparison.

THE FRAU: The camera swoops up to him: He seems so tall!

THE EXTRA: (The same angle that captured the Führer at his podium.)

ACHILLES: He leaves this place a shadow, whoever tries to stop me!

THE FRAU AS PENTHESILEA: Finally, the Queen stirs.

ACHILLES: Rise, lady.

PENTHESILEA: I live . . . But why?

ACHILLES: So that you can be my Queen,
If you will have me as your King.

PENTHESILEA: My enemy, also my King?

ACHILLES: Excellent woman, I will live out my life in the fetters of your beauty.

But first, tell me your name.

PENTHESILEA: Names can be forgotten.

If you forgot my name, could you still find my image in yourself? Can you still see me when you shut your eyes?

(He shuts his eyes.)

ACHILLES: You are so beautiful.

PENTHESILEA: Then my name is Penthesilea.

ACHILLES: You are so beautiful, Penthesilea.

(His eyes still shut. She begins to touch him on the face, the lips.)

PENTHESILEA: She doesn't need to ask his name.

ACHILLES: It is known in every country with a language.

THE FRAU: Cut.

Yes. Print it! Print—

(End of fragment.)

SCENE 17   Off Camera

The Frau in her armchair, smoking one of her cigars.

THE EXTRA: For the first time, the Man visits the Frau in her
   quarters.
THE FRAU: Speak.
THE MAN: It's Stefan.
THE FRAU *(Pretending not to know)*: Stefan . . .
THE MAN: The boy who brings your telegrams. The boy with
   five scenes in your magnum opus.
THE FRAU: Oh yes, the pretty pretty boy.
THE MAN: What if he were to come with us?
THE FRAU: To Africa.
THE MAN: You see everything that's happening. You know what
   he is. Let him come with us.
THE FRAU: You are the leading man. Why should you intervene
   on behalf of a supernumerary?
THE MAN: Because he acts well.

THE FRAU: You lie very badly for an actor.

I ask you again: Why should you intervene on his behalf?

THE MAN: Because we.

Because he and I—

THE FRAU: And you're asking me to reward an abomination?

THE MAN: I'm asking you to take him with us. I am asking you to save him.

THE FRAU: And I am telling you I can't.

THE MAN: You don't really believe it's an abomination.

You put it in your adaptation—Patroclus isn't even *in* the Kleist play.

THE FRAU: I added him to deepen the emotional journey.

THE MAN *(Bitterly)*: It has *worked*.

THE FRAU: You shouldn't have these distractions. Perhaps that's why your performance has been so dissipated.

THE MAN: I will do better.

THE FRAU: You had such potential when I found you.

Now, the love scenes, there is barely a flicker behind your eyes.

THE MAN: What If I were to . . . find that flicker?

(He moves in to kiss her, but the Frau turns her cheek to him.)

THE FRAU: I don't believe you.

THE MAN: I'm acting as hard as I can.

THE FRAU: You're not behaving like a man who wants something from me.

THE MAN: How does such a man behave?

(The Frau pushes him to his knees.)

THE FRAU: Ask me again.

THE MAN: How does such a man behave?

(The Frau pushes him onto his stomach.)

THE FRAU: Ask me again.

(Blackout.)

Roll film!

SCENE 18   On Camera

THE GREAT LOVE SCENE BETWEEN PENTHESILEA AND ACHILLES.

THE FRAU: Interior. Night.

(The following as a kind of foreplay:)

ACHILLES: Mosquitoes buzzing, wolves howling
PENTHESILEA: Incense censing
ACHILLES: Vaseline on the lens.
THE FRAU *(Shouting off)*: More Vaseline on the lens!
ACHILLES: Candles craven in the desert wind.
PENTHESILEA *(Smoldering, as before)*: Let me be food for your
    ravenous dogs.
        Let me be breakfast.
        Let me be dust.

ACHILLES *(Smoldering)*: Let me trail like a corpse behind your flashing-hooved horses.

 Let me be baggage.

 Let me be ballast.

PENTHESILEA: Let me be cinders.

ACHILLES: Let me be ash.

 Let me be nothing.

PENTHESILEA: Let *me* be nothing.

ACHILLES: No, me!

(They kiss.)

PENTHESILEA: Some grapes, my pet?

ACHILLES: Achilles belongs to no woman.

PENTHESILEA *(Shouting off)*: Some grapes for my new lion!

(The Extra enters the scene as Amazon 6, her face obscured by a plate of grapes.
 Achilles takes one of the grapes and poises it over his mouth.)

Wait, my love—caution.

(She snaps her fingers and Amazon 6 tastes a grape. She is immediately stricken, doubled over.)

AMAZON 6: Poison?

ACHILLES *(To Penthesilea, paying the Extra no mind)*: Who would do such a thing?

PENTHESILEA: They know you're here with me—it can only be them.

ACHILLES: Who?

PENTHESILEA: The High Priestesses.

 Powerful Amazons who would challenge this . . . attachment.

(Amazon 6 finally dies, unnoticed, the grapes spilling onto the floor.)

ACHILLES: I fear no one in this world but you.
You, who hold my heart between your teeth.
PENTHESILEA: This is no time for metaphor. You aren't safe here. Go back to your Greeks. Go back to your Boy. Go back before something terrible—

(End of fragment.)

SCENE 19   Off Camera

In a quiet corner of the set, the Boy approaches the Man. He seems to be looking for an answer from the Man.

THE BOY: I'm scared to ask.

   (The Man looks impassive at first, then smiles.)

   Yes?
THE MAN: Yes.

   (They embrace.)

THE BOY: What did you say to her?
THE MAN: Never mind that.
THE BOY *(Playful, jostling him)*: What did you say!
THE MAN: It was a . . . masterpiece of flattery.
THE BOY: You are always the seducer.

(They are about to kiss. Suddenly the Extra is there.)

THE EXTRA *(To the Boy)*: She's asking for you.
THE BOY: Me?
THE EXTRA: She needs you in costume for the Rose Festival.
THE BOY *(To the Man)*: My big scene.
THE MAN *(Squeezing his hand)*: You'll be fine.

(The Boy exits. Short pause.)

Why do you look at me like that?
THE EXTRA: Be careful.
THE MAN: She already knows.
THE EXTRA: Yes.
  But it will be better if you are discreet.

(The Extra starts to exit . . .)

THE MAN: You would say that.

(. . . but this stops her.)

THE EXTRA: What does that mean?
THE MAN: Why do you always go back to your room?
THE EXTRA: Why do I—
THE MAN: I see the light on in your room, late. Why don't you
  ever go out dancing with the rest of them? Why don't you
  go out looking for men, like the other Amazons?
  Do you have . . . someone?

(Pause.)

THE EXTRA: Once, I did.
THE MAN: What happened to her?

(Pause.)

THE EXTRA: Times are not the same anymore.

THE FRAU *(From off)*: Sister!

THE MAN: Does she know?

THE EXTRA: I have to go.

SCENE 20   On Camera

THE ROSE FESTIVAL: THE AMAZON PRIESTESSES, ROSE MAIDENS, AND CAPTURED GREEKS.

THE FRAU: Rose petals fill the air. Rose petals blind the camera!

THE EXTRA AS AMAZON 7: The Amazons dance a feverish victory dance

THE FRAU AS PENTHESILEA: But a lone figure remains still, in the center of the frame.

AMAZON 7 *(Dancing)*: My Queen, do you not enjoy the festivities?

PENTHESILEA: It is foolish to celebrate when Achilles rides free!

THE EXTRA: she says, while a voice-over tells the truth:

PENTHESILEA *(Recorded voice-over, her lips not moving)*: How can I fight the very man who holds my heart captive?

THE EXTRA AS AMAZON 7: Forgive me, my lady, but can even you find the immortal one's weakness?

PENTHESILEA: Get out of my sight!

(The Extra exits, head hanging.

The Extra immediately reenters as Amazon 8, with Patroclus in chains.)

AMAZON 8: My Queen. This prisoner knows Achilles!

(She throws Patroclus at the foot of the queen.)

He stays with the great man in his tent.

PENTHESILEA: Speak, boy!

THE BOY AS PATROCLUS: I know Achilles' weakness, yes. But it is my honor to keep it secret from those who would do him harm.

AMAZON 8: Tear the secret out of him!

(We hear the canned cries of other Amazons: "Destroy him! Bleed him! Cut off his arms! See if love will save him then!")

PATROCLUS: Do as you like. I will not speak.

PENTHESILEA: Why do you martyr yourself?

PATROCLUS: Because I love him.

THE EXTRA: And Penthesilea rises from her throne,
     Like a great bird stirred from sleep:

PENTHESILEA: "Love."

THE EXTRA: Close-up on her mouth, pronouncing the strange new word.

PENTHESILEA *(Almost inaudible)*: "Love"?

PATROCLUS: Yes, love can make the greatest suffering light as air.

THE EXTRA: She tries to hide him in the background, in soft focus . . .

PATROCLUS: You can end my life, but I am still closer to him than you will ever be.

THE EXTRA: . . . But even with his face dirtied, all the beauty on screen belongs to him.

PATROCLUS: Forgive me, Queen. I will tell you nothing.
PENTHESILEA: Then you are no longer useful to us.
Kill him.
AMAZON 8: Of course, my Queen.

(Penthesilea turns out for a close-up.)

PENTHESILEA *(Recorded voice-over)*: But can even death kill such a love as this?
THE FRAU: Cross fade from her face, pensive
THE MAN AS ACHILLES: To Achilles, riding full force toward his destiny.
THE FRAU: And . . . Cut. *(Off Camera now)* I think that is all for today.

(Everyone starts to leave. The following very rapidly:)

Sister.
THE EXTRA: Yes?
THE MAN *(To the Boy)*: What does she have you wearing?
THE BOY: "Fetters."
THE FRAU *(To the Extra)*: Get us a table at the inn.
THE BOY *(To the Man)*: You like?
THE MAN: I like.
THE EXTRA *(To the Frau)*: Steak and potatoes?
THE FRAU: Very rare.
THE MAN *(Whispering to the Extra)*: I think she forgot "please."
THE FRAU *(To the Boy)*: You, stay!
THE BOY: Stay?

(The Man winks at him. Then the Frau and the Boy are alone.)

Ma'am?
THE FRAU: You are good. You are not an actor—but, you are a very easy person to watch. I have been watching you.

THE BOY (*Unsure if this is a compliment*): Thank you.

THE FRAU (*"No, it is not a compliment"*): I have been watching you.

(*Pause.*)

THE BOY: What do you see?

THE FRAU: From my window in the inn I see the sun come over the mountains. I see the geese gather by the lake. And I see the private little movie you are making together.

(*Pause.*)

THE BOY: It is there, in your film, what we are doing. It is in your own film.

THE FRAU: Achilles and Patroclus are old companions.

THE BOY: It is between the lines.

It is in the close-ups, not the words.

And close-ups are what you do best.

THE FRAU: What are you saying?

THE BOY: I am saying: This is the story you are telling.

THE FRAU: Achilles loves *Penthesilea*.

THE BOY: And Patroclus?

THE FRAU: His was a heroic sacrifice. In any great love story there are . . . casualties.

THE BOY: Like a war.

THE FRAU: Why can't any of you understand! I am not interested in war. I am filming a love story!

THE BOY: Yes, you are.

I hope your Esteemed Friend will approve.

(*Pause.*)

THE FRAU: If you leave at once—if you leave the set at once, you can walk back to Bucharest without a triangle to wear.

THE BOY: But I thought—

THE FRAU: If you leave tonight, while he sleeps, he can continue to work for me. That is my gift to you.

THE BOY: And if I don't leave?

THE FRAU: If you leave tonight, while he sleeps, I will give you a hundred marks for your work and you can buy all the chocolate biscuits in creation.

THE BOY: Why do you hate me?

THE FRAU: Because you have stolen my film.

SCENE 21   Off Camera

THE EXTRA: The next day, a boy with blond hair delivers her
    telegrams.
THE FRAU (*Looking at the envelope*): News of Africa, I hope.
THE EXTRA: She gives him ten pfennigs, instead of chocolate.

(*The Frau reads. Light up on the Minister of Propaganda.*)

THE MINISTER OF PROPAGANDA: Esteemed Friend,
    Share this with no one *Stop*. We cannot authorize travel
    to Africa due to imminent conflict *Stop*. I urge you to stay
    in the country until otherwise informed *Stop*. There are
    greater things afoot than even your camera can envision
    Stop.
THE EXTRA: What is it?
THE FRAU: It's nothing. An invitation to a banquet.
    They want to give me an award.
THE EXTRA: Any news about the planes?

THE FRAU: Soon, he says.

(She realizes this isn't enough.)

Really, how long do they expect me to shoot close-ups?

THE EXTRA: What will you do about Patroclus?

THE FRAU: He only had one more scene to film.

(With ceremony) I was hoping that *you* might be up to the challenge.

THE EXTRA: Don't you think people will notice the difference?

THE FRAU: The lighting, the camera angles—I still have a few tricks up my sleeve!

THE EXTRA: But, when he sees me dressed in Stefan's costume—

THE FRAU *(A sudden realization)*: It will be beautiful.

THE EXTRA: I couldn't do that to him.

THE FRAU: Of course you can. This, sister, is what we call a break. The big death scene: Finally, a challenge worthy of your talent.

SCENE 22   On Camera

ACHILLES FINDS PATROCLUS, MORTALLY WOUNDED.

THE FRAU: POV shot, looking into the sky. The vultures circling, hungry. Sound in:

THE MAN AS ACHILLES: The hooves of his fastest steed, galloping to the rescue.

THE FRAU: Close-up.

ACHILLES: Begone, princes of filth! You'll not feast today.

(The Extra turns over, revealing her face. For the first time, the Man sees that it isn't the Boy. He struggles to stay in character.)

THE EXTRA: The vultures scatter, revealing the Extra in Patroclus's costume.

(Pause.)

ACHILLES: My boy, who has done this to you?

THE EXTRA AS PATROCLUS (*Barely able to speak*): Achilles?

ACHILLES: Don't try to speak. I'm here now.

(*Achilles cradles Patroclus.*)

THE EXTRA: She tries her best to hide her face.

THE FRAU: The entire scene filmed over her shoulder.

ACHILLES: This star-shaped wound. It is the work of an Amazon blade.

PATROCLUS (*Speaking with great effort*): Old friend . . .

ACHILLES: Rest, my boy.

PATROCLUS: Old friend, heed this warning.

THE FRAU: Cut to

PATROCLUS: His fist opens, slowly

THE FRAU: The camera peers into his hand. Extreme close-up on

PATROCLUS: A wild rose

Crushed

Like a blood clot.

THE FRAU: And the noble boy dies in his arms.

ACHILLES: Patroclus.

Old companion.

THE EXTRA: And though he looks down at me, that boy is still reflected in his eyes.

ACHILLES: I understand this warning.

But even your death cannot free me from her.

I must away to her. For there is no other—

(*Pause. As the Man now:*)

I can't.

THE FRAU: Cut.

THE MAN (*To the Frau*): Where is he.

THE FRAU (*Out*): CUT!

(Off camera now. Rapidly:)

THE MAN: What have you done.

THE FRAU: What do you mean what have / I—

THE MAN *(Overlapping)*: What have you done with him.

THE FRAU: It seems he left during the night. No one saw him.
(Looking at the Extra) What could we do but recast the part?

THE MAN: We had an agreement.

THE FRAU: I told you, I don't know where / he—

THE MAN: I DON'T BELIEVE YOU.

(Pause.)

I will go back.

THE EXTRA: No.

THE MAN: I will find him.

THE FRAU: Ah, the rigors of love.

THE MAN: WHAT DO YOU KNOW ABOUT LOVE.

THE EXTRA: Gentle.

THE MAN: Someone who tells a love story by drawing blood.

THE FRAU: You are endangering yourself.

THE MAN: You're so good at filming me like a statue.
Make your film with statues.

THE FRAU: Go then. Go! If you're fast you can snatch some of
the film, before they sweep him off the cutting-room floor.

(The Man spits at her feet as he leaves.)

SCENE 23   On Camera

**PENTHESILEA RETURNS TO REALITY, AFTER KILLING
ACHILLES IN A FIT OF MADNESS.**

*The Frau describes the camera's movements around her face. She is
in the scene at the same time. Barely moving, offering her face for a
beautiful close-up . . .*

THE FRAU: The camera first observes her through the parting
dust.

Something is wrong. She is too still.

The woman who lives her life drawn like a bow, suddenly still as a knife in the dirt.

Although her face is without expression, the camera's
attention seems to change it: Cut from her face to the
blood on her hands. Cut back, and the blank face seems
to reveal something new underneath. We seem to see the

moment when again she is more woman than beast. When she realizes what she's done.

The blood on her hands runs black-and-white.

The blood at her mouth.

Not

Her

Blood

Whose

Blood.

The camera, still now. As still as she.

Nothing moves, except something behind her eyes.

The delusions hemorrhaging from her head.

(The Extra enters quickly with a newspaper.)

THE EXTRA: Sister, read.

THE FRAU: We are filming.

THE EXTRA *(Out)*: Cut!

THE FRAU: *I* say cut.

Cut!

THE EXTRA: Read.

(Off camera now:)

THE FRAU *(Seeing the headline)*: "Germany Invades Poland."

THE EXTRA: Now you understand?

THE FRAU: Yes.

THE EXTRA: Given the circumstances—

THE FRAU: Yes, the film—

THE EXTRA: No, not / the film—

THE FRAU: The film is more necessary than ever.

THE EXTRA: We are at *war*—

THE FRAU: The world needs art, especially in wartime. When art fails to help us understand the world—

THE EXTRA: Is that what you do? Help us understand the world?

THE FRAU: I locate perfection and I put it in the center, and anything less stays at the edge of the frame! It's my job!

THE EXTRA: It *was* your / job.

THE FRAU: Others, they make it their job to locate imperfection and snuff it. But I prefer to say, "This is beautiful," or I say, / "This is not so beautiful."

THE EXTRA: You sound like them!—

THE FRAU: I say, "This is ideal," or I say, "This is not / ideal."

THE EXTRA: You sound like them!—

THE FRAU: I am telling another story!

An ancient story. Heroes. Beauty. Love.

Are these things useful to them?

THE EXTRA: —

THE FRAU: How can I not be useful to them?

(Accelerating now:)

THE EXTRA: Put down your camera.

THE FRAU: I can't do that.

THE EXTRA: Then you are an accomplice.

THE FRAU: No.

THE EXTRA: You held that boy's life in your arms and you dropped him. You are no better than Them.

THE FRAU: "Accomplice." You are the *ultimate* accomplice.

Always *observing*. Ordering my steak. Hiding in my shadow, as the rest of your kind are identified.

(Pause.)

THE EXTRA: What does that mean, "my kind"?

THE FRAU: Those outside of God's design.

(Pause.)

Yes. You . . . Aberration. You *Sister*. It is written on your face. It is written in all of your performances. You Amateur.

(The Extra winces, her hand touching her brow.)

THE EXTRA: Oh—
THE FRAU: What
THE EXTRA: My—
    My—
THE FRAU: Your what

(The Extra has dropped to her knees.)

THE EXTRA: I think it's my
THE FRAU: What!
THE EXTRA: My head it's my
THE FRAU: What do you mean / your
THE EXTRA: I don't . . . know or I'd
THE FRAU: What's wrong with your head
THE EXTRA: Behind my eyes—
THE FRAU: I don't know what to do—
THE EXTRA: Like a,
    like a—
THE FRAU: What should I—
THE EXTRA: Pain
THE FRAU: Marta?

(The Extra convulses.)

Marta! God!
    Someone! Help!

(The Extra lies very still.)

Marta?

(*Pause.*

   Then, suddenly:)

THE EXTRA: You believed me.
THE FRAU: *What?*

(*The Extra stands up, brushes herself off.*)

THE EXTRA: You *believed* me. You said my name!
THE FRAU: Are you mad?
THE EXTRA (*Wild, invigorated*): You never say my name, and now you use it like a magic word! "Marta." You see? Every one of us has a name.
THE FRAU: What are you talking about.
THE EXTRA: Every one of us who takes an arrow through the throat. Every one of them who disappears during the night. All of the Extras. Why don't you point your camera at them?

(*Short pause.*)

SPEAK.
THE FRAU (*Still rattled*): That was very . . . realistic.
THE EXTRA: You've taught me one thing: How to die.
THE FRAU: And yet you're still here.
THE EXTRA: What do you mean?
THE FRAU (*Grave*): The others, they died better.

SCENE 24   On Camera

PENTHESILEA'S GREAT SCENE OF DESPAIR. SHE IS VISITED BY THE GODDESS OF LOVE.

THE FRAU: Deserted by the crew, her camera sits alone on a tripod. Her camera, once agile, is rooted stupidly to the ground.

But it still sees

(As Penthesilea now:)

The pain.

Ares, God of War, split me in two with one of your thunderbolts.

End the pain.

THE BOY AS THE GODDESS OF LOVE: But it is not Ares who answers her prayers.

It is the Goddess of Love.

THE FRAU AS PENTHESILEA: Go away.

THE GODDESS OF LOVE: Child. You summoned me and now I've come.

PENTHESILEA: I didn't ask for you, I asked for my father, the God of War.

THE GODDESS OF LOVE: For one such as you, Love and War are forever entwined.

PENTHESILEA: Poetry can't help me anymore.

THE GODDESS OF LOVE: Poetry can always help.

Where does it hurt?

PENTHESILEA: Go away.

THE GODDESS OF LOVE: I can't hear you.

PENTHESILEA: YOU'RE THE ONE WHO GOT ME INTO THIS MESS AND NOW I WILL THROW MYSELF INTO THE RIVER SCAMANDER.

You're the cause. You're the.

(Penthesilea has spent all her energy on this outburst.)

THE GODDESS OF LOVE: Tell me, child. Where does it hurt?

(Without moving anything but her arm, Penthesilea indicates her head, her missing left breast, her groin.)

PENTHESILEA: Pain.

THE GODDESS OF LOVE: What can I do?

PENTHESILEA: Nothing.

THE GODDESS OF LOVE: But Aphrodite sings a wicked little lullaby

PENTHESILEA: And the soft notes fall on her like snowflakes:

THE GODDESS OF LOVE *(Singing)*:

Lay your pretty head in the dust
And when you wake, you'll have an oceanful of peacocks.

Take another drink of dust
And when you wake, you'll have a desertful of trout.
Lay your pretty head in the dust
And dream of red revenge and blood knots
And tribal beats and love-me-nots.

THE FRAU: And . . . cut.

THE GODDESS OF LOVE: Why do you always shout "Cut," just when the scene is getting interesting?

THE FRAU: I said Cut!

THE GODDESS OF LOVE: Don't you wonder what would happen if the camera kept running?

THE FRAU: Who are you?

THE BOY (*Breaking character*): Are you afraid it might find something real?

THE FRAU: This isn't in the script. None of this is in the script.

THE BOY: There isn't a script anymore.

THE FRAU: Cut.

THE BOY: There isn't a film anymore.

THE FRAU (*Closing her eyes, tight*): Cut!

THE BOY (*A statement of fact, not vengeful*): There isn't a me anymore.

THE FRAU: Get off of my set!

(*Blackout.*)

Get off of my set

(*Light returns, and the Frau is waking, with a start, in her armchair.*)

Get off of my
     Chair.

(The Extra looking on from a distance. As the lights rise, we see that she is wearing somber period clothing for the first time.)

THE EXTRA: It is the middle of the night.

It is her own room.

Outside the window, the boots of the SS go:

THE FRAU *(Whispered)*: Left-right, left-right,

THE EXTRA: Over the stones of the Pariser Platz.

Outside her window, she hears

THE FRAU: Glass breaking

THE EXTRA: All across the ancient part of the city.

The next day, the Frau builds a strong fire in the fireplace and feeds it her negatives. She does not look away, as the film is turned into strong black smoke that stays in her carpet and clothes for weeks. Everything you have seen goes up in flames.

(Continuous into:)

SCENE 25   Off Camera

A LIST OF SCENES THAT NEVER MADE IT ON CAMERA.

The Man and the Boy come out of the darkness to join the Extra. They too are wearing period clothing now.

THE MAN: They give Achilles a triangle to wear, so they will know him when they see him.

THE BOY: Patroclus hides in a forest for twenty days.

THE EXTRA: The Amazon quits her sister and goes home to see their father die, filled with stones.

THE MAN: A child on the street points at Achilles and shouts.

THE BOY: Patroclus eats the bark off of trees.

THE EXTRA: The Amazon orders a thousand whiskeys in a thousand empty bars.

THE BOY: Patroclus dies of the cold, far from his own country.

THE MAN: Achilles boards a train to a place of no return.

THE EXTRA: The Amazon does nothing but watch.

THE MAN, THE BOY AND THE EXTRA: Close-up
Mid shot
Long shot
Out.

(Blackout.)

EPILOGUE   Off Camera

Light slowly returns. The Frau on her deathbed many years later.

THE FRAU: The Frau lived forever
THE EXTRA: As she'd always threatened to.
THE FRAU: She outlived the war. She outlived the century itself.
THE EXTRA: And year after year, the journalists asked her why
    she'd destroyed the film.
        On this, she always declined to comment
THE FRAU: Preferring to direct their attention to her fierce new
    hobby, hang gliding.
THE EXTRA: She couldn't be pressed further, even with choco-
    late biscuits. And no one could have known that the nega-
    tives still looped through her dreams:
THE BOY: The boy with a look of surrender in his eyes.
THE MAN: The man who couldn't take his eyes off him.
THE EXTRA: The woman at the edge of the frame.

(The Extra looks to the Frau.)

And the woman at the center, staring into her own camera.

(The Extra, the Man, and the Boy surround the bed, watching her.)

THE FRAU: When she finally died, the cameras came to see it
THE MAN: To catch a last glimpse of her
THE BOY: Before an everlasting life, off camera.
THE EXTRA: And she found it impossible not to direct the cameramen from her deathbed.
THE FRAU *(Out, as if to the cameramen)*: Closer.

(During the following, the lights slowly dim to focus on the Frau, as if zooming to an extreme close-up. As the lights dim, the Boy, the Man, and the Extra are edged out of the "frame," one by one.)

Bring the camera close, or you won't find anything.
   I am not afraid to look like an old woman.
THE EXTRA: And a strange thing:
THE FRAU: Closer
THE BOY: The closer the cameras came . . .

(The Boy is outside of the frame now.)

THE FRAU: Closer
THE MAN: . . . The less they saw of her.

(The Man is outside the frame now.)

THE FRAU: Closer
THE EXTRA: Until once again, the Frau was alone at the center of the frame.

(The Extra is outside the frame now.)

THE FRAU: Bring it close enough to see behind my eyes. How else will you learn anything?

THE EXTRA: And her sister looked on, quietly, an Extra in the final scene of her life.

THE FRAU: Closer.

Closer.

Closer.

(Light fades.)

END OF PLAY

DORIS TO DARLENE, A CAUTIONARY VALENTINE

PRODUCTION HISTORY

Doris to Darlene had its world premiere at Playwrights Horizons (Tim Sanford, Artistic Director; Leslie Marcus, Managing Director) in New York City on December 11, 2007. It was directed by Les Waters. The scenic design was by Takeshi Kata, the costume design was by Christal Weatherly, the lighting design was by Jane Cox, the sound design was by Darron L. West, the original music was by Kirsten Childs, the music arrangement and production were by Victor Zupanc; and the production stage manager was Elizabeth Moreau. The cast was:

DORIS	de'Adre Aziza
VIC WATTS	Michael Crane
RICHARD WAGNER	David Chandler
KING LUDWIG II	Laura Heisler
MR. CAMPANI	Tom Nelis
YOUNG MAN	Tobias Segal

Doris to Darlene was written with the generous support of a NEA/TCG Playwright-in-Residence Grant at The Empty Space Theatre (Allison Narver, Artistic Director; Melanie Matthews, Managing Director) in Seattle, Washington, and a McKnight Advancement Grant from the Playwrights' Center (P. Carl, Producing Artistic Director) in Minneapolis, Minnesota.

CHARACTERS

Six Actors

DORIS, a girl singer, mixed-race, from sixteen to forty-one.

VIC WATTS, a record producer, white, from twenty-two to forty-seven.

RICHARD WAGNER, a composer, around fifty.

LUDWIG II, KING OF BAVARIA, eighteen. (To be played by a young woman.)

MR. CAMPANI, a dapper teacher, early forties.

THE YOUNG MAN, sixteen.

NOTE

While Doris and Vic Watts age more than twenty years over the course of the play, I encourage using actors toward the young end of this spectrum.

ON THE DOUBLING

All of the principals double in smaller roles from time to time. This should feel informal, playful—their disguises are by no means complete:

DORIS'S GRANDMOTHER is played by the actor who plays Mr. Campani.

THE RECEPTIONIST is played by the actress who plays Ludwig.

MISS LUFTUS is played by the actor who plays Wagner.

PROM DATE is played by Ludwig.

TALK SHOW HOST is played by Wagner.

BILLY ZIMMER is played by Vic Watts.

JOURNALISTS 1 AND 2 are played by Mr. Campani and the Young Man.

STABLE BOY is played by the Young Man.

PFORDTEN is played by Doris and PFISTERMEISTER is played by Vic Watts.

MAKEUP GIRL IS played by Ludwig.

ON THE THIRD PERSON

All of the characters have the ability to narrate the story from time to time. "Live" dialogue is indicated in **boldface**, like so . . .

> DORIS: And Doris stands there in her best dress thinking:
> **No way will Grandmother call me by some name some *man* gave me.**

I suspect that bolded and unbolded speech shouldn't actually sound very different. The narration should still be in character and should feel like part of the action. It is rarely delivered straight to the audience. This isn't a story that the characters have told before—it's still happening. (In fact, maybe it's a mistake to call it "narration" at all.) The third person language can be spoken directly from one actor to another, whenever this pleases.

ACT ONE

PROLOGUE

Doris has a portable record player and a record album under her arm. It is an early girl-group record. The Chantels would be good.

The Young Man and King Ludwig II are there as well. The three young people of the play, each in the dress of a different century.

YOUNG MAN: **This story is about where music comes from.**

KING LUDWIG II: **This story is about how you put it on paper, and how you take it back off again.**

DORIS: **This story is about people with music in their heads, and the people who put it there.**

(Doris takes the record out of its sleeve and puts it on the record player.)

LUDWIG: **Sometimes a song jumps across a century.**

YOUNG MAN: **It finds a new listener and lives again.**

(Doris lowers the arm onto the record. We hear the scratching.)

DORIS: **This story is about: How can you sing a song for someone you never even met?**

(Doris starts to dance to the music, like a girl alone in her bedroom. The Young Man and Ludwig watch her.
Light shifts. Continuous into:)

SCENE 1

LUDWIG: Doris.

YOUNG MAN: Doris.

DORIS: Doris is sixteen and she lives with her grandmother at the edge of a big city.

YOUNG MAN: Doris is sixteen and she longs for that big city, where pop music has just been invented.

LUDWIG: Doris is sixteen and she goes to school at Harper's Gulch High, where there is no music.

DORIS: But one morning she does not go to school.
One morning she walks till she can't see the house.

(The actor who plays Mr. Campani plays Doris's Grandmother.)

GRANDMOTHER: She can still feel her grandmother watching the speck of her on the horizon.

DORIS: Soon as she's out of sight she puts on her special red lipstick.
She catches the Number 9 bus to a building downtown.
The elevator stops at the penthouse, the doors open and pink and everywhere pink and ouch, the pink!

(The Ludwig actor steps in to play the Receptionist:)

RECEPTIONIST: **Welcome to High Wattage Studios. You got an appointment?**

DORIS: **My name is Doris and I'm here to see Mr. Vic Watts at ten o'clock sharp.**

RECEPTIONIST (*Looking straight at her*): An appraising pause.

DORIS: **Doris Unsworth?**

RECEPTIONIST (*Her hand shooting out to touch Doris*): **Oh *right*, the girl from the talent contest.**

DORIS (*Looking down at the hand*): Her fingernails are pink. Same pink as the walls, the carpet, the ashtray. She must have noticed Doris staring, cuz she says:

RECEPTIONIST: **Mr. Watts likes it pink. Mr. Watts wants his Think Space to look like cotton candy.**

DORIS: And Doris pretends to read one of the gossip rags while really she's watching the clock go 9:56, 9:57, 9:58, 9:59—

VIC WATTS: **No no no no no no no.**

(*Continuous into:*)

SCENE 2

Cigarette smoke drifts over the top of a tall black swivel chair. Vic Watts swivels around so we can see him for the first time.

VIC WATTS: **Doris Unsworth is no *good*. Doris Unsworth doesn't *sing*. Correction: Doris Unsworth sings but her name does not. What the public wants is Doris DuPont, Delicious Doris, Doo-Wop Doris, the Duchess of Doris. Doris Duke. Doris *Day*. (All the good ideas are used up.) Doris Duvall? Doris DuPont. The public wants alliteration and by God we'll give it to them. Or do away with plain ol' Doris all together and we get something like Darlene. *Darlene* DuPont. Darlene**

DuPont is a girl other girls want to *be*. You're turning a funny color, Darlene.

DORIS: Doris wonders what kind of man wears aviator glasses indoors.

VIC WATTS: **I never seen a black girl who blushed.**

DORIS: **My mother was black. My dad was from France.**

VIC WATTS: **Lucky for us, your face matches your voice.**

DORIS *(Thinking that was flirty but not sure)*: **Mr. Watts?**

VIC WATTS: **You're a pretty girl with a pretty voice and I think we can make something of you. How does that sound, Darlene?**

DORIS: And Doris stands there in her best dress thinking:

No way will Grandmother call me by some name some *man* gave me.

SCENE 3

DORIS: Soon as the door closes behind her, Doris hears:

VIC WATTS: Soft strange notes needling from Vic's hi-fi, soft. And strange.

(Underneath the following, we hear the early bars of Wagner's "Liebestod." We see King Ludwig II, young and pretty, in a waistcoat, with Wagner in a luxurious dressing gown.)

LUDWIG: Young King Ludwig II builds a dream palace in the mountains of Bavaria. The peasants are scandalized by the pink marble. Inside, Wagner sleeps very comfortably indeed. His sleep is quieted by the pink stone, which repels sound more effectively than all other colors.

RICHARD WAGNER: Wagner dreams of enchanted swans, and dragons, and swords with names.

LUDWIG: In the next chamber, King Ludwig dreams of taller mountains, and pinker palaces, and Wagner.

DORIS: Peeking through the keyhole, Doris sees:

VIC WATTS: Vic Watts has his eyes shut tight behind those glasses.

DORIS: Vic Watts doesn't listen to the music he makes for teenagers.

WAGNER: Vic Watts only listens to Wagner, whose music takes him far from himself. Or toward himself: he can't be sure yet.

DORIS: And Doris lets herself think a dangerous thought:

LUDWIG AND WAGNER *(Whispering in Doris's ear)*: **Maybe there's more to him than meets the eye.**

SCENE 4

VIC WATTS: Vic sends Doris back to Harper's Gulch in a long black car that smells like new.

DORIS: She makes it in time for fifth period

VIC WATTS *(As if planting these thoughts in her head)*: But the names of European capitals swim on the blackboard while she thinks, "What would it be like to step off a sharp-nosed silver jet into one of those European capitals on the arm of that little Machiavelli in sunglasses?" Together they'll sample the finest things of Europe:

DORIS: **The waffles of Belgium,**
    The Black Forest cakes,
    The fries of France!

MISS LUFTUS: Doris barely notices when old Miss Luftus asks her a question.

DORIS: **Huh?**

MISS LUFTUS: **Doris, perhaps you can daydream the capital of Luxembourg for us?**

DORIS: Doris turns the color of the pink walls at High Watt-age Studios.

The boys in the back row lock eyes, as if to say:

EVERYONE (*As students*): Who ever saw a black girl turn pink.

DORIS: Doris walks home from school. Glad to be home.

VIC WATTS: **Wait.**

DORIS (*Not hearing him*): Like she's been somewhere dangerous and now she's back safe.

VIC WATTS AND MISS LUFTUS: **Wait!**

DORIS: Back safe with a secret. Hand on the doorknob.

EVERYONE: **WAIT!**

DORIS: **My special red lipstick!**

She remembers just in time to wipe it off with tissue just as the door opens / and there

GRANDMOTHER (*Overlapping at "/"*): And there is Grandmother, there is her same old grandma not suspecting a thing.

DORIS: **Grandma.**

GRANDMOTHER: **Doris.**

DORIS (*It sounds funny now*): **Doris.**

GRANDMOTHER: **You look flushed.**

DORIS: **Cold out there.**

GRANDMOTHER (*Shaking her head*): **Who ever saw a black girl turn pink.**

DORIS (*Attitude*): **You did, I guess.**

GRANDMOTHER: **Where do you think you're going?**

DORIS: *Bandstand* **is on.**

GRANDMOTHER: **Not till you water my zinnias it isn't. They're parched.**

DORIS (*Quiet, almost to herself*): **I know how they feel.**

GRANDMOTHER (*But Grandma notices*): **You got a fire under your skin, poor girl. Just like your mom did.**

DORIS: **Not like her, like me.**

GRANDMOTHER: **Doris!**

DORIS: **Now on, you can call me Darlene.**

SCENE 5

DORIS: Vic Watts spares no expense on Darlene's first single.

VIC WATTS: **Give me a hundred violins, Barry. Gimme a millionteen tubas. Electric harpsichords. Little combo of Romanian gypsies for the bridge. Get those gypsies on a plane and bring them here. I want a wall of sound for our girl Darlene. I want ears bleeding. I want hearts bleeding. I want little teenage hearts hemorrhaging into the radio all across our great nation!**

DORIS: The lyrics prove to be a problem.

VIC WATTS: **It's not rocket science, Darlene.**
  "Shoppa loppa shoop shoop.
  He's sure the boy for me."

DORIS: "Shoppa loppa shoop shoop." "Shoopa loopa shop shop." What's the difference, it's all stupid.

VIC WATTS: **Respect, Darlene. There is a kind of genius in the stupidity of pop, Darlene, and we must respect that or we'll be out on the street with Nat King Whatshisname and all the fossils of yesteryear.**

DORIS: There are three other girls in the group, but only Doris sits in the control room with Vic. She feels a little thrill when she sees the envy in their faces.

VIC WATTS (*Putting headphones on her head*): **Listen to this playback, baby.**

DORIS: Sometimes hers is the only voice that makes it on the record.

(Together with a recording of herself:)

Herself repeated many times over.

(Together with ten recordings of herself:)

A chorus of Doris.

VIC WATTS: **One more take for me, baby. Can you do that for me?**

DORIS: **I'm tired, Vic.**

VIC WATTS (*Smooth*): **Tired's what happens when you do your thing, baby.**

DORIS: He touches her knee.

VIC WATTS: **Baby?**

DORIS: And she relents.

VIC WATTS (*Shouting off*): **Take forty-seven, boys!**

(*We hear the rhythm track start up, moving straight into:*)

SCENE 6

DORIS (*Into the mike*): Doris's voice starts in her diaphragm, passes through her larynx, travels into the microphone, through time, and out the woofers and tweeters of the future into the ears of a Young Man with a heartache, who wonders:

YOUNG MAN: What is it about these dilemmas that captivate his contemporary heart?

Tommy's from the wrong side of the tracks, Brenda wasn't invited to the party . . . How do these things put a lump in his cynical twenty-first-century throat?

DORIS (*Looking at him*): The Young Man is sixteen and he lives at the edge of a big city where girl groups are old news.

YOUNG MAN (*Not looking at her*): But he shuts his bedroom door and plays Darlene's songs like they're brand-new.

DORIS: Why is she his favorite? If he had the words, the Young Man might say:

YOUNG MAN: **What I love about her voice is its very lack of experience. Pure and clear, it functions as a girlish replacement for my own, less speakable desires.**

DORIS (*Their eyes meet for the first time*): But he doesn't have the words, not yet.

SCENE 7

Under the following, a not-very-soulful late '50s/early '60s song. Something with Doris Day would be good. Distant and tinny, as if over the radio.

GRANDMOTHER: Doris fixes the big bow on her prom dress while her date sits downstairs with Grandma.

(The Ludwig actor plays her Prom Date, a nerd.)

PROM DATE: **I know all the latest dances. I know the Frug, the Swim, the Mashed Potato, the Green Tomato, the Phat Phatoozie, the Special Sauce. I know the Locomotion, I know the Commotion. I know the Five Figure Promotion. Your daughter will have a good time tonight.**

GRANDMOTHER: **Doris is my granddaughter.**

PROM DATE: **Of course she is. Just you look so young. I can't believe you're a grandma.**

GRANDMOTHER *(Steely)*: Grandmother doesn't say anything.

PROM DATE: The cherry phosphates fizz in front of them, on coasters.

GRANDMOTHER: **Would I know your family, Steven? Are they churchgoers?**

DORIS: Doris descends, just in time, looking like a fancy cake.

PROM DATE: **Darlene, wow.**

DORIS: **Hi, Steven.**

PROM DATE: **Still can't believe you're going to your own prom, a big success like you.**

DORIS: **I'm just Doris, Steven. Doris from homeroom.**

GRANDMOTHER: **Yesterday she was Darlene.**

DORIS *(To Steven, ignoring Grandmother)*: **Whenever I walk into that school I feel like Doris again.**

PROM DATE *(Playful)*: **Well, I got a corsage here for Darlene.**

(Suddenly, the song she recorded with Vic comes on the radio. After the earlier song, it sounds comparatively expansive and soulful. Grandmother turns in the direction of the sound. Doris is spellbound.)

GRANDMOTHER: **Good grief, Doris, is that you?**
DORIS: The first time she ever heard herself on the radio.
GRANDMOTHER: **Is that Wagner he has you singing?**
DORIS: And she likes what she hears.
GRANDMOTHER: **Wagner with tom-toms?**
DORIS: **Mr. Watts says it's public domain, so.**
GRANDMOTHER: **It's filthy music.**
PROM DATE *(Suddenly interested)*: **Yeah?**
DORIS: Ten years later, Doris will remember the first time she heard her own voice.
GRANDMOTHER: Ten years later, Grandmother is dead and the song can't hurt her anymore.
PROM DATE: Ten years later, Steven still has the corsage he gave her, mummified in a little glass box.
DORIS: But here in the present, there's no time for reflection. Here in the present, everything starts to happen very fast.
VIC WATTS *(Off)*: **Show me the Billboards, Louie.**

(Light shifts.)

DORIS: The single tops the Pop charts for two weeks
VIC WATTS *(Walking on with the Billboard Charts)*: **Five weeks on the R&B.**
DORIS: Doris barely goes to high school anymore.
VIC WATTS: Vic signs her permission slips.
DORIS: Instead of French, she studies how to talk to the press.
VIC WATTS: She is a quick study.

(Light shifts.)

DORIS (*As if to the press*): **I am so privileged to be in this business. I thank God every day. I thank God and Mr. Vic Watts for showing me the power of music.**

VIC WATTS: **Ladies and gentlemen, they're all ready to do their thing. Introducing Darlene and the Daybreakers!**

(Doris turns to look at Vic and the song starts. We hear Wagner's "Liebestod" completely orchestrated like a '60s girl group song. Tom-tom drums, tambourines, handclaps, and Doris:)

DORIS (*Singing*):

> **Do you hear that song**
> **When he walks by?**
> **Makes me sing**
> **When he looks in my eyes . . .**

SCENE 8

The song fades down and we hear Wagner singing the same melody in an unsteady baritone. King Ludwig watches, rapt.

VIC WATTS: Before the song was Vic's hit single, it was notes from the pen of an even more difficult genius.

DORIS (*Pronouncing it very wrong*): Richard Wagner

VIC WATTS (*Pronouncing it sort of wrong*): Richard Wagner

WAGNER (*Pronouncing it perfectly, as if correcting them*): Richard Wagner sings the "Liebestod" for the first time in an unsteady baritone. He struggles to decipher his own mad scratchings.

LUDWIG: The young King Ludwig II watches. His courtiers try to ignore the pheasant waiting for them, fragrant, in the banquet room.

WAGNER: It occurs to Wagner that he is singing, quite literally, for his supper.

LUDWIG: The great man looks up from the page for a moment to explain: Isolde dies of love.

WAGNER: **In death she finds release, at last, like an orgasm.**

LUDWIG: The eighteen-year-old monarch looks at his feet and blushes.

WAGNER: **I'm sure you have heard the French term "*petit mort*." Well this is a *grand mort*.**

LUDWIG: Ludwig II rushes out to the terrace.

He mops his brow,

He breathes the night air,

He counts the swans in his man-made pond,

He reminds himself: **You are *King*.**

WAGNER: **My King—**

LUDWIG: The great man seems almost vulnerable, asking:

WAGNER: **My King, did you not enjoy the performance?**

LUDWIG: **On the contrary—**

I found myself so overwhelmed by its beauty that I could not bear to stay.

WAGNER: And something unheard of: Wagner blushes back.

LUDWIG: They stay on the terrace together, awake with the night air.

WAGNER: **My kindred,**

LUDWIG: Wagner says, touching him on the shoulder.

WAGNER: **My young kindred, who has never known love, but can recognize its notes.**

You will be a true lover of the arts.

LUDWIG: And, like a fairy tale, Ludwig waves his hand and brushes away Wagner's debt.

WAGNER: They go inside and eat the pheasant.

LUDWIG: (Which is really a pheasant stuffed with a goose stuffed with a guinea hen stuffed with a quince.)

WAGNER: **You live well, my friend. Very well indeed.**

SCENE 9

DORIS: Before she can even enjoy her number-one hit, Vic brings Doris a new song.

VIC WATTS: **I wrote it for you, baby.**

DORIS *(Looking down at the page)*: Doris reads the simple lyrics about a black girl with straight hair. Pretty black girl with white-girl hair and the guy who makes her want to sing, every time she looks in his dark glasses. *(Looking at Vic now)* And she thinks: This sure sounds familiar.

VIC WATTS: **Whaddaya think?**

DORIS: **How come it's the same.**

VIC WATTS: **What do you mean it's the same?**

DORIS: **All your songs got the same story. The girl is into a guy who everybody thinks is no good, but she can see on the inside he's really solid gold.**

VIC WATTS: **See, Darlene, every pop song is a little bitty drama and you only have 2.5 minutes to get through both acts. You got your conflict: The guy's no good. You got your resolution: Actually he's pretty good. See how that works?**

DORIS: **I just thought maybe there's a reason you like to write about the guy nobody likes.** *(Sly)* **I thought maybe you know that guy.**

VIC WATTS *(Looking at her)*: And Vic thinks for the first time: Maybe this is a prize worth fighting for.

DORIS *(Looking at him)*: And Doris thinks for the first time: Maybe he doesn't know how to win me.

VIC WATTS: **Tell me about your mom and dad. You never talk about yourself.**

DORIS: **Not much to tell.**

VIC WATTS: **Then it won't take long.**

DORIS: He was an exchange student. I guess nobody in France told him he wasn't supposed to get with a black girl. They were real young. And then they had me and I could never figure out *what* I was. Straight hair from Dad, and skin that tells you what I'm thinking behind it.

VIC WATTS: Oh yeah?

DORIS: I mean, the way I blush when I'm nervous.

VIC WATTS: You're blushing right now.

DORIS: And Doris blushes even more.

VIC WATTS: Whatta you got to be nervous about anyway?

(She leans in and kisses him.)

The guy's supposed to kiss the girl.

DORIS: This isn't one of your love songs.

VIC WATTS: Maybe it is, baby.

(As he kisses her back, the dark recording studio floats in.)

Easy on the mike, now. You're not Kate Smith singing the goddamn National Anthem.

DORIS: Where's everybody else?

VIC WATTS *(Handing her headphones)*: They'll be right there in your ear. I laid them all down yesterday, so you can sing it just for me.

DORIS: There in the dark, all Doris can see is her own reflection, suspended over him, in the glass of the recording booth.

VIC WATTS: Then Vic flips a switch, and it's like he's playing a hundred violins straight into her head.

(Pause. We don't hear the music at first, only Doris does—but we can see that there's music in her head.

Doris starts to sing into the mike, straight to Vic. The music starts to rise up as she sings, so that we come to hear what she's hearing.)

DORIS *(Rhythmically spoken intro)*:

> They say he's too cool to love me right
> They say he acts like the prince of night
> But if they could look in his eyes, they'd see
> Oh gosh, oh golly, that boy loves me.

(Singing now:)

> Guess he likes the way I do my hair
> When he holds my hand the other girls stare
> But I don't really care,

> *No-whoa-whoa-whoa-whoa-whoa*

> No I don't really care,

> *Whoa-whoa-whoa-whoa-whoa-whoa.*

> I don't really care,
> Everything around me fades
> Cuz I'm too busy staring
> Into his deep, dark shades.
> I can see our future,
> I know I know I know we got it made
> Yeah the future is ours now—

(She stops singing, but the backing track continues, the melody soaring.)

> **Sorry.**

VIC WATTS: **Why'd you stop? Don't it feel good?**

DORIS: **"The future is ours." Just—sounds a little cocky is all.**

VIC WATTS: **Sounds pretty goddamn good is what it sounds.**

(During the following, Vic takes her face in his hands.)

DORIS: She doesn't tell Vic the real reason she stopped:
  She can feel his power, and she can feel her own power,
  and it's lifting her up so high she's scared to look down.

SCENE 10

YOUNG MAN: The Young Man walks into class with Darlene in
  his ears.

*(We hear the same song, faint now, as if it's bleeding out of the
Young Man's headphones.)*

MR. CAMPANI: The first day of school, and the new teacher tells
  him to take off his headphones.

(The song suddenly goes out.)

YOUNG MAN: **This is Music Appreciation, isn't it?**
MR. CAMPANI *(Not unkind)*: **You'll appreciate the music I choose,
  when I choose.**
YOUNG MAN: The new teacher, Mr. Campani, is different. The
  students are scandalized by his pink bow tie.
MR. CAMPANI: Mr. Campani wears argyle socks and does not
  slouch.
YOUNG MAN: Mr. Campani does not say "doesn't." He says "does
  not." You can see your reflection in his shoes.
MR. CAMPANI: He looks like he came into this world clean and
  he stayed that way.
YOUNG MAN: The boys in the back row lock eyes with one
  another, as if to say:
EVERYONE *(As boys)*: **"I know what he is."**

MR. CAMPANI: Mr. Campani is flamboyant.

YOUNG MAN: But Mr. Campani is *shrewdly* flamboyant: Not a body flapping against all social codes, but a body that knows punctuation. *(We see the following)* His wrist flies to his brow to indicate the hot sufferings of Werther; two fingers at his throat for consumptive Violetta, her headvoice resurrected for one last hurrah. He acts out all the great opera scenes for us. But although he says:

MR. CAMPANI: **I was once a singer**

YOUNG MAN: . . . He never sings us a note.

MR. CAMPANI: **At first I was scared of opera, like you**

YOUNG MAN: He says, seeming to read our thoughts.

MR. CAMPANI: **But when I saw Wagner's *Götterdämmerung*, I was so overwhelmed with emotion that I ran up the aisle and vomited in the lobby, right there on the red carpet.**

YOUNG MAN: The teacher looks him straight in the eye, as though recognizing him for who he is: A romantic, a kindred upchucker, a queer.

MR. CAMPANI: **Have any of you ever felt something like that, watching a performance?**

YOUNG MAN: The Young Man looks down at his college-rule paper and blushes.

MR. CAMPANI *(Looking straight at the Young Man)*: **Anyone?**

SCENE 11

We hear a talk show jingle. Rising chimes.

VIC WATTS: Vic goes on a TV talk show with a man who talks even faster than him.

TALK SHOW HOST: **In case you just tuned in, we've been talking to Detroit's boy blunder, record producer Vic Watts.**

That's right, the whiz kid himself, here with his canary of the moment, the lovely Miss Darlene DuPont.

DORIS: Doris sits there thinking, "Canaries don't sing as good as nightingales."

VIC WATTS: Thanks for having us, Stu.

DORIS: "Canaries just look pretty and die fast."

TALK SHOW HOST: Vic, I want the folks out there in teevee land to get a taste of that crazy ear candy you're feeding the kids these days.

VIC WATTS: It's your show, Stu.

TALK SHOW HOST: If I may read a quick sample:

(He puts on spectacles, theatrically.)

I believe this is Darlene's new single "Gosh, Golly, He Loves Me."

(He reads very dry—no rhythm, no enthusiasm.)

"Guess he likes the way I do my hair.
When he holds my hand the other girls stare.
But I don't really care.
No whoa whoa whoa whoa whoa.
No, I don't really care.
Whoa whoa whoa whoa—"

DORIS: That's not how it sounds. Vic / makes it—

TALK SHOW HOST: Just a minute, sweetheart. It's not finished yet:

(Very official again:)

"Whoa whoa whoa whoa whoa whoa."

(He pauses importantly, looks at Vic.)

Now is that what you call a lyric, friend?
DORIS: Vic keeps it cool.
TALK SHOW HOST: **The way you rhyme "whoa" with "whoa." You need a rhyming dictionary for that?**
DORIS: Vic acts real cool, but Doris can see him dig his fingernails into the armchair till it leaves marks.
VIC WATTS: **My songs are for dancing to. My songs are for falling in love to. They weren't meant for reading. You need the mix. You need the sweet sound machine. That's where I come in. So do me a favor and read that again, friend.**
TALK SHOW HOST: **Sorry?**
VIC WATTS: **Just read me that over from the start: "Guess he likes the way I do my hair . . ."**

(A reluctant pause.)

TALK SHOW HOST: **"Guess he likes the way I do my hair . . ."**
VIC WATTS: **Real nice, now just keep on keeping on like that.**

(Talk Show Host repeats "Guess he likes the way I do my hair" over and over.)

First off you add the rhythm track. Lay some hands on me, baby.

(Doris starts to do handclaps.)

You got a sweet sound, Stu. Maybe you can come work for me when they cancel your show.
TALK SHOW HOST *(Uncomfortable)*: Ha ha.

VIC WATTS: **Once you lay that down, you add some more rhythm: Some tom-toms, taste of Africa.** *(Vic starts stomping his foot, in rhythm)* **The high hat, taste of Detroit.** *(Doris makes the sound of a high hat)* **Now what we're gonna do is dub that together on the rhythm track and add a whole mess of chicks going:**

VIC WATTS AND DORIS:
> *Ooh Ooh, Ooh*
> *Ooh Ooh, Ooh . . .*

VIC WATTS: **And to that you add some even messier chicks going:**

DORIS:
> *Ah Ah, Ah*
> *Ah Ah, Ah . . .*

(It has become a rousing, catchy tune now—majestic even:)

DORIS:	VIC WATTS:	TALK SHOW HOST:
Ah Ah, Ah	**Ooh Ooh, Ooh**	*Guess he likes the*
Ah Ah, Ah	**Ooh Ooh, Ooh**	*way I do my hair*
Ah Ah, Ah	**Then you add a rainstorm,**	*Guess he likes the*
Ah Ah, Ah	**you add a glockenspiel, you**	*way I do my hair*
Ah Ah, Ah	**add a Javanese gamelan, you**	*Guess he likes the*
Ah Ah, Ah	**lay on a track of the goddamn**	*way I do my hair*
Ah Ah, Ah	**president going, "Ich bin ein**	*Guess he likes—*
Ah Ah, Ah	**Berliner," you add some echo**	
Ah Ah, Ah—	**you add a hundred violins—**	

(Vic Watts ends the "song" abruptly—dramatically, like a conductor ending Beethoven's Fifth.)

VIC WATTS: **And that, my friend, is a motherfuckin' top-ten hit.**

(Looking out:)

Can I say that on TV?

SCENE 12

LUDWIG: King Ludwig moves Wagner to his dream palace in the mountains of Bavaria. Exotic birds festoon the trees; trained bears dance the latest steps in the great courtyard.

(Wagner ascends his tower for the first time.)

WAGNER: Wagner shuts himself in the tallest tower, where he begins his great *Ring* cycle.
LUDWIG: The friendship grows
WAGNER: The friendship verges on immoderacy.
LUDWIG: **My lion of culture!**
WAGNER: **My speckled little rooster!**
LUDWIG: **My artist, my everything! Keeper of our future!**
WAGNER *(Distastefully)*: Ludwig's advisors . . .

(Doris plays Pfordten and Vic Watts plays Pfistermeister. Perhaps they each have a monocle in a different eye?)

PFORDTEN: Pfordten
PFISTERMEISTER: Und Pfistermeister
WAGNER: . . . Suspect that the King is growing too close to his resident genius.
LUDWIG: One night, at a state dinner, Wagner calls the King
WAGNER: ***Mein junge,***

LUDWIG *(Moved)*: "My boy."

PFISTERMEISTER: Old Pfistermeister narrows his eyes,

PFORDTEN: Old Pfordten tugs his mustache.

WAGNER: **I meant no impudence, dear sirs.**

LUDWIG: . . . While Ludwig pretends to be offended.

WAGNER: Whenever they aren't watching, Wagner puts his feet up on the damask as an army of servants takes down his demands.

LUDWIG: **Whatever you desire, you shall have it!**

(It would be good if the look of this evoked Vic's "I want hearts bleeding" speech.)

WAGNER: **Give me a hundred piccolos. Give me a million-teen timpani.**

LUDWIG: **You ask too little!**

WAGNER: **Give me a hundred cannons and a hundred soldiers to light them. Horses with a sense of syncopation. I want war, I want Waterloo! They say when the smoke cleared on the battlefield, no one could tell who won. It will be the same when the music ends in the concert hall: No one will know who won!**

SCENE 13

GRANDMOTHER: With her arthritis, it takes Doris's grandmother five minutes to walk out to the mailbox.

DORIS: She receives three bills, a coupon book, and a letter from High Wattage Studios, which she waits all morning to open.

VIC WATTS *(Speaking out; cordial in a slick way)*:
Dear Mrs. Unsworth,
I am writing to congratulate you on raising such an exemplary granddaughter. It's clear that Darlene

grew up with a true feminine ideal in the house. If you see her too seldom these days, it is simply because we are busy preparing her for the world: Voice coaches, image advisers, posture consultants, stylists—all for one special young lady.

I thank you also for your letter dated June the 16th and respectfully disregard its rather quarrelsome tone as the well-intended concerns of a doting guardian. Darlene has also asked me to request that you stop attempting to contact her by telephone, as the rigors of her concert tour demand a stress-free environment. *(He holds up a photograph of Doris)* I am enclosing an autographed 8x10 glossy of Darlene so that she can be right at home with you even while she's off on the ride of her life.

Cordially,
Vic Watts
Dictated but not read.

GRANDMOTHER: Grandmother rips the letter into many small pieces.

DORIS: But she takes the glossy picture of Doris and puts it in a beautiful frame. She puts it where she'll see it every day and think:

GRANDMOTHER: **Where'd he put the girl I knew?**

(Grandmother turns to see Doris, just as Doris turns away.)

What tall tower has he trapped her in?

(Light shifts. Continuous into:)

SCENE 14

Doris opens her eyes.

VIC WATTS: **Happy birthday, baby.**

DORIS: Vic gives Doris a Rolls for her sweet seventeen.

VIC WATTS: Doris doesn't know what to say.

DORIS: **Big red bow!**

VIC WATTS: **Who ever saw such a shiny thing, huh baby?**

DORIS: **Like the flyest hearse I ever seen.**

VIC WATTS: **It's a funny way of thinking, but yeah.**

DORIS: And he plants a minty

VIC WATTS: **Smooch**

DORIS: On her lips. She opens her eyes on the kiss and sees:

VIC WATTS: His eyes shut tight, just like when he listens to Wagner.

DORIS: And he seems like such a *boy* to her all of a sudden—this mad genius who everyone is scared of but not her. She does the math in her head: Six weeks we've been together. Six weeks and three days.

VIC WATTS: **Baby.**

DORIS: **Mmnh?**

VIC WATTS: **Have a look in the glove compartment.**

DORIS *(Playful)*: **What's in there—gloves?**

VIC WATTS: **Just look.**

DORIS: **A ring?**

VIC WATTS: **Happy birthday, baby.**

DORIS: **A diamond—that means . . .**

VIC WATTS: **You're my sound, baby. You're my *voice*.**

DORIS *(Embracing him)*: **Oh, Vic!**

VIC WATTS: **If it weren't for you, how would I say anything.**

DORIS: But right in the middle of their perfect moment, the Santa Ana wind sweeps through the Valley and catches Vic's toupee like a kite / and—

VIC WATTS: And suddenly boy producer Vic Watts looks like he's right on the brink of a midlife crisis.

DORIS: **Vic?**

VIC WATTS *(Recovering the toupee)*: **Shit. Shit.**

DORIS: **Vic, it's okay, my hair's falling out too.**

VIC WATTS *(The toupee back on now)*: **I don't know what you're talking about.**

DORIS *(Going to him, tenderly)*: **All the teasing, all that dye. It comes out on my comb every morning.**

VIC WATTS: **What are you talking about? I got a full head of hair.**

DORIS: And for the first time since he gave her a new name, she sees: Vic's got a dangerous talent for making things so, just by saying it.

SCENE 15

WAGNER: **I want a babbling brook to inspire me! I want a mountain to echo my notes back to me a hundredfold! I want a bird that sings Brahms in my ear till I sleep! No, Bach—I detest Brahms.**

LUDWIG: Word spreads of Wagner's state-sponsored excess. The Munich journalists write:

(Campani and the Young Man play the Journalists.)

JOURNALIST 1: **"Is he to forge Germany's bold new art form in the flames of his own voluptuary?"**

LUDWIG: And, more succinctly:

JOURNALIST 2: **"Perhaps he will write his next opera on the virtues of effeminate decadenza?"**

LUDWIG: And, most succinctly:

JOURNALISTS 1 AND 2: **"What ever happened to the *suffering* artist?"**

WAGNER: And yet, even in this excess, Wagner is not happy.

LUDWIG: **Even smothered in damask und dahlias?**

WAGNER: Wagner is unhappy.

(Ludwig follows Wagner during the following:)

LUDWIG: Every day, he paces the vast wilds of the palace, looking for the inspiration they once offered. But he can no longer find the footprints of the gods. The birds in the thick fir trees no longer possess the power of language. There are no more swords waiting to be named.

WAGNER *(Hushed, fearful)*: There is no more music in his head.

(Continuous into:)

SCENE 16

VIC WATTS: Vic Watts likes it dead quiet.

DORIS: He builds a soundproofed palace in Malibu and shuts Doris inside with him. The neighbors are scandalized by the pink stucco.

VIC WATTS: Songless birds festoon the trees. Bodyguards creep about the grounds, silently. Ten-foot hedges keep the sunlight out.

DORIS: Doris doesn't sing anymore.

VIC WATTS: **Sit back and enjoy retirement, baby.**

DORIS: She hasn't sung a note since that day at the studio Vic said:

(Light shifts. We hear a British Invasion–type song.)

VIC WATTS: **Get a load of this.**

DORIS: **What is it?**

VIC WATTS: **The Wemberly Whigs.**

DORIS: **Wigs?**

VIC WATTS: **W-H-I-G. It's British or something. We'll give them a new name.**

DORIS: **You signed them?**

VIC WATTS: **They're *now*, they're new. They sound like . . . *new*.**

DORIS: **They sound like they're playing in a garage.**

VIC WATTS: **All the guys at the studio think it's ginchy.**

DORIS: **What's "ginchy"?**

VIC WATTS: **It's you about six months ago, baby.**

(Light shifts. Music out.)

DORIS: Now, instead of singing, she looks at her gold records hanging on the wall.

VIC WATTS: The only thing allowed to break the silence is Wagner's "Liebestod," which Vic plays to fall asleep.

(We start to hear the "Liebestod," needling quietly on a record player. The slow, languorous beginning.)

He sleeps soundly, dreaming of gunplay, and bodyguards, and Wagner.

DORIS: But Doris lies awake.

(Pause. The music.)

Dead awake, at two A.M.

VIC WATTS: Finally she stumbles down Vic's seventy-six pink marble stairs to make herself a bologna sandwich.

DORIS: **Quiet in this house, always so *quiet.***

VIC WATTS: The crumbs dropping down on Vic's ice white baby grand.

DORIS: **So quiet I want to break something just to hear the sound it makes.**

VIC WATTS: Tomorrow he will ask her about the crumbs—

DORIS: But she doesn't care. Catching her reflection in the dark window, she asks it: Had Vic Watts really believed he could make a star of her?

VIC WATTS *(Directly to her)*: Had she really believed that he believed?

DORIS: Did love blind him so completely that he thought she could eclipse those other girls? Sarah, with four and a half octaves; Martha, who could shape a song and make it hers.

VIC WATTS: Or had Vic *wanted* an ordinary voice? A mediocre talent that would depend on his decorations. *(Directly to her)* A girl who would follow him anywhere, who would never leave.

DORIS *(Directly to him)*: And so she leaves, just to prove him wrong. Middle of the night, with nothing but the clothes on her back.

VIC WATTS: She leaves the gold records on the wall:

DORIS: **His name on them, not mine.**

(We hear the "Liebestod," but it is slowly overwhelmed by the girl group version.)

VIC WATTS: Vic sleeps right through it, his toupee on the night-stand.

DORIS: In the car, through the night, ninety-miles an hour, all the way to Michigan, Doris sings her voice out.

(All we hear is the girl group version now—classical yields to pop.)

SCENE 17

YOUNG MAN *(With headphones)*: The Young Man plays Darlene so loud that the bells and locker slams fade away, and the dreaded high school becomes nothing but a music video for her song.

MR. CAMPANI: Sometimes, the Young Man follows Mr. Campani.

YOUNG MAN: He starts to take detours from his own dull day in order to walk ten paces behind his teacher:

(We see this.)

Down the long hall from Teacher's Lounge to First Period;
    On to lunchtime and his cigarette breaks behind the stadium;
    Down, after school, to the white Toyota Celica with the bumper sticker that reads:

MR. CAMPANI: **"If it's not baroque, don't fix it."**

YOUNG MAN: The Young Man is propelled, not deterred, by the possibility that his teacher will turn around and discover him there, twenty steps back.

(They both stop walking, a suspended moment. But Campani doesn't turn to look at him.)

MR. CAMPANI: But part of him knows: He'll have to risk more if he wants to be discovered.

(Light shifts.)

YOUNG MAN: For now, the Young Man must be satisfied with the lectures, when he closes his eyes and pretends Mr. Campani's words are just for him:

(Mr. Campani speaks out, in a light of his own. We are his students.)

MR. CAMPANI: Even when I'd just started singing, I could tell Wagner was different—before I read a single note. At the top of his manuscripts, Johann Sebastian Bach wrote the initials "I.N.J." *In Nomine Jesu.* "In the name of Jesus," he wrote on the blank page, hopefully. *In Nomine Jesu*, as if to say: I am not making this to bring myself fame. This is dedicated to something outside of myself.

(We see Ludwig and Wagner now in another part of the stage.)

In giving myself over to divinity, I become it, it takes possession of me, it writes in my hand.

(Wagner lifts his quill.)

At the top of his manuscripts, Richard Wagner wrote, simply:

WAGNER *(Writing)*:	MR. CAMPANI:
Richard Wagner	**"Richard Wagner."**

(Continuous into:)

SCENE 18

WAGNER: Wagner has written nothing on the page but his own name.
LUDWIG: Night after night like this. Ludwig sits at the dinner table alone, and the pheasant grows cold.

WAGNER: Wagner wets and rewets his pen. His candle has almost spent itself. He idly spins a globe, touching the purple paper of the African continent.

LUDWIG: He tears the hair from his head in salt-and-pepper pelts, contemplating the problem of Act Two:

WAGNER: **What would a dragon sing if it could sing?**

LUDWIG: As the composer retreats from the world, his patron rushes headlong into it: Hunting, horseback riding, all the pleasures of the sprawling estate.

(The Young Man plays the Stable Boy in the following:)

WAGNER: Wagner watches from the tower as Ludwig fastens a tiny bell around the stable boy's lovely neck.

LUDWIG: **A trinket for you, my boy. A token.**

STABLE BOY: The stable boy asks **what is it for?**

LUDWIG: **We would not want you taking any birds by surprise.**

STABLE BOY: They were students together, capturing bullfrogs and making them race. But now the young man kneels and kisses the emerald ring on his finger.

LUDWIG: Even as the boy takes him in his mouth, Ludwig cannot help but look to the highest window of the highest tower:

WAGNER: A light

LUDWIG: A candle

WAGNER *(Looking down at his paper)*: Wagner turns away from the window and the cheaper pleasures it frames.

LUDWIG: The same old question on his lips:

WAGNER: What would a dragon sing if it could sing?
      (Looking up) **Of course: It would sing fire!**

(As Wagner starts to write furiously, we hear the orgasmic final minutes of the "Liebestod.")

LUDWIG: As the stable boy brings him to the edge of ecstasy, Ludwig leaves his slight body for a moment and flies up to that faraway window.

WAGNER: *Wer stort mir den Schlaf?* Wagner writes, his cursive unfurling like a skyfull of tails.

LUDWIG: Ludwig presses himself against the glass

WAGNER: But Wagner does not look up from his work.

(They are very close now, inches apart, but Wagner doesn't see him.)

LUDWIG *(With great ardor)*: **I experience life, but without perception.**
You perceive life, but without experience.
Together, could we not be complete?

(Lights shift. The Stable Boy becomes the Young Man before our eyes.)

YOUNG MAN: Just as the King climaxes, the Young Man wakes up in his bed, his sheets sticky with the dream. A biography of Wagner lies open, beside his pillow.

SCENE 19

We still see the Young Man as Mr. Campani speaks out.

MR. CAMPANI: **"Liebestod."** *Liebe* and *Tod.* **Love and death. Unified in one word, one action, one song. The long-delayed climax of Wagner's opera. The soprano has paced herself like a long-distance runner and, after four hours, she can finally spend the rest of her huge voice. "Do I alone hear this melody?" she sings.**

Tristan lies dead at her feet, but she looks out into the audience and sees him resurrected. "Do I alone hear this melody?" The onlookers don't hear anything, and they pity her. But Wagner allows *us* to share in her madness. His orchestra plays the music in her head.

We all know what it's like to have a song in our head no one else can hear. To walk around all day humming a commercial jingle. To look at someone and hear a hundred violins.

(The school bell rings. Mr. Campani looks in its direction.)

Oh for some violins.

YOUNG MAN: And as the tide of students carries him to third period, the Young Man turns back and sees: Mr. Campani mouthing the words of the song.

WAGNER: But the song is not only in a classroom with linoleum floors. It is also in the palace of King Ludwig II, where Wagner sings, squinting at his own black markings.

VIC WATTS: It is also in the studio of Vic Watts, who takes Wagner's black markings and adds tom-tom drums; he adds a tire chain, for rhythm; he adds four backup singers and he adds / Doris

DORIS *(Overlapping)*: Doris turns the black markings back into a song that plays as she comes downstairs in a prom dress, smitten with her own perfected voice. / It plays

YOUNG MAN *(Overlapping)*: It plays in the bedroom of a Young Man, who learns that this dumb pop song says more about desire than he knows how to say. The music teaches him himself. And the next time he is in Mr. Campani's class, the Young Man raises his hand to ask a question.

DORIS *(Looking at Vic)*:	LUDWIG *(Looking at Wagner)*:
Some loves are on the verge of extinction.	Some loves are on the verge of extinction.

YOUNG MAN *(Looking at Campani)*: Others are just beginning.

DORIS: And her song will outlast them all. It plays everywhere. It plays everywhere *but* the pink stucco palace of Vic Watts, who only listens to classical music, who plays the "Liebestod" over and over, with his eyes shut tight, probing it for the secrets of genius.

(A simultaneous event:
Ludwig watches Wagner, writing the song.
Doris watches Vic Watts, bent over his record player.
Lights slowly fade on everything but:
The Young Man, with his hand raised, looking at Mr. Campani.)

YOUNG MAN: **Mr. Campani?**

(Mr. Campani turns and sees him. Violins. The final, shimmering bars of the "Liebestod." The song is all around them, and us. Blackout.)

ACT TWO

SCENE 1

The Young Man raises his hand, just as he did at the end of Act One.
(But the classroom looks ordinary now, fluorescent. No violins.)

YOUNG MAN: **Mr. Campani?**

MR. CAMPANI: **Yes, the young man with the hair in his eyes.**

YOUNG MAN: **Me?**

MR. CAMPANI: **I'm afraid I've forgotten your name.**

YOUNG MAN: **Jacob.**

MR. CAMPANI *(Looking straight at him)*: Jacob wants to ask why
Mr. Campani never sings for them, but he hasn't got the
nerve.

YOUNG MAN: **I wondered, just— Did Wagner want to do that
to people? I mean— Make them run up the aisle and
throw up? Is that what he thought music is supposed
to do?**

MR. CAMPANI: **I suspect, young man, that you already know
the answer.**

YOUNG MAN: Yes?

MR. CAMPANI: Any composer . . . any *artist* hopes to make the audience lose their lunch.

Now did you have a real question for me?

YOUNG MAN: How does it do that, the music?

MR. CAMPANI: I have devoted the last twenty-five years to the study of opera, and truly I do not know.

SCENE 2

LUDWIG: Winter, and Ludwig races across the snow on a crystal-spangled sleigh shaped like the swan from *Lohengrin!*

WAGNER: While Wagner writes.

LUDWIG: Spring, and he hunts on a mountaintop fashioned tree-by-tree after the one in *Die Walküre!*

WAGNER: While Wagner writes.

LUDWIG: Summer, and he swims in a grotto fashioned rock-by-rock on the one from *Tannhäuser!*

WAGNER: While Wagner writes.

LUDWIG: Ludwig has not only built a theater for Wagner's operas, he has rebuilt all Bavaria in their image. And himself, the heroic tenor!

WAGNER: Ludwig's advisers . . .

PFORDTEN: Pfordten

PFISTERMEISTER: Und Pfistermeister

WAGNER: . . . Are not amused.

PFORDTEN *(Simmering)*: He has rebuilt all Bavaria in Wagner's image.

PFISTERMEISTER *(Simmering)*: The royal coffers are almost empty.

WAGNER: While the King is busy with fantasies

PFORDTEN: Pfordten

PFISTERMEISTER: Und Pfistermeister

PFORDTEN AND PFISTERMEISTER: Hatch an evil plan.

WAGNER: They begin to assemble a list of the King's eccentricities:

PFORDTEN: **The King is so shy that, at state dinners, he has the musicians play so loudly that conversation is impossible.**

PFISTERMEISTER: **Every morning when he wakes, the King bows to the birds outside his window, and is heard to remark:**

LUDWIG: **Fill me with song, feathered friends.**

WAGNER: One night, while Ludwig stares across the darkness at Wagner's tower, a letter is slipped under his door.

PFORDTEN AND PFISTERMEISTER: **"My dear King,**

LUDWIG (*Reading*): **"Your Majesty's interest in music has devolved into an advanced stage of mental disorder, impacting Your Majesty's apprehension of reality. Suffering from such a disorder, freedom of action can no longer be allowed. Your Majesty is declared incapable of ruling, which incapacity will last for the length of Your Majesty's life.**

    "Sincerely,

PFORDTEN: **"Pfordten**

PFISTERMEISTER: **"Und Pfistermeister."**

(Ludwig drops the letter.)

LUDWIG (*Looking to Wagner in the tower*): There is only one place for him to run.

SCENE 3

DORIS: Doris drives through the night to the house she grew up in.

GRANDMOTHER: Grandmother makes peppermint tea.

DORIS: **Oh Granny**

GRANDMOTHER: Grandmother dabs her runny mascara with a hankie.

DORIS: **It felt like I was drowning.**

GRANDMOTHER: Same one she used to dry her own daughter's tears, so many years ago.

DORIS: **We didn't even talk anymore.**

GRANDMOTHER: **Well, you can talk soon.**

DORIS: **What do you mean?**

VIC WATTS: Just then, a pair of headlights shoots through the flowered curtains.

DORIS: **Who's here?**

GRANDMOTHER *(With difficulty)*: **I'm sorry, Doris.**

DORIS: **You told him I was coming?**

GRANDMOTHER: **He's your husband now. God knows I tried to stop things from going this far—but he's your husband now and you got to work things out, you're bound to him.**

DORIS: **What kind of caveman law is that?**

VIC WATTS *(From outside)*: **Darlene?**

GRANDMOTHER: **Your wedding vow, Doris.**

VIC WATTS: **Darlene!**

DORIS *(Shouting outside)*: **How'd you get here so fast?**

VIC WATTS: **Private jet, baby.**

DORIS: **Well you can turn it right back around.**

VIC WATTS: **Open this door or I'm knocking it down.**

DORIS: **You couldn't knock out a tooth with that pansy-ass fist of yours!**

VIC WATTS: **Then I'll pay somebody to knock out your teeth, baby. Then you'll be too ugly to leave me.**

DORIS *(Turning back to Grandmother)*: **Why are you making me do this alone?**

GRANDMOTHER: **When your own mom and dad left you alone, I was there for you, Doris.**

VIC WATTS: **Darlene!**

DORIS (*Shouting outside*): **That's not my name!**

GRANDMOTHER: **One hit song, and you left this house and never turned back.**

VIC WATTS: **Darlene!**

GRANDMOTHER: **No one to get my groceries, no one to get my medicine.**

DORIS: **I fell in love.**

GRANDMOTHER: **With him? Or with what he made you?**

DORIS: **With *him*.**

VIC WATTS: **Darlene!**

GRANDMOTHER: **I'm sorry, Doris.**

VIC WATTS: **DARLENE!**

(*Grandmother becomes Mr. Campani right before our eyes. Continuous into:*)

SCENE 4

MR. CAMPANI (*Imposing, as if to the students*): **Die Götterdämmerung. The only opera with *two* umlauts.**

YOUNG MAN: **Mr. Campani takes the class on a field trip to the local opera house.**

MR. CAMPANI: **Die Götterdämmerung. The most bladder-punishing of all operas, the first act alone runs two and a half hours. Even with a King's patronage, it took Wagner four years to finish.**

(*In another part of the stage, we see Wagner composing at his desk:*)

WAGNER: **Dissonance: The strings at seconds and sevenths. The brass—**

(Wagner is not sure what to do next.)

MR. CAMPANI: Act Two ends with the hair-raising "Vengance Trio": Under the influence of a love potion, Siegfried has abandoned Brünnhilde; now the valkyrie plots her revenge, and the music shares her taste for blood. "So be it," she sings. "Let his death atone for the shame he has brought me!"

YOUNG MAN: Three minutes into the "Vengeance Trio" of Act Two, the Young Man wonders why his stomach hasn't demanded a mad dash up the aisle. Is he not a true opera lover like Mr. Campani?

MR. CAMPANI: The Young Man's eyes wander from the stage, off to:

YOUNG MAN: The chandeliers,
   The fur coats

MR. CAMPANI: The *boys*.

WAGNER: **A flurry of accidentals from the brass, rupturing the major chord.**

(Wagner is stuck again. He chews his pen, staring at the page.)

MR. CAMPANI: The first time the Young Man has seen any of these sturdy-named classmates in evening wear.

YOUNG MAN: Teddy Duncan, Kip Fairfax, Pace Morrison.

(Billy Zimmer is played by the Vic Watts actor.)

BILLY ZIMMER: Best of all is Billy Zimmer

YOUNG MAN: Immediately to his right, wearing a yellow tuxedo shirt with brave irony

MR. CAMPANI: The top two buttons left undone, seemingly out of oversight, offering a glimpse of chest hair.

BILLY ZIMMER: (This is Billy Zimmer's third year as a sophomore.)

WAGNER (*A breakthrough*): **The trumpets sound a broken chord. The timpani wake with a rumble.**

YOUNG MAN (*Pulse racing, but he barely moves*): Emboldened by the Vengeance Trio, the Young Man shifts his knee ever so slightly toward the knee of the excellent Billy Zimmer on his immediate right, thanking God for putting the two of them alphabetically together on Mr. Campani's alphabetically determined seating chart—

(Suddenly slow, expansive:)

WAGNER: **From the strings, an augmented fifth**

MR. CAMPANI: For several seconds they are

YOUNG MAN: Knee to knee

WAGNER: **The strings, plucking**

BILLY ZIMMER: Trouser on trouser

WAGNER: **The trumpets, double-tonguing**

MR. CAMPANI: The Young Man holds his breath.

WAGNER: **Addolorato?**
    Affrettando!

YOUNG MAN: Aware all over his skin

WAGNER: **Accelerando,**
    Accelerando,
    Accelerando!

(The Young Man stands suddenly.)

MR. CAMPANI: . . . Until he dashes up the aisle, just in time to heave upon the lush red carpeting of the lobby.

(Continuous into:)

SCENE 5

The papers flying off Wagner's desk.

WAGNER: **Accelerando,**
      Accelerando!

LUDWIG *(Off)*: **Maestro, are you in there?**

WAGNER: Reluctantly, Wagner looks up from his "Vengeance Trio."

LUDWIG: **Open the door at once!**

WAGNER: The violins still ringing in his head.

LUDWIG: **Open this door—I command you!**

WAGNER *(Turning to see Ludwig)*: **My King. Why do you visit my tower so late?**

LUDWIG: **Because I mean to throw myself from it.**

WAGNER: **Are you as mad as they say?**

LUDWIG: **They mean to take my music from me—they mean to take my life from me!**

WAGNER: **So you will take it first.**

LUDWIG: **There is no other course, old friend. Step aside.**

WAGNER: **Forgive me, my King, but I will not.**

LUDWIG: **Why do you keep me from a glorious death?**

(Short pause. Then, with dawning horror:)

    Is it because I am your bank?

WAGNER: **My King, no—**

LUDWIG: **You would not want to lose your satin curtains, your dressing gowns.**

WAGNER: **I would not want to lose my greatest *listener*.**

LUDWIG *(Moved)*: **Take heart, old friend. Your music will surround me in the next world.**

(Ludwig makes a dash for the window, but Wagner holds him back.)

WAGNER: And Wagner sees: He is the author of the boy's madness.

LUDWIG: **Why do you block my way? Do you not believe in the everlasting soul?**

WAGNER: **I don't know, my boy.**

    No one knows what kind of music waits for us after death.

LUDWIG *(Dumbfounded)*: **But . . . in *Parsifal*, the soul flies up on the wings of a dove. In *Lohengrin*, the swan rises from the lake. Brünnhilde leaps into the fire and the world is born anew!**

WAGNER *(Touching Ludwig on the cheek)*: **My poor boy: You merely fund my operas, you are not a character in them.**

LUDWIG: For Ludwig, it is the ultimate betrayal.

(Light rises on Mr. Campani, speaking out:)

MR. CAMPANI: **. . . And when Pfordten and Pfistermeister arrived to take the young King to the asylum, he did nothing to resist.**

WAGNER: **My boy . . .**

(Light remains on Wagner as he watches Ludwig leave.)

MR. CAMPANI: **But Wagner must have realized that what he said was not altogether true . . . For it is often difficult to separate the music lover from the music.**

(Continuous into:)

SCENE 6

Outside Grandmother's house. Vic is sitting on the sidewalk in a shark-skin suit, smoking a cigarette. A few hours later, and his rage is spent. Doris approaches.

DORIS: **All that huffing and puffing. Good thing we built this house outta brick.**

(Vic is looking at his feet, deflated.)

You came all this way on that jet, you must have something to say.

VIC WATTS: **Are you coming home or what?**

(Pause. He realizes this isn't enough.)

I . . . want you to come back home please.

DORIS: **I'm home right now.**

VIC WATTS: **Why you gotta act like that, Darlene?**

DORIS: **What, like I got a head of my own?**

VIC WATTS: **I got you a walk-in closet. I got you a toy fucking poodle. You want a kid or something? We could have some of those too.**

DORIS *(Abrupt)*: **Why'd you stop making my songs?**

VIC WATTS: **They stopped selling.**

DORIS: **So that's all it was about: How many people would buy it?**

VIC WATTS: **Or another way of saying it is: How many people would listen. And nobody's listening to you anymore, Darlene. You got good diction, you got good moves. But four white boys from Liverpool have more soul than you.**

DORIS (*Shaken*): **You . . . picked me, Vic. You told me I had it.**
VIC WATTS: **Come on, baby. Let's go home.**

(Vic walks away. She doesn't move.)

MR. CAMPANI: **Why is it difficult to separate the music from the music lover?**

(We see Doris watching him go.)

The human body changes the very sound of an orchestra. When Wagner's great opera house at Bayreuth was completed, he tested the acoustics by filling all nine hundred seats with soldiers from the local garrison. He could not be sure how his music would sound if there was a single empty seat. Think of that: A piece of music is really a duet between the instrument and the listener's body!

(Buzz. The class bell brings us back to fluorescent reality. Doris is gone.)

Ah, our own special brand of music.
   (As if to departing students) **Goodbye. Goodbye. Enjoy your freedom!**

(The Young Man approaches with books in his arms.)

YOUNG MAN: **Mr. Campani?**
MR. CAMPANI: **Ah, my young kindred, I enjoyed your paper very much. "Love as Malady" in *Tristan*, right?**
YOUNG MAN (*Confidentially*): **Mr. Campani, I did it.**
MR. CAMPANI: **You did what?**
YOUNG MAN: **I threw up at the *Ring*. Just like you!**

MR. CAMPANI: That is . . . bracing news.

YOUNG MAN: I have to ask—

MR. CAMPANI: I hope that wasn't part of your research. Truth be told, I sometimes find your prose a bit confessional.

YOUNG MAN: I don't want to talk about the paper. I have to ask you something.

MR. CAMPANI: You're certain you want my advice—a grown man who wears a bow tie?

YOUNG MAN: I wanted to ask . . . *(Even more confidential)* What happens to people like me?

MR. CAMPANI: People like you.

YOUNG MAN: People like us.

MR. CAMPANI *(Amused by the euphemisms)*: Music lovers?

YOUNG MAN: Yes.

MR. CAMPANI: You want me to tell you that a young suburban homosexual can grow up to be a beautiful swan.

YOUNG MAN: You sound so . . .

MR. CAMPANI: Glib? I'm sorry.

But tell me why someone so young should be so concerned about his future.

YOUNG MAN: Because it has to be better than here. I don't like myself here.

MR. CAMPANI: Maybe you should run away.

YOUNG MAN: What?

MR. CAMPANI: Maybe you should change your name.

YOUNG MAN: Is this, like, reverse psychology?

MR. CAMPANI: In opera, people are always running away to become themselves.

YOUNG MAN: And what happens to them then?

MR. CAMPANI: They get lost, and then they get more lost.

Sometimes they follow talking birds. Sometimes they drink magic potions. Sometimes they leap into fire. But always, they look for love.

YOUNG MAN: And do they find it?

MR. CAMPANI: **It depends on the composer.**

YOUNG MAN: **What do you mean?**

MR. CAMPANI: **My voice teacher liked to say: Italian music is like a kiss on the mouth. German music is a kiss on the forehead. French music is a kiss on the neck.**

(Pause.)

YOUNG MAN: **What kind of music is this?**

(Mr. Campani kisses him on the forehead.)

(Disappointed) **People in Wagner kiss—I mean really kiss.**

MR. CAMPANI: **But a kiss in Wagner is never just a shabby little lip-lock. It is always a kind of transcendental . . .**

YOUNG MAN: **Consummation?**

(Short pause.)

Aren't you attracted to me?

(Pause.)

MR. CAMPANI: **Yes.**

YOUNG MAN: **Don't you want to have sex with me?**

(Pause.)

MR. CAMPANI: **Yes.**

YOUNG MAN: **Then why don't you?**

MR. CAMPANI: **My young kindred, are you so eager for your life to turn into an opera?**

YOUNG MAN: **Yes!**

MR. CAMPANI: Then I have an operatic proposal for you: Go find someone your own age. Drink magic potions. Leap into fire. And after that, if I still hold some . . . interest for you, we can have another discussion.

YOUNG MAN: There's nobody here.

MR. CAMPANI: What about that Rimmer fellow?

YOUNG MAN: Billy Zimmer?

MR. CAMPANI: Yes of course, Zimmer.

YOUNG MAN: Billy Zimmer's a thug.

MR. CAMPANI: Some people find thuggery rather . . . magnetizing. It's a mysterious but well-known phenomenon.

(Short pause.)

YOUNG MAN: Mr. Campani?

MR. CAMPANI: Yes.

YOUNG MAN: What's your first name?

MR. CAMPANI: In opera, it is very bad form to answer that question.

YOUNG MAN: You're so weird.

(The Young Man exits.)

MR. CAMPANI: And Mr. Campani, who is indeed weird, thinks of Wagner's Lohengrin, and Puccini's Calaf, and all the opera knights who keep their names secret. He thinks: It is always this secret that gives them their power.

SCENE 7

We hear the "Liebestod," sounding less like fifty violins and more like a scratchy old record. Vic Watts is watching the record spin in a dark room.

DORIS: Twenty years after the divorce,

VIC WATTS: Twenty years after the studio closed,

DORIS: Twenty years after she stopped answering to Darlene, Doris gets a call about a TV documentary.

VIC WATTS: It's the story of Vic Watts and his girl singers and they want her to spill it.

(Light shifts. Quite bright now, like klieg lights:)

And spill it she does.

DORIS *(As if to the interviewer)*: **I thought hey, great, we'll live together, we'll make records together. How could I have known everything would go dark? All of a sudden I married Vic and—*wham*.** *(She makes the gesture of doors slamming in her face)* **Darkness.**

(The Ludwig actor plays the Makeup Girl.)

MAKEUP GIRL: The director whispers something to the makeup girl, who comes running to Doris.

DORIS: Doris asks her what she's up to with that powder puff.

MAKEUP GIRL: **No one can see your pretty eyes under all that, Mrs. Watts.**

DORIS: **Miss Watts.**

MAKEUP GIRL: **No one can see your eyes under all that, Miss Watts.**

DORIS: **Sorry, honey. I haven't been on television since it turned color. I guess I don't know what looks good.**

MAKEUP GIRL: Miss Watts needs extra powder when they ask if she still sings.

DORIS: **Never. Not even in the shower.**

MAKEUP GIRL: And, as she holds still for the powder puff, she sees, over the Makeup Girl's shoulder . . .

VIC WATTS *(Putting on aviator glasses)*: . . . **A familiar face.**

DORIS: Still wearing those glasses, as if they'll ward off old age.

VIC WATTS: Twenty years.

DORIS: Twenty years.

(Doris and Vic look each other in the eye, for the first time in the scene.)

DORIS AND VIC: They do not cross the room to say hello.

SCENE 8

MR. CAMPANI *(Out)*: **It might have seemed like magic—but the great innovation of Wagner's opera house was simply to turn out the lights. The emperors, kings, and queens used to go to the opera to be seen, splendid, in their box seats. Now, thanks to Wagner, they sit in the darkness with the rest of us.**

Wagner did not want us to see the kings, or the conductor's wild arms, or even the orchestra, which he submerged for the first time, in a "pit." Which he did not call a "pit," as we do today, but rather a "mystic gulf" between audience and stage.

By snuffing the candles, by blacking out the orchestra, Wagner rendered the audience inseparable from the performance. Darkness, you see, is all the permission we need to lose ourselves. I think perhaps we are always looking for an excuse.

(In a dark part of the stage, the front seat of the Young Man's car. He is there with Billy Zimmer, each of them with a bottle of Michelob. Sounds of a nearby freeway.)

YOUNG MAN: **'87 Thunderbird.**

BILLY ZIMMER: "Ooh."

YOUNG MAN: **All-pleather interiors.**

BILLY ZIMMER: "Aah."

YOUNG MAN: **Rusty hubcaps.**

BILLY ZIMMER *(Referring to the air freshener)*: **Smelling tree.**

YOUNG MAN: **It's new-car smell.**

BILLY ZIMMER: **Pretty butch, pretty Whitesnake video, remember? Redhead on the hood of that car, rolling around like some kinda fuck bunny. Just like this car, spitting image.**

(Pause.)

You ever have hair like those guys with the hair? Winger. *Kix*.

YOUNG MAN *(Playing cool)*: ***Years* before my time.**

BILLY ZIMMER: **Wall o' bangs, Aqua Net to the skies.**
    Hey, you trying to call me old?

YOUNG MAN: **No no I just wanted to hear what you were like—growing up.**

BILLY ZIMMER: **Yah, hair was big the first time I was a sophomore. But our school's like a decade behind the rest of the world.**

(Awkward pause.)

So, what kind of music do *you* like.

YOUNG MAN: **You know, the whole women-on-meds genre. Karen O. Cat Power.**

BILLY ZIMMER: **More like women *off* meds.**

YOUNG MAN: **And sometimes, you know, girl groups.**

BILLY ZIMMER: **Girl groups?**

YOUNG MAN: **Just sometimes.**

BILLY ZIMMER: **Like Destiny's Child?**

YOUNG MAN: **No. Wait.**

BILLY ZIMMER: **What?**

YOUNG MAN: **Just a second.**

(The Young Man puts his headphones on Billy's head. We hear Doris's song.)

They're called Darlene and the Daybreakers.

There's four of them, but Darlene's the only voice on most of the tracks. I copied it from 45s—they're pretty rare now.

BILLY ZIMMER: **It's pretty okay.** *(He takes off the headphones and the music goes out)* **Ironic-okay.**

(Short pause.)

YOUNG MAN: **It's good to see you out of school. Like we can be different, you know?**

BILLY ZIMMER: **Come on, you** *love* **school. I've seen you.**

Did the Vulcan mind link with that opera 'mo.

YOUNG MAN: **I did not.**

BILLY ZIMMER *(Mimicking Jacob)*: **"Why did Wagner want people to throw up?"**

YOUNG MAN: **It's just . . . his class is better than the others.**

(Short pause.)

I guess you know why I called you, why we're here.

BILLY ZIMMER: **Cuz we haven't graduated to the back seat yet?**

YOUNG MAN: **I meant up here on the** *hill*—**don't be glib, I mean—**

This is like the hardest thing I ever did.

BILLY ZIMMER *(More flirty than mean)*: **What, you want some kinda reward?**

YOUNG MAN: **Um. No.**
BILLY ZIMMER: **Wait. Don't move.**

(He kisses the Young Man. This lasts four or five seconds—not reticent.)

Surprise.
YOUNG MAN *("Wow")*: **Ha.**
BILLY ZIMMER: **Yeah. Yeah.**
> **Before we do any more, maybe we should sort out the particulars.**
YOUNG MAN: **Huh?**
BILLY ZIMMER: **Finances?**
YOUNG MAN: **Finances.**
BILLY ZIMMER: **It's twenty if you're gonna blow me and more depending for what.**

(Short pause.)

YOUNG MAN: **You want me to pay you.**
BILLY ZIMMER: **The dads and granddads pay.**
> **Spend time with a novice, you bet.**
YOUNG MAN: **I don't have any money.**
> **I've got to— Just a second—**

(The Young Man opens the car door to throw up.)

BILLY ZIMMER: **Okay now that's gross.**
> **Okay. You're gonna be okay. Okay?**
> **When yer done with that you can drop me outside the movieplex.**

(The Young Man gets up, woozy.)

YOUNG MAN: **Sorry.**

BILLY ZIMMER: **You know you're not half ugly—might've discounted you.**

YOUNG MAN: **Why do you**

BILLY ZIMMER: **What.**

YOUNG MAN: **"Dads and granddads."**

BILLY ZIMMER: **Not like it's a *career*. But it's money, and it's not flipping burgers or four years in combat boots. TV's always telling you:**

(In the manner of an earnest talk show host:)

"Don't debase yourself. Gotta respect yourself. *Apply* yourself."

YOUNG MAN: **So?**

BILLY ZIMMER: **So they just want to keep you from a good thing.**

(The Young Man counts the crumpled bills in his pocket.)

YOUNG MAN: **I've got seven dollars. What's that get?**

BILLY ZIMMER: **Kiss goodbye?**

YOUNG MAN: **—**

BILLY ZIMMER: **Hey hey, don't be so sensitive!**
Keep your seven bucks—I'll give you a virgin burn, free of charge.

YOUNG MAN: **What's a virgin burn?**

BILLY ZIMMER: **I'll show you.**

YOUNG MAN: **No, I don't want to know.**

BILLY ZIMMER: **Whatever.**

YOUNG MAN: **I don't want to know.**

(The Young Man starts the car.)

SCENE 9

Back at the television studio. Doris and Vic as they were, eyeing each other across the room.

DORIS: Pretty soon it's Vic's turn in the hot seat.

MAKEUP GIRL *(Powder-puffing Vic)*: Mr. Watts has even more makeup on than Miss Watts.

DORIS: The interviewer lobs him some easy ones first.

VIC WATTS *(As if to the interviewer)*: **Sure I like today's music. Prince can write a song. Bananarama's got it. Name like Bananarama, you'd better goddamn have it.**

DORIS: But then she goes off the script.

VIC WATTS: **The love of my life?**
I thought we said nothing personal.

DORIS: But the interviewer leans forward in her chair.

VIC WATTS: **The love of my life . . .**

DORIS: And Doris holds her breath.

(Short pause.)

VIC WATTS: **The music.**
(Looking straight at Doris) **It was always the music.**

MAKEUP GIRL: And then the strangest thing.

DORIS: Doris starts to sing.

VIC WATTS: After twenty years of

DORIS: Nothing

VIC WATTS: She opens her mouth

DORIS: And sings the song he wrote to make her love him.

(Under the following, we might hear an echo of the second single, "Gosh Golly He Loves Me." Not the vocal, but the rhythm track and melody.)

And it's a little bit ugly
And a little bit pretty
And a little bit frail
And a little bit strong
And a little bit magic
Like waking up one day and learning you can shoot
 lasers out your eyes or lightning out your fingers.

VIC WATTS: And as producers and makeup girls swirl around her, Doris won't stop singing, as if to say:

DORIS: **It wasn't the music you loved. And it wasn't me. It was something a little bit both.**

SCENE 10

We see Wagner watching Ludwig leave, as before.

LUDWIG: Three days later, they find Ludwig's body at the bottom of the lake where he counted swans and dreamed of enchanted swords.

WAGNER: No one knows what happened for certain.

LUDWIG: Some say he escaped the asylum and drowned himself. Others say he was murdered.

WAGNER: But Wagner knew better. Ludwig had always imagined himself as a character in *Lohengrin*, more than any of the other operas. It seems impossible that he could have entered the dark water that night without thinking of the final scene of *Lohengrin*.

(During the following, Ludwig walks into the lake and drowns. Serene, as if reassuring himself with an old bedtime story. We hear music from the final scene of Lohengrin.*)*

LUDWIG: Lohengrin recognizes the swan as the young man enchanted many years ago, prisoned in an animal's body.

He loosens the chain 'round the swan's neck.

The swan sinks into the lake, and in its place appears a boy in shining silver.

Lohengrin lifts the boy from the water and places the crown on his head again, and he is silver.

(Continuous into:)

SCENE 11

The classroom.

MR. CAMPANI *(Out)*: Maybe Ludwig believed that he too would be lifted out of the lake, restored. This man who dedicated his life to making Wagner's fictions real. But as his lungs filled with water, the King must have known for the first time that music doesn't always tell the truth. One thing is for certain: Ludwig died of romanticism.

(The bell rings, loud. Light returns.)

He would not survive long at this school, that much I am sure of.

(The Young Man approaches Mr. Campani.)

Ah, young Master Jacob.

YOUNG MAN: It happened again.

MR. CAMPANI: **Again?**

YOUNG MAN (*Touching his stomach*): **All over the car.**

MR. CAMPANI: **You must be a true music lover.**

YOUNG MAN: **Don't joke.**

MR. CAMPANI: **Have you considered Pepto Bismol?**

YOUNG MAN: **I said don't joke.**

MR. CAMPANI: **Yes of course—a budding aesthete couldn't be caught smiling.**

YOUNG MAN (*"Listen"*): **He wanted me to pay him.**

MR. CAMPANI: **Billy Zimmer? Oh dear. He's wilier than he looks.**

    Did you pay him then?

YOUNG MAN: **What?**

MR. CAMPANI: **Did you go through with it?**

YOUNG MAN: **Are you kidding?**

MR. CAMPANI: **I thought you were looking for experience.**

YOUNG MAN: **That's sick, that's / sick—**

MR. CAMPANI: **No, my kindred, just realistic.**

YOUNG MAN: **You're a bitter old man. Life has been disappointing to you and now you're trying to make me like you!**

MR. CAMPANI: **Ah, splendid: Fifteen-year-old psychoanalysis.**

YOUNG MAN: **I'm *sixteen*.**

(*Pause.*)

I thought you—

    The last time, you said, we could have another discussion . . .

(*Pause.*)

MR. CAMPANI: **I don't think that's a / good—**

YOUNG MAN: **You said that / we could—**

MR. CAMPANI: **I was mistaken.**

Now, if you'll excuse me, I have thirty dispassionate papers on *Rigoletto* to grade.

(Mr. Campani busies himself. A moment where the Young Man has nothing left to lose.)

YOUNG MAN: **Mr. Campani?**
Why did you stop singing?

(Mr. Campani is arrested by the question.
Doris appears. She watches the rest of the scene, unnoticed by the Young Man and Mr. Campani.)

DORIS: **Because I wasn't ever going to be great.**
MR. CAMPANI: **Because I wasn't ever going to be great.**
YOUNG MAN: **You mean you shouldn't do something unless you're great at it?**
MR. CAMPANI: **That's what I thought then. And you're right, I was . . . disappointed.** *(With difficulty)* **Some voices grow, with every role, with every challenge. Mine did not. When I was your age I was at Juilliard and ten years later my career was over. But I already loved it too much.**

(Ludwig appears. He watches the rest of the scene, unnoticed.)

YOUNG MAN: **What do you mean?**
LUDWIG: **Once you let music take you over, you can never be cured.**
MR. CAMPANI: **Once you let music take you over, you can never be cured. So many things have happened to me since I gave up singing. New careers and new lovers, new cities.** *(Referring to his age)* **New lines. But I don't know if anything has compared to looking out into the dark, singing someone else's words to a roomful**

of strangers. I don't think I'll ever be that . . . important again.

(Wagner and Vic Watts approach from different directions.)

YOUNG MAN *(To Mr. Campani)*: **I think you're important.**

WAGNER *(To Ludwig)*:	VIC WATTS *(To Doris)*:
Maybe that's why it's so easy to hurt you.	**Maybe that's why it's so easy to hurt you.**

MR. CAMPANI *(To Young Man)*: **Maybe that's why it's so easy to hurt you.**

(Pause.)

YOUNG MAN: **Would you sing for me?**

MR. CAMPANI: **Right here? Right now?**

YOUNG MAN: **Please.**

MR. CAMPANI: **It's not like riding a bicycle. The voice demands constant attention.**

YOUNG MAN: **What are you scared of?**

MR. CAMPANI: **What if nothing comes out?**

DORIS: But after all those years, the urge to sing again is strong.

LUDWIG: And it is hard to disappoint the look in the eyes of his biggest fan.

WAGNER: And Mr. Campani plants his feet, and takes a deep breath, and starts to sing the "Liebestod" in a beautiful, unsteady baritone.

(Mr. Campani starts to sing. His voice is ravaged, but he still sings with great precision. And hints of the voice he once had.)

YOUNG MAN: The Young Man watches.

WAGNER: The way the older man's eyebrows reach for the high notes.

VIC WATTS: The way he rises up on the balls of his feet.

DORIS: This man whose shoes are always shined.

LUDWIG: Finally his body has lost some of its control.

WAGNER: It has become a servant to the music.

LUDWIG: And, as he listens to this song about a great love finally consummated, the Young Man wonders if his kiss will be returned.

DORIS: Part of him wants the song to last forever.

YOUNG MAN: Part of him wishes he never heard the song that got him into all this trouble.

(Light shifts. Continuous into:)

SCENE 12

Lights rise slowly on the record player that Doris brought on at the beginning of the play. A record spins on it, scratching softly. The end of the record, or the beginning.

MR. CAMPANI: The "Liebestod" jumps back down Mr. Campani's throat and stays there until he is a young man with a great singing career ahead of him, and the song doesn't sound nearly as sad.

YOUNG MAN: The Young Man backs out of Mr. Campani's room and goes back to junior high. He plays Doris's song on his headphones, loud, hoping it will teach him something about love. But he no longer knows where the song came from.

DORIS: The song plays in discount stores and workout videos and on a TV documentary where Doris appears with words on the bottom of the screen to remind people who she is.

VIC WATTS: Before long, the song slips off the gold record on the wall in a quiet living room in Malibu. Skips off the record and climbs back into Doris's mouth / and

DORIS: And music fills the quiet house again. Doris backs up the aisle in a wedding dress and Vic takes the ring off her finger and her heart is unbroken.

VIC WATTS: The song she's sung so many times plays over the radio for the very first time, and the song climbs back up the microphone cord in Vic's studio, / and

DORIS: And the Number 9 bus takes Doris back to her grandmother. She grows smaller and smaller with every day, and eventually she grows so small that her mother and father take her back again.

VIC WATTS: And the "Liebestod" waits patiently all this time, black notes on paper. It sleeps on paper for a hundred years / until

LUDWIG: Until King Ludwig climbs out of the swan pond and shakes his long hair dry. The water exits his lungs and his lungs fill with air and the air carries the song out of his mouth / and

WAGNER: And into the mouth of Wagner, who sings it for the first time in an unsteady baritone while the courtiers think of the pheasant, fragrant, in the next room.

LUDWIG: The pond dries up. The swans fly back to their natural habitat. The pink marble climbs off its foundation and crawls back to a Venetian quarry, and the grass grows taller and taller.

WAGNER: Wagner forgets the name Ludwig and moves back to his family and destitution. The gold coins fly out of his purse, the fine silk falls off his body. But his pen moves faster with every day, and his ideas grow fresher, and his old body stands taller and taller.

LUDWIG: King Ludwig takes off his crown and forgets the name Wagner, and he is a young boy who dreams of swans and his heart is unbroken.

WAGNER: The black notes of the "Liebestod" skip off the paper and back into Wagner's head, where they wait to be written. But they don't wait for long. They fly out of his head and out into the world, where they become days he hasn't lived yet, and hearts he hasn't broken, and birdsong he hasn't heard: All the newborn, excited atoms of a song before the artist plucks it out of the air.

(Wagner's pen lifts off the paper and up into the air, where it pauses for an instant.

At the same instant, Doris lifts the needle off the record.

Blackout.)

END OF PLAY

THE AMATEURS

PRODUCTION HISTORY

The Amateurs had its world premiere at the Vineyard Theatre (Douglas Aibel and Sarah Stern, Artistic Directors) in New York City on February 27, 2018. It was directed by Oliver Butler. The scenic design was by David Zinn, the costume design was by Jessica Pabst, the lighting design was by Jen Schriever, the original music and sound design were by Bray Poor; and the production stage manager was Rachel Gross. The cast was:

LARKING	Thomas Jay Ryan
BROM	Kyle Beltran
HOLLIS	Quincy Tyler Bernstine
RONA	Jennifer Kim
GREGORY	Michael Cyril Creighton
THE PHYSIC	Greg Keller

The Amateurs was originally commissioned by South Coast Repertory (Marc Masterson, Artistic Director) in Costa Mesa, California, and written with support from Goodman Theatre (Robert Falls, Artistic Director) in Chicago, Illinois. A staged reading of *The Amateurs* was developed and presented at Goodman Theatre's New Stages Festival on November 14, 2015.

CHARACTERS

LARKING	*He plays God.*
BROM	*He plays Noah.*
HOLLIS	*She plays Noah's Wife.*
RONA	*She plays Shem and Shem's Wife.*
GREGORY	*A set designer.*
THE PHYSIC	*Also plays Henry's Apparition.*

SETTING

ACT ONE: Fourteenth-century Europe.

ACT TWO: The present.

ACT THREE: Fourteenth-century Europe.

In Acts One and Three, there might be a wagon, or the suggestion of a wagon—something that can act like a stage but isn't a stage. The special effects for the play-within-the-play should be in line with what fourteenth-century technology could accomplish with the aid of great effort and ingenuity.

NOTE

If there needs to be an intermission, it should fall between Acts One and Two, with no break between Acts Two and Three. But no intermission would be even better.

Oh happy people of the future, who have not known these miseries and perchance will class our testimony with the fables!

—LETTER FROM PETRARCH, DURING THE BLACK DEATH

Our suffering has returned us to an earlier period of art, before the invention of the idea of good taste . . . We have been taken back to a time when griots told stories in Africa, when old wives invented fairy tales, when audiences felt pity and terror.

—EDMUND WHITE, DURING THE AIDS EPIDEMIC

Are we full or empty at the end of tragedy?

—BERT O. STATES, *THE PLEASURE OF THE PLAY*

ACT ONE

PROLOGUE

God addresses us. He has a long white beard held in place with string.
(God is not a very good actor, but he has a powerful voice.)

GOD:

> I, God, who all the world have wrought,
> Heaven and earth—and all from nought!—
> Now see my people, in deed and thought,
> Are lost in sin so bold:
> Some in Pride, Ire and Envy,
> Covetousness and Gluttony,
> Some in Sloth and Lechery,
> And other ways manifold!

(There is a parade of the Seven Deadly Sins, in crudely arresting masks.)

PRIDE:

> They call me Pride (of course I'm first)—
> I swell and swell until you burst.

GLUTTONY:

> Bursting suits me mighty fine,
> For Gluttony is my name:
> My father he was a bacon haunch,
> My mother she was the same.

PRIDE: Look now, here's Wrath:

WRATH:

> I walk on a bed of knives,
> I sleep with my hands balled tight,
> From hellfire I was born—
> Return with me to Hell you might!

PRIDE: Now welcome Sloth:

> *(Sloth is the shortest of the Sins. He doesn't project his voice
> enough.)*

SLOTH:

> I was born on a long slow summer's day . . .
> That's already more words than I want to say.

GLUTTONY: Here's Lechery now:

LECHERY:

> Like Gluttony, my cousin,
> I live to eat and eat
> But Satan knows I savor
> A different sort of meat!

ENVY:

> I am Envy: Fear my jealous stare,
> For those of you who sit out there
> Have took from me my rightful chair!

(The Envy actor flips his mask, deftly, and now plays Covetousness.)

COVETOUSNESS:

> And Covetousness, his closest kin:
> I'm more inclined to want the chair
> Than hate the person sitting in.

THE OTHER SIX DEADLIES:

> If you have liked us all half well
> We'll see you very soon in Hell!

(The Seven Deadlies start to exit. Envy lags behind. Wrath breaks character, but her mask is still on.)

WRATH: Henry?

(Envy falls to his knees, dazed.)

ENVY: My mouth.
WRATH: Henry get up.
ENVY: Tastes like.
WRATH: Get up, they'll know.

(Gluttony breaks character, calling to Wrath from the wings.)

GLUTTONY: Hollis!
ENVY: My ears are wet.
GLUTTONY: Keep away from him—it's the plague!

WRATH: He's my *brother*, Rona.

(God reappears, on high now: He can tell something is amiss, but the show must go on.)

GOD:

>I repent full sore that ever I made man,
>By me he sets no store, who am his sovereign.
>I will destroy therefore beast, man, and woman,
>Who sit in evil's thrall:
>Vengeance will I take—
>In earth, for sin's sake—
>My anger will I wake
>Against both great and small!

(Lights narrow to a spot on Wrath—whose real name is Hollis—watching her brother die.)

HOLLIS: Henry?
ENVY: Tastes like blood. Hears like blood.

1

Gregory speaks out to us, rapidly. His Sloth mask sits nearby.

GREGORY: Two of every kind, he says.
And I say *every* kind?
And he says what are you deaf?
And I say no Mr. Larking
And he says two of every kind, is that a problem?
And I say well kind of well yeah
And he says well well well why?
And I say two of every kind is a lot, like what about insects
And he says what *about* insects
And I say well they're so *small*—you won't see all the detail 'less you're down front. I'll be three days just on the prongies and no one will know.
The prongies? he says.
The, *(Makes an impatient gesture for antennae)* I say.
"Antennae," he says.

Like I said, I say.

And Mr. Larking says,

Don't you think I do invisible work too? The way I keep my voice warm and my body sharp as a knife? The audience might not know but it makes a difference.

(Beat.)

Plus the elephants, I say.

Elephants? he says.

And I tell him how it's quite the opposite problem than insects: If I paint them smaller than a real elephant no one will believe. It'll take 'em right out of the illusion.

And he says Gregory you idiot,

You precious little idiot

(Which did not put me in a generous spirit)

He says no one west of the Tiber ever laid eyes on a real elephant so how do they know how big?

And I say it's worse then, cuz all they know is the *legend*, and legend has to be bigger than real.

And he says you'll figure something out.

And I say I thought I was an idiot

So I had him there.

(Beat.)

And Larking says, like he's a new person all of a sudden, he says,

"You're not an idiot, Gregory. At least not when it comes to making things that look like things. For that, you're the best man I know."

(A proud pause.)

So I paint us two dogs (start out easy)
    Two lambs
    Two aardvarks
    Two possum
    Two by two by two by two
    And I stopped before elephants cuz I was tired.
    And it was good.

(Beat.)

That's my joke—like the Bible?
    "And it was good," like I'm God
    Which I'm not.
    Mr. Larking is God.
    Mr. Larking says he gets to be God cuz he's got the best
voice.
    I'm not allowed to play a part
    On account of my looks.
    I only get parts where my face is covered.

(Gregory picks up a lightning bolt he's been whittling.)

But when it comes to the scenery
    And clothes to wear,
    And tricking the eye,
    I'm Him.
    I'm God.

(Continuous into:)

2

Larking enters, still in his God costume. Gregory whittles.

LARKING: What's that supposed to be.
GREGORY: You know. *(Pointing it like a lightning bolt)* "Pow."
LARKING: Why isn't it all silver?
GREGORY: Who says lightning's silver?
LARKING: Or gold then.
GREGORY: Where am I gonna find paint like metal?
LARKING: Steal it.
GREGORY *(?)*: Steal for God.
LARKING: From the monks, maybe. They paint pictures on their walls. Must have gold for the halos.
GREGORY: You are low, Larking
LARKING: Says the holy idiot. *(Taking in Gregory's work)* How much longer?
GREGORY: All of it?
LARKING: Two of every kind.
GREGORY: A month?
LARKING: You have two weeks.
GREGORY: Two weeks!
LARKING: Then we start performing *Noah's Flood*.
GREGORY: We've never made it all the way through.
LARKING: Exactly. We have to practice or it won't be ready for the Duke.
GREGORY: When they don't like us, they throw things.
LARKING: That's how we get better.
GREGORY: Sometimes it's worse than throw things.
LARKING: How could we know Henry would die on us right there in the Prologue?
GREGORY: I have nightmares. The whole town running after us, yelling Kill 'em all! Send 'em to Hell with him!

LARKING: We're actors. They bury us outside the city walls—
and that's if they like us. So we've got to be the best they've
ever seen, if we want to live.

GREGORY (*Back to work, shaking his head*): Two weeks.

LARKING: We'll be ready. I know my lines and the others have
less.

(*Rona comes in, dressed as Shem's Wife.*)

GREGORY: Hi, Rona.

RONA (*To Larking, ignoring Gregory*): Are you hiding?

LARKING: Why would I be hiding?

RONA: Cuz you know you deserve a thrashing.

(*Larking kisses her neck, but she breaks away.*)

LARKING: What've I done now.

RONA: Saw you looking at her.

LARKING: At who, at Hollis? I wasn't.

RONA: How do you know At Hollis then?

LARKING: I was looking at her, like, "You should focus on God
while He's talking."

RONA: Mm.

LARKING: You know how she goes other places in her head, during a scene?

RONA: I hate her. Always thinking deep thoughts.

LARKING: Her brother died, Rona.

RONA: "Her brother died." And she wanted our best blanket to
bury him!

LARKING: Hardly "bury."

RONA: Blankets are for the living.

LARKING: Shhh.

(*Hollis enters now, carrying all the masks in a basket.*)

RONA: Hi, Hollis.

HOLLIS: Hi. *(To Gregory)* Have you seen Sloth?

GREGORY: Over here.

(Hollis picks up the Sloth mask and exits. Immediately:)

RONA: I hate her.

LARKING: Hate is a strong word.

RONA: I hate you.

(He tries to kiss her again. She recoils from his God beard.)

Take that thing off, it reeks.

LARKING: Soon as we get to the river, we'll do a washing.

RONA: You mean I'll do a washing.

(For a second, just the sound of Gregory sanding his lightning bolt.)

Can't Hollis take some of his lines?

LARKING: You like lines.

RONA: Ever since Henry's dead I have to be both Shem *and* Shem's Wife. "Greetings, Husband." *(Turning her head, suddenly in a lower voice)* "Greetings, Wife." I look insane.

GREGORY: I can say lines.

LARKING *(Still to Rona)*: It's only till we find a new Henry.

RONA: Won't be easy. He had the best voice of all of us.

(Beat.)

LARKING: Why are you so cruel.

RONA: If I wasn't, you'd get bored.

(Brom passes through.)

BROM: Have you seen Hollis?

RONA: Why?

BROM: I want to show her . . .

(He opens his cupped hands a little: There's a tiny point of light inside.)

Last firefly of the season.

RONA: Let it go, you fool.

BROM: Why?

RONA: Each one is the soul of an unbaptized infant!

(Brom looks into his hands, skeptical.)

They fly around, still looking for God.

BROM *(Defiant)*: Henry always said they meant hope.

(He exits.)

RONA: And look how that worked out.

LARKING: You're terrible.

RONA: Truthful.

(He starts to kiss her neck, her hair.)

GREGORY *(Referring to the lightning bolt)*: What about yellow?

(Rona looks at Gregory. Larking still kissing her.)

Yellow's close to gold.

RONA *(To Larking, whispering)*: He's saying something.

(Larking looks at Gregory.)

GREGORY: We got yellow.

(Rona snorts.)

Why don't she like me?

LARKING: Rona? She doesn't like anybody.

RONA: It's true—you all disgust me. *(To Larking)* I know a place we can go.

(She leads Larking off. Gregory pretends to zap them with the lightning bolt, a little half-hearted.)

GREGORY: Ker-pow.

(Then a clap of real thunder, leading into:)

3

Noah pleads to the heavens. (Brom, as Noah, wears a fake beard now. Hollis and Rona stand nearby, holding poses as Noah's Wife and Shem's Wife.)

NOAH:

Lord over all, comely King of the sky—
Noah, thy humble servant, am I!
Lest that I and my children shall fall,
Save us from sin and bring us to thy hall
In heav'n.

(God appears up in the clouds.)

GOD:

Noah, my friend, my servant free,
Righteous thou art, I rightly see!
A ship soon thou shalt make for thee
Of tree both dry and light.

> Three hundred cubits, 'twill be long,
> And fifty of breadth, to make it strong;
> Of height? Fifty. And met thou fong; /
> Thus measure it about.

(Rona holds her pose, but whispers to Hollis:)

RONA *(Overlapping at " / ")*: "Fong," what's "fong"?
HOLLIS *(Sotto voce)*: Rhymes with strong.
NOAH *(Trying to stay in character)*: Quiet, Wife! God is talking.
HOLLIS: She was talking to me—

GOD:

> Destroyèd all the world shall be!
> Save thou, thy wife, and thy sons three.

RONA *(Muttering to Hollis, amused)*: "Three"—I count none.

GOD *(For Rona's benefit, but still in character)*:
> And all their wives also with thee,
> No matter how shrill and unsavory.

NOAH:

> Ah, Lord, I thank thee loud and still,
> That I, to you, art in such will;
> Thy bidding, Lord, I shall fulfill,
> On behalf of all mankind.

(He strikes a penitent pose. Beat.)

RONA *(Muttering)*: Doesn't rhyme with "ill."
LARKING: Rona!
RONA: Seems like it should rhyme, like the others.
> Or do you like how it ends all incomplete.
> Is that your *thing*, not completing.

(The actors stand there: Are we still talking about the lines?
Should we keep going?
    Gregory starts to lower lightning bolts from the sky. Creak
creak creak creak.)

LARKING: Not now, Gregory!

4

Hollis and Rona by a stream. Hollis washes the Noah costume, Rona
washes the God costume.

RONA: Sounds kind of nice I think— An escape, almost
HOLLIS: Rona don't say that
RONA: Why not
HOLLIS: 'Cause it's blasphemous.
RONA: I mean maybe not for forty *days*
    But don't you think all that water—?
HOLLIS: I guess—
RONA: Pure, sky-given water to wash away the rats and the sores
    and the bedpans?
HOLLIS: That whole big boat was a bedpan.
RONA: True.
HOLLIS: I mean, *elephants.*
RONA: Never seen an elephant.
HOLLIS: Me either but you can imagine.

(Beat.)

    Rona do you think I'm good?
RONA: As in, not evil?
HOLLIS: Good I mean in the play good?
RONA: You deliver the story of the scriptures to the people.

HOLLIS: But I mean, do you believe I'm *her* when I'm up there on the wagon?

Do you believe I'm Noah's Wife?

RONA *(Does not compute)*: But you're not her.

HOLLIS: Never mind.

RONA: You're pretty, if that's what you're / asking

HOLLIS: That's not what / I'm

RONA: In a—untilled field kind of way.

HOLLIS *(I think?)*: Thanks.

(Little beat.)

RONA: I'm sorry about Henry

HOLLIS *(Taken aback)*: Oh

RONA: I never had a brother, so I don't really know

But you probably loved him?

(This is as warm as it gets with Rona. Something relaxes between them, for a moment.)

HOLLIS: Can I ask you something?

Are you . . . ?

(She looks at Rona's stomach.)

RONA: *No*—

HOLLIS: How do you even know what / I'm asking

RONA: I know what you're asking and no.

HOLLIS: Is it Larking's?

RONA *(Rapidly)*: No— *(Realizing she's given herself away)* How did you?—Does it show?

HOLLIS: The way you are with him. You were always so . . . *(She doesn't say slutty)*

And now the past few weeks you're like the Blessed Virgin. The Blessed Virgin but with more um anger.

RONA: Do you think he knows?

HOLLIS: I think I know more in my little pinky than Larking does.

　　Sorry. I know he's / your—

RONA: It's okay. It's not like I'm in love with him.

HOLLIS: But it's his.

RONA: I don't know.

HOLLIS: *Rona.*

(Rona looks down at her washing.)

Rona, who?

5

Light up on Gregory, wide-eyed.

GREGORY: I'm almost finished painting the grasshoppers and the silverfish and the earwigs and the mites, two by two by two by two, and my arm knew it was working hard when I hear a voice behind me and that voice is a lady and that lady is Rona and she says *Shh Boy Shh Boy Shh.*

　　And I say if you're looking for Mr. Larking he's not here

　　And she says *I'm not looking for Mr. Larking*

　　And I say

　　Oh

　　And she says put your hand on me here.

　　And I say my hand hurts on account of painting the earwigs

　　And she says maybe it's better if we don't talk.

(A beat, as he takes in the ramifications of this.)

So we don't.

6

. . . And back to the stream. Hollis has stopped her washing.

RONA: It was Henry.

HOLLIS: You and Henry?

RONA: Your poor dead brother Henry laid with me, it's true.

HOLLIS *(Genuinely baffled)*: Henry never so much as looked at you.

RONA: All an act.

He was at war with himself. At war with his true feelings.

HOLLIS: Did he know that he—that you were—?

RONA: *(Touching her stomach)*: I've only known three weeks, and he's been gone . . .

HOLLIS: Twenty-nine days

RONA: Yes exactly

HOLLIS: Your cheeks were dry, when we left him by the road.

RONA: Shock. It was all so overwhelming

HOLLIS: Was it.

RONA: I mean, knowing that I was carrying his seed. Or I mean not *knowing* yet, I didn't *know*— But I think on some level I think I knew I think.

(Hollis gives her the side-eye.)

But now, how wonderful: Henry lives on! In me! And you'll want to help me raise him of course, little Henry

HOLLIS *(A touch ironic)*: Or Henrietta

RONA: I'm not sure that's a pretty name, but yes. And you'll help protect me from harm since I'm the mother of your own dear nephew.

HOLLIS: But I don't understand, what makes you so sure it isn't Larking's?

RONA: The cards told me.

HOLLIS: You and your magic. Those cards don't know everything.

RONA: Actually, they do Hollis

Actually that is the *definition* of the cards

That they are tapped into the oldest part of the *universe*
and thus that they see everything.

(Beat.)

Also, Larking isn't always able to, you know

HOLLIS: *Oh*

RONA: Well mostly almost never actually.

HOLLIS: All bark and no bite.

(Rona stifles a giggle. Hollis sees Larking coming.)

Look, here he is now

RONA: Oh no

HOLLIS: That big strapping slice of man-meat

RONA: Hollis don't

HOLLIS: Mr. Bark And No Bite

RONA: Hollis!

LARKING *(Smarmy)*: Ladies.

You look like you're having fun.

RONA: Here.

(Rona holds out the God beard. It's sopping wet.)

Go hang it from a tree.

7

Dark storm clouds signal the arrival of the Flood.

GOD:

> The flood is nigh, as well you see;
> Therefore tarry you nought—
> Aboard the vessel you ought!

NOAH: Come Shem, my son, come Wife, come all aboard!

> *(Rona plays Shem and Shem's Wife. She does her best, even though she hates it:)*

SHEM: Wife, come with me, if you fear the flood.
SHEM'S WIFE *(Demure)*: Here I am, Husband. Humble wife of Shem, I follow where my husband goes.

> *(Noah and his family board the Ark. Only Noah's Wife remains behind.*
>
> *The animals follow, two by two: A kind of painted canvas scrolls by, showing each species as it is named. If we are alert, we might make out Gregory in the wings, turning the crank that sets the canvas in motion.)*

SHEM:

> Sir, here are lions, leopards in,
> Horses, mares, oxen, and swine;
> Goats, calves, sheep, and kine
> Here sitten thou may see.

NOAH:

> Take here cats and dogs too,
> Otter, fox, ermine also;

Hares hopping gaily can go
Have grass here for to eat.

NOAH'S WIFE:

And there are bears, wolves set,
Apes, owls, marmoset,
Weasels, squirrels, and ferret;
Here they eat their meat.

SHEM'S WIFE:

Yet more beasts are in this house:
Each and all from lynx to louse
Here a ratton, here a mouse.

(The scrolling canvas stalls. No mouse.)

Here a mouse.

(Still no mouse. Hissing, sotto voce:)

Here a fucking mouse, Gregory.

(Gregory gives the machine a kick. Two mice glide forward, smoothly.)

(Placid again) . . . For 'ere they travel together.

NOAH:

And here are cocks, kites, crows,
Rooks and ravens, many rows,
Storks and spoonbills, heaven knows,
Each one in his kind.

Wife! Why stands thou there?

(Noah's Wife turns to him.)

Why doesn't thou join me on the Ark?

(Noah's Wife drops character and speaks directly to us, as Hollis. Continuous into:)

8

Tight spot on Hollis. A step outside of time.

HOLLIS: Why?
Don't know why.
Never had to know *why*.
I'm only told, "Hollis, stand next to the sheep,"
Or, "Hollis, slaughter the Innocents,"
Or, "Hollis, birth the Christ child."
Never know why, just do.
If I started asking Why
I'd have to wonder why they welcome us to town by
Dumping bedpans on our heads
And why they say goodbye with tar and feathers;
I'd have to wonder why did poor Henry catch the plague
And not Rona
When Rona deserves it so much more;
And why couldn't we bury Henry
Even a foot down even
Instead of throw him on the wormy pile with the rest.

After all that, maybe it's better just to hear,
"Hollis, stage left," or
"Hollis, stage right," or
"Hollis stop breathing through your mouth,

You dumb slag, I can't hear my own speech."
There's no Why to worry over.
Still,
It's a lot of time,
Up here,
Time to tell yourself stories.
And now it's stuck in my head, that "Why."
What was *her* Why,
Noah's Wife,
Lady with no name.
"Wife! Why doesn't thou join me on the Ark?"
And maybe she's thinking:

(She delivers the following to Noah, though he can't hear her:)

What if the animals smell bad?
What if the lions eat me?
What if I don't want to leave my home?
What if everyone I know is already dead and gone and
Lying in a wormy pile?
What if I don't trust God anymore.
What if I don't trust *you*, Husband.
What if you're the devil in disguise?

(Lights snap back to normal. Noah calls out to her, more impatient now.)

NOAH: Wife! Why stands thou there?
    Why doesn't thou join me on the Ark?
NOAH'S WIFE: Coming, Husband.

9

Larking, Rona, Brom and Hollis around a campfire. Something a little too paltry is roasting on a spit. (A squirrel or two?) Gregory sits farther off, feeding real doves in a cage. An argument already underway:

LARKING *(To Hollis)*: How do I know it won't happen when you're up there in front of the Duke? How do I know you won't just / float out of your body again

HOLLIS *(Overlapping)*: I won't. I wasn't—

LARKING *(Continuous)*: and off to la-la land.

HOLLIS: Because I won't.

LARKING *(A bit much)*: And you call yourself an *actor*. You have one job: Remember the words, and say them audibly!

RONA *(To Brom, sotto voce)*: Sounds like two jobs.

HOLLIS: But that was the problem

LARKING: What

HOLLIS: I remembered the words *too* well. I remembered so well they felt like mine.

LARKING *(Does not compute)*: Felt like yours.

HOLLIS: He asks me why don't I come on the ark, so I started thinking why. How do I feel about this ark?

LARKING: There's that word again, "feel." You don't feel. You get on the boat, because that's what it says in the fucking Bible. Or would you put words in your creator's mouth?

GREGORY *(Not looking up from the doves)*: Shouldn't say "fucking Bible."

HOLLIS: So, there's no reason I'm not on board yet.

LARKING: No.

HOLLIS: I'm just a little slower than the others.

LARKING: Yes.

HOLLIS *(Not okay)*: Okay.

LARKING: Great.

(Silence. Brom turns the thing on the spit.)

HOLLIS: Except there's the line / where he—
LARKING: Forget about the fucking line!
RONA *(Faux-innocent; making trouble)*: Forget about the Bible?
LARKING: The line isn't in the Bible, I added the line.
BROM: But you just told her don't put words in / God's mouth.
LARKING: Except for me. The director can put words in God's mouth.
GREGORY: Seems confusing
BROM: Sure does
RONA: Yeah.

(A beat. Then, suddenly huge:)

LARKING: MUTINY! MUTINY!
RONA: You're spitting on me.
LARKING *(To Hollis)*: Look what you started, a fucking revolution. This is why they don't let women onstage.
RONA *(Quoting his own words back to him)*: Her brother *died*, Larking.
LARKING: Two months ago! Are we supposed to crawl into his grave with him? No, we have to practice so that His fucking Highness doesn't figure out you're a bunch of talent-free goons.
GREGORY: Shouldn't say "fucking Highness."
LARKING *(Still to Hollis)*: Don't you get it? This is our salvation! The Duke's resident players, safe behind his walls. But you know what, if you'd rather join Henry—you can just lie down like him and let the sickness take you. But I prefer to stand up and hitch the wagon and keep on living.

(Hollis looks down at her feet. The calm before the storm.)

HOLLIS: Let the— "Let it take you"

LARKING: I'm just saying that at / some point

HOLLIS: You're saying it's Henry's *fault* he's dead

LARKING: I'm saying there was a point where he stopped fighting, / we all saw

HOLLIS: The point at which he was breathing blood, I think it was.

BROM: Never mind him, Hollis

HOLLIS: He's saying my brother / deserved it

RONA: Your brother, always your brother. / What about all the others—

HOLLIS: Oh, now he's just my / brother

RONA: It's the same with half of everyone we've ever known.
Half of everyone's in the ground now.

BROM *(Muttering)*: Or not in the ground.

HOLLIS: Exactly: Who's to remember my Henry, on a pyre of everyone we've ever known? In a month, you'll have all forgotten him. And in another year, we'll be forgotten too.

(Beat.)

GREGORY *(To the caged doves)*: Coo coo. Coo coo.

(The others look at Gregory.)

LARKING: We'll be in Bergen by noon. There's a square big enough for the wagon and the scaffold. We'll give them *Cain and Abel*, and the *Fall of Man*, and maybe *Before the Fall*.

RONA: *Before the Fall* is boring.

HOLLIS *(Under her breath)*: Paradise— Who can relate.

LARKING: And we'll finish with *Noah's Flood*.

(A sudden insurgence:)

RONA: What?

BROM: No!

HOLLIS: Every time we've tried it, it's been

BROM *(Grim)*: Memorable.

LARKING: The Duke needs something new. Something timely. He expects us in December, and already the leaves are turning—

BROM: December, that's three months—

LARKING *(No time at all)*: Three months to make the greatest thing he's ever seen.

RONA: The greatest thing. I'd settle for another actor.

BROM: Did you ever think of . . . ?

(Brom looks at Gregory. Then they all look at Gregory.)

GREGORY: Coo coo.

BROM: Never mind.

10

In different corners of the woods, Rona, Brom and Larking all pray to their separate saints. Rona lays her tarot cards out in front of her.

RONA: St. Felicitas, make me a virgin again.
　　I know I'm asking a lot.
　　But St. Felicitas,
　　I believe you have the power to pluck the infant out
　　And close me up
　　And make me pure.

BROM: St. Teresa, who defeated her temptations,
　　Help me forget Henry.
　　I know God took him back to wash him clean of me,
　　And so no one will know how we sinned,

But St. Teresa I still think of him.

St. Teresa, help me find somewhere safe for my thoughts to rest.

Help me not to love a ghost.

LARKING: St. Dominic, help them act well.

Help them be worthy of God's word.

Help them not embarrass me.

I prayed to St. Cosmas last night but St. Dominic, they need *double* the help.

St. Dominic, sit on their shoulders and whisper the lines in their ears when they need you.

RONA: St. Felicitas, make me a virgin

BROM: St. Teresa, make me forget

LARKING: St. Dominic, make them *actors*.

11

The heavens open. Gold and silver lightning bolts. Maybe Gregory turns a crank that rolls a barrel with rocks inside, for thunder. Noah's Wife peers out the window of the Ark.

NOAH'S WIFE:

> The flood comes flowing in full fast,
> From every side it gush-eth past!
> Now all the world is full of flood
> O'er every tree we see in sight.

NOAH:

> This window will I shut anon,
> Into the chamber will we be gone,
> Till this water, O Mighty One,
> Be stopped up by thy might.

(Noah shuts the window. Two seconds of silence. When he opens the window, the rains have stopped.)

> Now forty days are fully gone!
> Send out a dove I will anon.
> If earth, tree, or stone
> Be dry in any place,
> It is a sign, sooth to sain,
> That God hath done us grace.

(Noah releases a real dove. Then Gregory lowers a look-alike dove, made of wood, from the flies.)

NOAH'S WIFE: Ah, how fast it returns!

(The dove holds an olive branch in its mouth. Gregory's struggling with the ropes—it's heavy.)

NOAH:

> Lord, thou hast comfort me today,
> For by this sight we may well say
> The flood begins to cease.
> O gentle dove—

(The dove smashes, spectacularly, to the ground. Gregory tries to lift it, unsuccessfully.)

HOLLIS *(Sotto voce)*: What did you / do!
GREGORY *(Sotto voce)*: He kept saying make it bigger!

(Noah, trying to ignore the chaos, solemnly continues his speech.)

NOAH:

> O gentle dove, you brought with haste
> A sturdy branch from some far place.

(Hollis is looking frantically for the missing branch. Sweat forming on Brom's brow.)

> Hold it aloft, beloved Wife
> To signal the end of all our strife!

(Hollis can't find the branch, so she mimes holding it aloft. Gregory drags the leaden dove offstage, muttering:)

GREGORY: Bugger bugger bugger bugger bugger bugger bugger . . .

NOAH:

> Lord, I thank thee for thy might
> Thy bidding shall be done in hight.

(Larking enters in costume. At first we think he's God, but he starts clapping sarcastically.)

LARKING: Wonderful.

HOLLIS: What're you looking at *me* for, it was Gregory!

LARKING *(To Brom)*: And *you*. If there's no olive branch, you don't stand there like a block of petrified wood in search of its mother forest. You press on, speaking loud and clear!

HOLLIS *(A brand-new thought)*: Or. What if we were to *acknowledge* what's happening?

LARKING: You mean make it up?

HOLLIS: Rather than pretend it's all going to plan.

BROM: What do you want me to do, improvise in rhyming couplets?

> "I see our dove has fallen fast . . ."

HOLLIS *(Helpfully)*:

> "Our troubles surely not have passed."

BROM: Shut up.

12

Everyone asleep by a dying campfire.

HENRY'S APPARITION *(Looking at Hollis)*: One night, by the fire, Hollis dreams she sees her brother in the hissing smoke.

HOLLIS: Henry, is that you?

HENRY'S APPARITION: Miss me, little sister?

HOLLIS: I do. I do miss you.

HENRY'S APPARITION *(Stark, but not ghostly)*: I come from beyond the river of the dead, with a warning.

HOLLIS: If it's about Rona I already know.

HENRY'S APPARITION: Rona?

HOLLIS: That you laid with her

HENRY'S APPARITION *(Genuinely confused)*: I never laid with Rona

HOLLIS: I knew it, thank God

HENRY'S APPARITION: And it's a little disappointing that you *believed* her / frankly

HOLLIS: I'm sorry I'm sorry, she's such a tramp. Give me your warning.

HENRY'S APPARITION: I have come all this way to tell you:

Do not replace me, for the man who replaces me will bring you worse than flood.

HOLLIS: We don't have a choice. We aren't just missing Shem— you were Isaac, and the Angel Gabriel, and Mak the Sheep Stealer . . .

HENRY'S APPARITION: I was versatile.

But the warning stands: Beware the man who would wear my robes and say my lines.

(A beat.)

HOLLIS: In plays, people are always wearing disguises.

How do I know you're my own brother
And not the devil?

HENRY'S APPARITION: My darling sister,

(He touches her on the cheek. Scary-soft:)

The devil has bigger fish to fry.

(Lights shift. Hollis wakes. An unfamiliar man is standing over her [played by the same actor who played Henry's Apparition]. We'll call him the Physic. It is snowing lightly.)

PHYSIC: Miss? Hello, miss?

HOLLIS *(Vague with sleep)*: Henry?

PHYSIC *(Gentle)*: Not Henry.

HOLLIS: Who are you?

PHYSIC: It started snowing—I was passing by.

HOLLIS *(What next)*: Snow in October.

PHYSIC: I didn't want you and your friends to freeze while you slept.

(Hollis stands, recovering her wits.)

HOLLIS: The fire's out.

PHYSIC: I'll help you light it.

HOLLIS *(Almost to herself)*: A conscientious traveler, what next.

PHYSIC: Sorry?

HOLLIS: I will do it, thank you. Now good night.

(The Physic's eyes pass over Rona.)

PHYSIC: You have a pregnant woman with you.

HOLLIS: How do you know that? No one knows that.

PHYSIC: I'm a doctor. A physic.

HOLLIS: Never met a physic.

PHYSIC: . . . Or I used to be.

HOLLIS: What, you kill too many people?

(She was joking, but she sees that it's true.)

PHYSIC: They want miracles, and that is beyond my training.

(Someone snores nearby, loud.)

Who's that?

HOLLIS: Oh, that's God. *(Seeing the Physic's face)* Larking—he's called Larking. But he has a way of staying in character.

(They watch him. Another extra-loud snore.)

He's even louder awake.

PHYSIC: Are you all a family?

HOLLIS: Yes and no. We're players.

PHYSIC: I saw a play once. I didn't care for it. The snake was funny not scary. And when he offered Eve the apple, everyone shouted, "Don't take it! Don't eat it!" but she pretended like she didn't hear us.

HOLLIS: We have lines, we aren't allowed to say just anything.

PHYSIC: The theater is strange. Somehow a hand in a green stocking is a snake, but a real woman isn't a woman—not when she pretends she can't hear us.

HOLLIS *(After a beat)*: Our snake is better than a stocking. We have a kind of coil that can go long or short, like a real snake.

PHYSIC *(A touch ironic)*: Magic.

HOLLIS: There's a man who does the effects for us. He has a mind like a child, but he's the best with effects.

(He looks down at Rona again.)

PHYSIC: Who plays Eve, you or her?

HOLLIS: Rona.

PHYSIC: Of course.

HOLLIS: ?

PHYSIC *(Referring to her pregnancy)*: She tasted the apple and was banished from the garden.

HOLLIS: We're all of us banished.

(Beat.)

You can't hide with us, if that's what you're thinking.

PHYSIC: I'm not hiding. What makes you think I'm hiding?

HOLLIS: You were a physic and now you're not. You haven't slept. *(Off his look)* Bags under your eyes. You're traveling alone and no one travels alone. And you stop to tell me it's snowing out of the kindness of your heart?

PHYSIC *(A beat)*: When the baby comes, I can birth it.

HOLLIS: I was midwife to my mother when my sisters came.

PHYSIC: If any of you gets sick, I can / give you—

HOLLIS: Heal us, like you healed the others? You're not magic.

PHYSIC: I'm not sure anyone is magic anymore. Except maybe your man and his retractable snake.

(Beat. Then, suddenly frank:)

HOLLIS: What is happening?

PHYSIC: You mean

HOLLIS: Why is God doing this?

PHYSIC *(Shrug)*: He's angry with us.

HOLLIS: We've angered him before. But never to the point of . . . extermination.

PHYSIC *(Referring to the Flood)*: Never?

HOLLIS: Or just the once. And he promised to never again /
send the—
PHYSIC: And now He has broken His promise.

*(It's hard to tell if that was sympathy or tough love. The Physic
stands.)*

I am sorry I have nothing to offer you.

(He starts to go.)

HOLLIS: Wait.
Sleep until morning.

(Some darkness and distance between them.)

The birds aren't up yet—you have a little while.
Sleep and I'll tend the fire.

13

*The Physic takes something from a sack and holds out his hand to
Gregory. The others are huddled in another part of the stage.*

PHYSIC: Know what this is?
GREGORY: Nail.
PHYSIC: Not just.
GREGORY: Rusty nail?
PHYSIC: This nail came from the one true cross.
GREGORY: You mean the cross that Jesus?—
PHYSIC: The very.
GREGORY: Looks too new.
PHYSIC: That's on account of its powers.
It can heal the sick, if you pray right.

GREGORY: Nah.

PHYSIC: Nah?

GREGORY: Makes no sense.

PHYSIC: Nothing magic makes sense—that's why we call it magic.

GREGORY: I mean: Why does it *bring* life if it's what took life from Him?

PHYSIC: Oh, you're a smart guy.

GREGORY: Uh-huh.

PHYSIC: How it works is you drive the nail into a wall or a board, whatever's around. You pray, and it bleeds for the person you want to heal. It bleeds so they don't have to, see?

(Gregory nods, solemn.)

Maybe objects do penance, like people. They have to right what they made wrong.

GREGORY *(After a beat)*: It's a stretch.

PHYSIC *(Moving to put it back in his pocket)*: Guess you don't want it then.

GREGORY *(Quickly)*: I do I do.

(The Physic gives him the nail. He glances over at the others.)

PHYSIC: What do you think they're talking about?

GREGORY: You.

PHYSIC: Put in a good word for me?

GREGORY: I don't get a vote.

PHYSIC: Think they'll let me stay?

GREGORY: Well, we're short a man.

(The Physic's ears prick up.)

I wasn't supposed to say that.

PHYSIC: Out with it.

GREGORY *(Reluctant)*: There's roles to fill before we get to Travo. That's where His Highness lives.

PHYSIC: His Highness

GREGORY: The Duke who sponsors us. Mr. Larking says if we find favor enough, he'll retain us in court, which means—

PHYSIC: Shelter from the plague.

(Gregory nods. Beat.)

How come they won't let you vote?

GREGORY *(Matter-of-fact)*: Because I'm an idiot.

PHYSIC: Says who?

GREGORY: Him.

(Larking returns just then, with the others trailing behind.)

LARKING: Physic!

PHYSIC *(Standing)*: Yes.

LARKING: Are you a barber as well?

PHYSIC: Only a physic.

(Larking exchanges a look with the others. Then back to the Physic.)

LARKING *(Very rapidly, with impeccable diction)*: Repeat after me: "Six sick hicks nick six slick bricks with picks and sticks."

PHYSIC: "Six sick hicks nick slicks"— I'm sorry.

RONA: Tsk.

BROM: Can you sing?

PHYSIC: A little. What sort of song?

GREGORY *(Childlike)*: A happy song.

(The Physic clears his throat. They're all staring. A feeling like this could be a train wreck.)

PHYSIC: All right then.

(But he starts to sing beautifully, in perfect Latin—a pretty, upbeat melody.)

> Vita brevis breviter in brevi finietur
> Mors venit velociter quae neminem veretur
> Omnia mors perimit
> Et nulli miseretur
> Et nulli miseretur.

(Maybe Gregory joins in with makeshift percussion—a hammer and a plank—helping the song build to a rousing conclusion.)

LARKING: I'll be buggered. A singing physic.

GREGORY: What do the words mean?

BROM: "Life is short, it will end soon.
 Death comes quickly and spares no one."

HOLLIS *(To the Physic)*: That's a happy song?

PHYSIC: It is if you don't know Latin.

LARKING: On behalf of all of us, Doctor, welcome.

RONA, GREGORY AND BROM *(Generally)*: Welcome. Welcome.
 Good luck. You'll need it.

LARKING: First you'll learn Shem. There's his robe, and his leather sandals.

(The Physic regards Hollis, who hasn't spoken a word.)

PHYSIC *(To Hollis)*: You lie low, miss.

HOLLIS: I was outvoted.

PHYSIC *(Lightly)*: Last night you were my angel. Now you're my chief prosecutor.

HOLLIS: We still don't know your story, sir. We only know it ended badly.

BROM *(To the Physic)*: It isn't personal.

HOLLIS: It isn't?

BROM: It's her brother's shoes you're filling. Her brother Henry.

(We see Brom's face, but the others don't.)

She loved him.

(The Physic goes to Hollis.)

PHYSIC: We won't forget him.

HOLLIS: I doubt that.
 I worry we are built for forgetting.

14

In different corners of the woods, Rona, Brom and the Physic pray to their separate saints.

RONA: St. Felicitas, maybe you didn't hear me before,
 When I asked you to make me a virgin again.
 Or maybe I was asking too much.
 But St. Felicitas, if I must have a child
 Then make him a boy, St. Felicitas.
 Make him a son.
 I don't want a lemon-faced girl.
 I want a boy who climbs trees and drives off demons. /
 St. Felicitas

BROM: St. Teresa, make me well.
 I couldn't make my thoughts clean
 I couldn't stop thinking of him and
 The poison has found a home inside me and feasted there.

(Brom takes off his shirt. There are large, black, egg-sized buboes under his arms: the plague.)

Make me whole, St. Teresa.
   Not only for myself, but for those who have trusted me.

(The Physic makes sure he's alone, then starts to roll up his long sleeve. There is a little leather box on his arm, tied in place with a skein of leather straps. He says the Birkhat Ha-Gomeyl.*)*

PHYSIC: Barukh atah Adonai Eloheinu melekh ha'olam . . .

(Rona takes a rose branch and makes a fist around it. She winces.)

RONA: St. Felicitas, take this pain and give me a son in return.
BROM: St. Teresa, take this pain and make me well in return.

(He takes out a long metal pin.)

PHYSIC: . . . ha'gomeyl lahayavim tovot, sheg'malani kol tov . . .
BROM: St. Teresa, take this pain.

*(Just as Brom raises the pin to lance a boil, lights shift sharply to: Gregory, driving the Christ nail into the set.
   Bang. Bang. Bang.)*

GREGORY *(To the nail)*: You be right there till I need you.

15

Rehearsal. The players ready their masks for the Seven Deadly Sins parade. The Physic has been given Henry's dual role of Envy and Covetousness.

ENVY:

> I am Envy: Fear my jealous stare,
> For those of you who sit out there
> Have took from me my rightful chair.

(The Physic removes his Envy mask, and flips it over.)

COVETOUSNESS: And Covetousness, his closest kin—

LARKING: Remember upside down, not just backwards.

PHYSIC: I'm sorry.

LARKING: Don't be sorry. It's the hardest part on account of it's two-in-one.

RONA *(Under her breath)*: Yeah, who ever had to do that.

PHYSIC *(For Hollis's benefit)*: I'm sure Henry was much better.

HOLLIS: You'll be fine.

LARKING *(To Physic)*: The key is find a different voice for Covetousness— Maybe he's a higher pitch *(Says this in a higher pitch)*, so we can tell him from Envy.

PHYSIC *(Trying a high voice)*: And Covetousness, his closest— *(Bailing)* I'm sorry.

RONA: I never knew the difference, Envy and Covet.

BROM: Envy is for people, Covet is for things.

RONA: "Thy neighbor's wife"? She's a person not a thing.

LARKING: Not when your neighbor's coveting her.

(Rona rolls her eyes.)

PHYSIC: How come I play both?

LARKING: We'd look pretty foolish as the Six Deadlies.

RONA: Lucky we don't look foolish.

(She dons her ridiculous Gluttony mask, pointedly.)

LARKING *(To Physic)*: Even with Gregory we're only six. *(Gregory is nearby as he says this)* I don't like letting him onstage at all, but at least he's in a mask.

RONA: Maybe he should wear it all the time.

LARKING: Okay, you maggots, let's put it all together. From the top.

(The others put their masks on. Even though it's just rehearsal, the room changes a bit—the temperature lowers. As before, a parade of the Seven Deadly Sins:)

PRIDE (BROM):

> They call me Pride—of course I'm first
> I swell and swell until you burst.

GLUTTONY (RONA):

> Bursting suits me mighty fine,
> For Gluttony is my name:
> My father he was a bacon haunch,
> My mother she was the same.

PRIDE (BROM): Look now, here's Wrath.

WRATH (HOLLIS):

> I walk on a bed of knives,
> I sleep with my fists balled tight,
> From hellfire I was born—
> Return with me to Hell you might!

PRIDE (BROM): And look, now Sloth.

SLOTH (GREGORY):

> I was born on a long slow summer's day . . .
> That's already more words than I want to say.

GLUTTONY (RONA): Here's Lechery now:

LECHERY (LARKING):
> Like Gluttony, my cousin,
> I live to eat and eat
> But Satan knows I savor
> A different sort of meat!

ENVY (PHYSIC):
> I am Envy: Fear my jealous stare,
> For those of you who sit out there
> Have took from me my rightful chair!

(The Physic removes his Envy mask, readying to switch characters. Suddenly a seventh actor appears—an Extra Man, already in the mask of Covetousness. He wears a black robe and stands very straight.)

EXTRA MAN: And Covetousness, his closest kin.

(They turn to see him.)

> I'm more inclined to want the chair
> Than hate the person sitting in.

(An awful little pause.
> *Brom counts heads:)*

BROM: One two three four five six seven.
LARKING: Seven
GREGORY: But we're six
LARKING: Says the genius. *(To the Extra Man)* Who's that playing a joke on us?

(No answer.)

RONA *(A brave face)*: It's the boy who pawed me in the tavern the other night. Isn't it. What if I give you a dance after all?

EXTRA MAN: You're far too easily had to be coveted.

RONA: Larking, defend me.

LARKING *(Pretty lame defending)*: If you're looking for a job, friend, we're full up.

EXTRA MAN: No one remembers me?

(The masked figure turns to Hollis.)

Not even you?

(Beat.)

BROM *(Very quiet)*: Henry?

HOLLIS: This is an evil prank—
   Show your face at once.

EXTRA MAN: Hasty hasty.

(The Extra Man's hands slowly rise to his mask. He takes it off: There is nothing underneath but a black void.)

Now you know me.

(Hollis faints.)

I took one of you before.
   Who will be next?

(Beat.)

BROM: I will.

GREGORY: No!

BROM: The sickness has me already.

LARKING: And you kept it a secret?

BROM: I thought, if I prayed—

LARKING: You idiot, you've killed us all.

BROM *(To the Extra Man)*: Take me and not them.

EXTRA MAN *(Amused)*: You think I strike deals?

BROM *(Willful)*: Me and not them.

(He holds out his hand to the Extra Man.)

I am ready.

(Blackout. End of Act One.)

ACT TWO

The actor who plays Gregory comes out in contemporary clothes. His manner is very different now.

THE PLAYWRIGHT: Hi. Hello there. I'm the playwright, I wrote this play. And the Vineyard Theatre thought it might be a good idea if I talked to you for a little while about, well, *(Gestures to the stage around him) Why.* It seems that a few ticket holders have been, um, voting with their feet I guess you would say? And I suggested we could just lock all the doors maybe, or like lightly shame people as they're trying to leave, but they said No. No, they said. We are all adults and it would be better if you could maybe just contextualize things a little.

(Beat.)

Now of course I'm not really the playwright—you've seen me already. I'm Michael Cyril Creighton, I play Gregory, but now I'm going to be the playwright for a little while.

I've studied him in rehearsal for weeks, studied his nervous tics, his twitches, all his many tics and twitches and I am up to the challenge. *(Referring to his clothes)* This is a faithful reproduction of his drab, post-hipster Brooklyn uniform. He favors plaid. *(Pointing out a spot)* Ramen stain.

Hopefully you aren't allergic to these sorts of shenanigans—some people are, which is okay. I think I even am, a bit. We'll work through it together. *(Looks up at the stage manager's booth)* The lights are a little . . . *(The house lights rise a little)* Thank you. *(To us again)* That was planned of course. To help this feel like a frank little detour. "Come with me, as we raise the house lights and look one another in the eye."

I'm going to start by telling you about Mr. Shear's sixth-grade Health class and some of the things that happened there. This was, what, 1989? 1990? One of the things I learned in Health class was how poorly informed I was, relative to other twelve year olds. I remember one day, my frequent tormentor Damon McCutcheon leaned over and said, "Jordan, do you know what a condom is?" And I didn't know, so I quickly answered, "Yes I do I totally do and it's *disgusting*." And Damon McCutcheon said, "You don't know what it is, do you." By now a crowd was forming. And I explained, with as much confidence as possible, that a condom is what women wear when they're having their woman times. Everyone jeered, including Mr. Shear, and they lifted Damon McCutcheon up on their shoulders like a hero and carried him off to fifth period.

One day Mr. Shear was given the task of making us terrified of AIDS. He must have done a good job of this, because six years later, when I finally got a boyfriend, I wouldn't do *anything*. No oral no nothing. We pressed our bodies together uselessly while we kissed, like Pyramus and Thisbe against the wall only without the wall, and our sweaty torsos made that unfortunate farty sound when they slapped together and apart. Months and months of this, all because Mr. Shear had scared me into thinking if I got a drop of Alex Supolski's virgin cum on my hand I was as good as dead. No, that's glib: The fear was real. It was constant and it was real.

The scariest thing Mr. Shear told us about AIDS was not Kaposi's sarcoma, or the hundred-percent mortality rate, though those were scary. The scariest thing was the story of Gaëtan Dugas, the French-Canadian flight attendant who was believed, at the time, to be Patient Zero. Right away, some things that were questionable to us:

Male flight attendants,

French-Canadians,

Names with the sound "gay" in them.

Of course, Mr. Shear pronounced it GAY-shun Doo-GAY, not Gaëtan Dugas. Gaytian DuGay had sex with monkeys in the jungles of Africa, then he flew to the jungles of New York City to have sex with *you*, if you let him, and then the next morning he said "Welcome to the world of AIDS" before swishing out of your life forever. Gaytian DuGay, as if daring the twelve-year-old boys to send a chorus of "gay, gay, gay, gay" echoing around the classroom. And they did, they dared—and that word stuck in my throat for years.

Later in college, after months of bad sex with Alex Supolski had given way to no sex at all, I was walking through the Castro district with some friends. It's 1997 now. And probably we were seeing *Vertigo* at the beautiful old movie house, or buying a Portishead CD—the sort of quaint, tangible things people did in the '90s. And we passed by a funeral home—I think it was sandwiched between a nightclub and a store for little scraps of Lycra to wear on gay cruises—and I remember saying, Look at that, how funny that there's a funeral home right in the middle of all this, I thought this was like a party neighborhood, how *funny*. And my friend Holmes—who was a lesbian who had been arrested at several protests—my friend Holmes says,

What are you talking about, Jordan?

What are you *talking* about?

A hundred thousand people died here. The other *day* they died here. Did you think it was just a place people went to buy little scraps of Lycra to wear on gay cruises?

Because I was safe in Mr. Shear's Health class in 1990, safely learning to be scared, I forgot how people had struggled and fought and died, and were struggling and fighting still. I had never even met anyone with AIDS. Unless you count Mr. Goldsworthy.

Mr. Goldsworthy was a nervous, wholesome man who wore pleated khakis and was probably, no definitely younger than we thought he was. He was married to his high school sweetheart. In his free time, Mr. Goldsworthy coached the debate club and the boys' tennis team. I was on both teams, and a star on neither. The varsity tennis kids did an impression of him that went something like:

(Mr. Goldsworthy appears in a pool of golden light, played by the same actor who played Brom. He is wholesomely handsome in a sweater vest.)

MR. GOLDSWORTHY *(Lisping)*: "Come on, boys, let's get nice and sweaty."
PLAYWRIGHT: And an alternate version, which went like:
MR. GOLDSWORTHY *(Lisping)*: "That's it, boys. Snap those towels."
PLAYWRIGHT: The variations were endless, and always well-received—as long as lots of "S"s were involved.

Mr. Goldsworthy made us keep daily journals in debate class. And one day, while we were journaling, Mr.

Goldsworthy stepped out of the classroom. And my friend Bryan O'Keefe and I—I can't believe we did this—we crept over and read Mr. Goldsworthy's own journal, which was lying open on the desk. We didn't have to look long. At the bottom of the page, in perfect cursive:

MR. GOLDSWORTHY *(No lisp)*: November 4th 1993. I can't wait to see Bruce tonight, to explore the city and each other.

(Mr. Goldsworthy's light goes out.)

PLAYWRIGHT: First of all, "Bruce." Gayest of all names. Then, "Explore the city and each other"—even then I recoiled from the bad poetry of it. But also my heart secretly soared at the thought of this adult escape. If Mr. Goldsworthy could find somewhere, far from the junior varsity tennis team, somewhere truly *(No lisp)* nice and sweaty, then perhaps I could find my way there too some day.

Did Mr. Goldsworthy leave his journal open *hoping* that someone would find it, and out him, and his life would change? If so, we failed him, Bryan O'Keefe and I. We kept his secret, and he stayed in the closet, putting on his pleated khakis every morning. But a few years later, I was home from college and I saw Mr. Goldsworthy at a movie theater. Or someone who looked like Mr. Goldsworthy, only his hair was dyed purple, and he had a tongue piercing, and he looked ten years younger than I remembered. He looked younger than I've ever felt. He seemed barely to remember me, and certainly he no longer needed me to liberate him. He looked young and happy and gay, and six years later he died from AIDS.

(A longer beat. Has he lost his way?)

The question playwrights are always asked is, "Where did the play come from?" And we are annoyed at this question.

Probably because we're afraid that the minute we start answering it, we'll be making the whole thing smaller. This is all to say that I didn't sit down to write a play about Mr. Goldsworthy, or the bubonic plague, even. No, for some reason I was interested in a small strange scene from the fourteenth century morality play *Noah's Flood*.

(The Brom and Hollis actors enter, costumed as Noah and Noah's Wife.)

Especially the moment when Noah turns to his wife and asks:

NOAH:

> Wife! Why standst thou there?
> Why doesn't thou join me on the ark?
> Come in, on God's half! Time it were,
> For fear lest that we drown.

PLAYWRIGHT: To which she replies:

NOAH'S WIFE:

> Yea, sir, set up your sail
> And row forth with evil hail,
> For without any fail,
> I will not out of this town!

PLAYWRIGHT: Yikes. And that's just the beginning, because Noah keeps asking—he begs, he pleads, and still she refuses. Not just refuses—she boxes him on the ears, she spits on him, she curses God. Normally, people in morality plays behave like good little stick figures. They come out and say their name—"I'm Prudence," or "I'm Wrath"—and they are prudent, or they are wrathful, and they get off. Like a school play where the kids play vegetables. But here was this woman who stops the whole narrative cold, acting out a story that can't be found anywhere in the Bible. Driven by a motive that is at best inscrutable and at worst, well—

HOLLIS: Crazy.

PLAYWRIGHT: Thank you. I mean who in their right mind doesn't get on a big boat their husband has been instructed by *God* to build, when the water is rising and everyone without a boat is already floating dead and bloated at your feet?

(Hollis raises her hand to ask a question, but the Playwright doesn't notice.)

You could argue that Noah's Wife is simply comic relief, of a not-very-feminist sort. After God's long shaming sermons, the players had to make people laugh to keep them from wandering away from the pageant wagon, to keep them from canceling their medieval subscriptions. And what's funnier than an angry housewife shaking a rolling pin over her head? But I prefer to think of this little passage in *Noah's Flood* as a milestone in the emergence of *character*. An early effort to show a person with real features—with wrinkles with warts with a soul. The beginning of "I." Now, why might we be seeing this right at the height of the bubonic plague?

(Brom clears his throat. The Playwright turns back to the actors, remembering they're still there.)

Yes! You have an answer!

BROM: Actually I was just wondering if we could—

PLAYWRIGHT: Oh sorry, yes, that's all for now. Thank you both.

BROM: Yup.

(Brom and Hollis start to exit.)

PLAYWRIGHT: See you in a few. *(To us, a little sanctimonious)* You know, I think we can never thank them enough.

BROM (*Muttering, almost offstage*): You can thank us by paying us more.

PLAYWRIGHT: What's that?

BROM: Nothing.

(*And they're gone.*)

PLAYWRIGHT: It's important to mention that, in the Middle Ages, people didn't think of themselves as "I" in the same way we do today. The concept of the individual as we know it hadn't been invented. It took people like Giotto and Tolstoy and Freud and Seuss to form our broad, quilty idea of the self. We'll never know exactly how people thought of themselves back then, but we do know they had no Tumblr pages, no diaries for the most part, no sense that they could climb up out of poverty and own a huge company. Their teacher, if they had one, didn't tell them, "You're *special*, everyone is special." They told them that kings and queens are special and other people are serfs.

What, then, do we know about these noble amateurs making theater in the dark of the fourteenth century? We know that they were keenly aware of the brevity of life. Every time they said goodbye, it might be *goodbye*. Every play they started writing they might not live to finish. So, what if Noah's Wife wasn't just a cheap ploy to keep the audience from leaving? What if, having watched everyone they knew be tossed on an anonymous heap by the side of the road, they were uniquely compelled to show us a human being as an individual? (*Looking off into the wings*) Do we have the cards?

(*No answer.*)

And by we I mean you?

RONA (*Offstage*): Coming.

(The actors who play Larking, Rona and the Physic come out, wearing sandwich boards with paintings on the back. They are slightly ornery about having such a mule-like role in Act Two, but the Playwright doesn't seem to notice.)

PLAYWRIGHT: We can see this increasing interest in the individual very clearly in Western painting. First we have a Byzantine Madonna—

(Larking's sandwich board says "Byzantine" on the front. Larking turns upstage, revealing:)

Not without her human qualities, but still less a person than an icon. A tuning fork for our faith. Then, a hundred years later, we have Giotto . . .

(Rona turns upstage so that her "Early Renaissance" board reveals:)

See how the eyes are filled with new intelligence, new mystery. (By now, the first lamps of the Renaissance are being lit, even though the plague is still raging across Europe.) Then, a hundred-plus years later, we have:

(The Physic, whose board is marked "Late Renaissance," turns around to reveal:)

. . . Leonardo and the High Renaissance. The formal pose has melted into a scene of domestic normalcy. Playful, particular—and seemingly painted by someone who's seen an actual *baby* before. Now, Mary is more concerned with her child than with our worship.

What happened here? It wasn't just that painters had grown more adept at perspective, at mixing pigments. They had become more interested in *people* as the main event, not as players in a predetermined divine script.

Something had spurred them to think, "Maybe there's no one in charge, maybe we can act for ourselves, maybe we can go off . . . script.

(He notices that Quincy Tyler Bernstine, the actor who plays Hollis, has appeared again in the wings.)

QUINCY: Excuse me, Michael?
PLAYWRIGHT: I'm sorry, are you speaking to me?

QUINCY *(Slight eye roll)*: Sorry, I mean Jordan.

PLAYWRIGHT: Am I running long?

QUINCY: Well, yes, actually, but I really just wanted to say that I have a story that might be helpful.

PLAYWRIGHT: Helpful?

QUINCY: I mean, from an actor's perspective.

PLAYWRIGHT: "Helpful."

QUINCY: . . . As you're trying to bring all of these themes together? Coherently?

PLAYWRIGHT *(Defensive)*: Do you mean the sixth-grade Health class and AIDS? I'm totally going to tie it back in.

QUINCY: Totally. But if I could just tell them this thing that happened when I was doing a show—

PLAYWRIGHT: Is this the time you threw up on Trigorin?

QUINCY *("And thanks for telling them")*: No.

PLAYWRIGHT: Sorry. Go ahead.

QUINCY: Yeah?

PLAYWRIGHT: They're all yours.

QUINCY: Uh. So. *(Really looking at us now)* Hi. I'm Quincy. A few years ago now, I was doing a production of *A Christmas Carol* down in Louisville, Kentucky, and I was playing Mrs. Cratchit. Mrs. Cratchit doesn't have as much to do as Mr. Cratchit. Bob. I mean there were a few things for me to invest in, like, you know, I had to pay attention to my kids, to create specific relationships with our many Cratchit children. I think we had eight or nine kids, maybe more— they really wanted to give the local kids a chance onstage— and I had to create, you know, specific relationships with all of them—figure out who did their homework, who was the bad seed, who liked to torture insects. And of course there was the intense situation with Tiny Tim, who was played by the cutest little five-year-old girl, she was great. Her name was Hero, which was sort of perfect—she was always keeping me from getting lost backstage. I personally don't enjoy a Tiny Tim who milks me for sympathy, and this girl she had a kind of fiery little will, she was kind of spunky and wonderful and, uh. Really played against the disability.

Now, did you know that Mrs. Cratchit doesn't even have a first name?

PLAYWRIGHT: Just like Noah's Wife—

QUINCY: Yes, although in the Jewish tradition, she is called Naamah, and sometimes Emzara.

PLAYWRIGHT: Wow.

QUINCY: But you knew that, from all the research you did.

PLAYWRIGHT *(He didn't)*: Totally. From the research, for the play.

QUINCY: So yeah, originally she didn't have a first name, and the same is true of Mrs. Cratchit. In some of the more feminist-leaning adaptations, people have decided to call her Emily. Thoughtful. But in this version, not only did I not have a name, but the show had been cut down to a sleek intermissionless ninety minutes, and so guess whose scenes had been hacked to pieces? Yes. Mine. And on top of that the director made us all sing Christmas carols during the transitions—just to, you know, make it accessible— so we would all come out in a big group and sing "God Rest Ye Merry Gentlemen" while the turntable was turning, which was problematic for me because I can't sing but also because well, *why*. Why was I singing to the audience and, more importantly, who was doing the singing? Who is the "I"? Is it me, Quincy (who can't sing) or is it me, Emily Cratchit, and does Emily Cratchit with all of her kids have time to leave the house and sing "God Rest Ye Merry Gentlemen" to . . . whom? I mean who am I and who is the audience? Who are you? Please don't answer. It's not that kind of play.

So when it came time to sing, I was so paralyzed I couldn't make a sound because I didn't know who I was or why I was there, so I would just:

(She mouths the words to "God Rest Ye Merry Gentlemen" enthusiastically.)

And then one night while I was doing that, this weird little idea came to me. What if . . . .? What if this whole *Christmas Carol* business, this whole situation where Scrooge gets redeemed, gets taught the true meaning of Christmas by supernatural beings was actually engineered and controlled by . . . ME. EMILY CRATCHIT. What if this whole thing had been my idea, what if I was the most supernatural being of all, what if I had done some secret spells in my kitchen to raise the ghost of Marley, to raise the ghosts of Past, Present, Future— What if Emily Cratchit was actually a witch, what if I was the *author of this whole experience?* I mean, c'mon, who has the strongest motive for getting Ebenezer to reform his ways? Whose idea was this whole thing anyway? Marley's? God's? The Christmas spirits? Boring. I was a real live flesh-and-blood human woman, nay MOTHER, with eight or nine kids, one of whom had a serious disability. I had the motive! My husband needed a fucking raise, and by God I was going to do whatever I could to make that happen. For our Family. For my brave little Tiny Tim who never once felt sorry for herself/himself. Even if that meant casting some spells, raising up some ghosts to scare the shit out of my husband's boss.

So this was my "invisible" work. I, Quincy, aka Emily Cratchit, was going to take control of the narrative from the inside, even if no one knew I was doing it. By God, I was going to have some motherfucking agency. Now I could walk onstage with a sense of purpose! I knew who I was—I was the witch who was in charge of this whole play. I could sing loudly! And if I sang off-key it didn't matter because I wasn't trying to sound pretty I was trying to scare the shit out of you, to get you to take a look at yourselves, to take yourselves on (as my therapist likes to say) before for it was *too late*.

One night before the show I was sitting on the couch sharing a Snickers bar with the Ghost of Christmas Past and I told her my secret. I was afraid she would think I was crazy but instead she said, "Interesting Choice." And after that, she always gave me a meaningful look while we were singing "We Wish You a Merry Christmas" at the end of the play, as if to say: "Nice work, Goody Cratchit," and I would nod silently to her, from under my bonnet: "Thank you, Christmas Past, fellow Master of the Black Arts."

I guess my point is that I had to find a way to give myself a sense of purpose and wholeness onstage. I desperately needed a narrative that helped me not feel so powerless. And so, to sum this all up—

PLAYWRIGHT: Yes, good—

QUINCY: I think this voicelessness—this *namelessness* I had been suffering from, I mean it isn't your brother dying from the Black *Death* maybe, but I think it still relates to the powerlessness we sometimes feel as mortal human creatures. Because let's face it if you ever stop to think about it, this whole situation, this whole Being a Person, is really just chaos and dissipation and fragmentation, and, well, basically a death march basically.

(Beat.)

Sorry, that got a little—

PLAYWRIGHT *(Newly energized)*: No, no!—I mean that was *dark*— but this is good

QUINCY: Yeah?

PLAYWRIGHT: Because those fourteenth century players telling the story of Noah's Ark—maybe they were also trying to make their roles a little less nameless, in the hope that they would feel less nameless themselves. And in that effort, the first *characters* were born. From Noah's Wife to— *(He looks to Quincy)*

QUINCY: Namaah—

PLAYWRIGHT: —To Namaah. From Mrs. Cratchit to Emily Cratchit, Secret Witch. From Mr. Goldsworthy to Robert Goldsworthy, secret lover of Bruce.

Yes: It's possible that the reason we're looking at this fourteenth century epidemic in the first place is because of a different epidemic, and the efforts of some ramen-stained, plaid-wearing person to understand the things it extinguished and the things it inspired, and whether he even has the *right* to be inspired by it, having only feared. To understand whether Mr. Goldsworthy left his journal open hoping to be saved. Or did he leave it open to save me, because that's really what he did.

What, then, to take from this little detour? I suspect we can boil it all down to a single (if multitiered) question:

Confronted with a crisis, what is the artistic impulse?

Is it to dive headlong in, and record suffering for future generations?

Or is it to make us forget the crisis? To fill us, either by beauty or laughter, with the will to live.

Or or or, is it a rejection of art entirely, a mere fight for survival? A turning away from the luxury of fiction.

And if it's art we choose, then which is art:

An ark to carry us over the waters?

Or a nail that bleeds for us, so that we can be healed?

Yes.

Yes.

Yes.

Yes.

Yes.

(He takes us in for a moment, then turns upstage. The nail that he put in the wall earlier, as Gregory, has started to bleed.)

Yes.

(Quick fade. End of Act Two.)

ACT THREE

1

The Playwright changes back into his Gregory costume:

GREGORY: Back to the open road.

  Back to lice in your hair and no running water and go to bed when the sun goes down. It makes that other century seem fond and faraway.

  When last we left them, the players had a visitor—

(Light on the Extra Man entering, as before.)

And Brom made a sacrifice—

(Light on Brom holding his hand out, as before.)

And it was all a little much for Hollis—

(Light on Hollis fainting, as before. The Physic rushes to her side.)

There now, you're all caught up. And now I surrender my omniscience. (I feel lighter already.) Fourth wall up— You're on your own.

(Light shifts. Gregory runs to join the others, who are gathered around a hole in the ground. Larking is delivering a eulogy of sorts:)

LARKING: Brom spoke clearly. He remembered his lines.

He was the strongest actor, next to me. *(An amendment)* He was the strongest actor.

I don't know much else, except that he was from the north and he could mend shoes and he kept to himself. He never complained of the cold.

GREGORY: Probably 'cause he was from the north.

LARKING *("Shut up")*: Thank you, Gregory.

Brom never spoke of his family, or his loves. He had a job and he did it. I expect to see him in Heaven, if I make it there.

(Larking throws the first shovelful of dirt. The Physic and Hollis stand slightly apart from the others:)

PHYSIC *(Scoffing)*: Heaven.

HOLLIS *(Taken aback)*: Do you see him elsewhere?

PHYSIC: My mother told me, "Asher, Heaven and Hell are the same lie. They're to keep people from living while they've the chance." I was six.

HOLLIS: I'm sorry

PHYSIC: For what

HOLLIS: That you inherited her blasphemy.

(Beat.)

"Asher."

(The blood drains from his face. He's revealed himself.)

It's a Jewish name. And that's why you were running away.

PHYSIC: In my town, they think the Jews are responsible.

HOLLIS: For the plague? They are giving you a lot of credit.

(*In earnest*) I've heard of your people poisoning wells and stealing children, but nothing so . . .

PHYSIC: Godly?

(She nods. A beat.)

They made a house.

HOLLIS: They / made?—

PHYSIC: A plain wooden house, by the river. It was a house for Jews.

HOLLIS: To live in, separately?

(He shakes his head.)

PHYSIC: There were no windows, which should have been sign enough. All the Jews of the town were made to go inside. Then they lit the torches. Everyone stood across the river and watched it burn. They wanted to make sure the Jews didn't change shape and escape.

HOLLIS: But then how did you?—

PHYSIC: I've kept it secret, for years. Jewish doctors can't treat Christian patients. *(She nods: of course)* So it was easy to escape. I simply had to stand there on the bank and . . . watch.

HOLLIS: Then you weren't running from the townspeople when we met you.

PHYSIC: No. I was simply running. Probably I will always be running.

(Beat. Hollis glances toward the others at Brom's grave.)

HOLLIS: Did we dream it?

PHYSIC: Six people don't have the same dream. And that's Brom down in that hole, in any case.

HOLLIS: I don't believe that's him down there.

PHYSIC: "Heaven."

LARKING *(To the others)*: Hitch up the wagon.

(Larking comes from the grave now, wiping the dirt from his hands.)

PHYSIC: Please— Keep my secret.

HOLLIS: Why should I?

PHYSIC: Please.

(Larking is there.)

LARKING: We can still make it by the solstice if we hurry.

HOLLIS *("We're not still going?")*: It is mountains away. It is *countries* away.

LARKING *(As he exits)*: Then you'd better start walking.

2

The Duke's palace. Larking, Rona, Hollis, Gregory and the Physic are met by the Duke's officious Major-Domo (played by the actor who played Brom). They are freezing.

MAJOR-DOMO: You are the players?

LARKING *(Bowing)*: We are.

GREGORY: Are you the Duke?

LARKING: Gregory—

MAJOR-DOMO: I am the Duke's Major-Domo, I oversee the operations of the palace.

We are full up for the holidays, but there's two cots in there for you to fight over, and hay for the rest. If you want to wash there's a pump by the stables.

LARKING: And firewood?

MAJOR-DOMO: There's woods all around, aren't there.

(Larking is chastened—a new look for him.)

Two Tuesdays next is the night before Epiphany, that's when you'll perform for His Excellency. He's expecting something more memorable than last year.

LARKING: What was wrong with last year?

MAJOR-DOMO *(Deadpan)*: He doesn't remember.

RONA: Oh—

(Rona has a sudden dizzy spell. Larking steadies her.)

MAJOR-DOMO: What's the matter with her.

HOLLIS: She hasn't had much to eat today.

MAJOR-DOMO: Could've fooled me. Fat cow.

(Hollis and the Physic lock eyes.)

GREGORY: She's not, she's beautiful.

MAJOR-DOMO: Eye of the beholder, they say.

LARKING: Excuse me, but when do we get an audience with the Duke?

MAJOR-DOMO: An audience with the Duke?

LARKING: For the sake of preparation.

MAJOR-DOMO *(Preposterous)*: An audience with the Duke!

LARKING: . . . So that we may pay our respects, take any requests His Excellency may have—

MAJOR-DOMO: No one sees the Duke except his doctor, his chamber boy, his scribe, and his food taster. Even his wife and daughters are on quarantine. The littlest took ill one morning and she was in the ground by sundown.

HOLLIS: How will he see the performance?

MAJOR-DOMO: There is a loose brick in his bedchamber for spying on visitors of state. He will remove the brick and watch your performance, as a prisoner watches the sky through a slit in his cell.

HOLLIS: It doesn't sound very *festive*.

MAJOR-DOMO: If the Duke favors you, he will give you a message through me. That is your audience with him.

GREGORY: Do you have paint?

MAJOR-DOMO: Excuse me?

GREGORY: White paint is best, but orange could also be good.

LARKING: Gregory, you idiot—

MAJOR-DOMO (*Happy to contradict Larking*): We'll see about some paint for the gentleman. (*As he exits*) The Duke does enjoy spectacle.

LARKING (*Turning to Gregory with contempt*): Paint?

GREGORY: It's for an idea— How Rona could play the other two sons, not just Shem.

RONA: Oh good, more lines.

HOLLIS (*A beat*): I think it's colder in here than outside.

PHYSIC: I'll get the firewood.

HOLLIS: I can help.

LARKING: We'll draw straws for the cots.

HOLLIS: Let's give Rona one.

LARKING: Why should she have it, just like that?

RONA (*Throwing Hollis a look that says "Don't give me away"*): Straw's good enough for me.

3

Dress Rehearsal. Dark clouds signal the arrival of the Flood.

GOD:

> The flood is nigh, as well you see;
> Therefore tarry you nought—
> Aboard the vessel you ought!

(Larking steps out of the scene and watches from the wings. Maybe he mouths the words from time to time. The Physic has taken over the role of Noah.)

NOAH: Come Shem, my son, come Wife, come all aboard!

SHEM: Wife, come with me, if you fear flood.

SHEM'S WIFE: Here I am, Husband. Humble wife of Shem, I follow where my husband goes.

NOAH: Shem, gather your brothers, younger and youngest.

SHEM: Brothers, come hither!

(Shem pulls a cord on his costume that releases his two "brothers," wooden cutouts of Ham and Japhet that fall to either side of his shoulders. Rona throws her voice, acting as the other brothers. Somehow she has four roles now.)

HAM: Here I am Father, your second son Ham.

JAPHET: And I, your third son Japhet.

HAM: Shall we aboard as well?

JAPHET *(A kind of echo—pretending to do both voices at once)*: . . . As well?

NOAH: Quickly, my sons.

RONA: This is . . . / awful.

LARKING: Don't stop. Now counter, so that Hollis can move into place.

(Rona and the Physic counter. Hollis moves into place as Noah's Wife.)

And Noah says,
NOAH: Wife!

(Rona touches her stomach.)

Why stands thou there?
RONA: Oh no.

(Her water has broken.)

HOLLIS: It's not—
RONA: Yes I think
LARKING: What is it now?
RONA *(To Hollis)*: It's coming.
LARKING: What's coming?

(They don't say anything.)

What?

(Blackout.)

4

Lights up abruptly. The Physic is delivering Rona's baby. It is not going well. The others assist, as well as they can. Gregory is (secretly) a nervous father.

PHYSIC: Apply the sard stone!
GREGORY: Apply the sard stone!
LARKING: I'm not deaf!
PHYSIC: Hurry.
LARKING: Where?
GREGORY: In your hand!
LARKING (*"You idiot"*): . . . Do I *put* it?
PHYSIC: Her inner thighs.

> (*Rona screams, wracked with a painful spasm. Larking rubs the large, blood-red stone on her thighs.*)

> "Oh happy stone, work your magic."

LARKING: Like this?
PHYSIC: No—closer to, you know
LARKING: What
RONA: My cunt, you idiot.
LARKING: This is weird.
HOLLIS: Here, I can—

> (*Hollis takes the stone and places it between her legs.*)

PHYSIC:

> "Open up, you dark gates,
> Just as the gates of Hell opened
> For Christ the redeemer and all the harrowed souls!"

> (*Rona screams.*)

LARKING: I can't look.
HOLLIS: It's normal, this is normal.

PHYSIC:

> "Just as those Hellish doors opened,
> Open now, so that the child may come out intact,
> And that this mother's life be saved also."

LARKING: Is it working?

PHYSIC: It isn't *instant!*

(Rona grunts something indecipherable but angry.)

What'd she say?

HOLLIS: "Men are worthless," I think.

PHYSIC *(To Rona)*: Don't worry, I've done this before

RONA *(Through clenched teeth)*: Coulda fool may—

HOLLIS *(Translating)*: "Coulda fooled me."

PHYSIC: I got it.

RONA: Hollis

PHYSIC: Keep pushing

RONA: Where's Hollis / I want Hollis

HOLLIS: I'm here, Rona, I'm right / here

PHYSIC: Keep pushing, it's past ready

GREGORY *(Nervous dad)*: "Past ready," what's that?

PHYSIC: It has to come out—

You can see the top of its head there?

LARKING *("Ew")*: Oh yeah

GREGORY: Has to come out or what?

PHYSIC: It's just—time.

(Hollis clocks that he's being evasive—she knows enough about childbirth to be scared.)

RONA *(Exhausted)*: How long have I been doing this now? It feels like all my life.

LARKING: It was dark when you started and now it's getting dark again.

HOLLIS: Rona, push

RONA: I'm so tired

PHYSIC: Rona, you / have to

GREGORY: Rona, push.

RONA *(Through her teeth)*: Fuck!

PHYSIC: Rona, you're a tough crazy lady, / I know you can // do this for me. Do it for your baby, /// I know you want to give your baby a chance don't give him back to God just yet, take him for yourself first! Hold him in your arms!

RONA *(Overlapping at "/ ")*: Fuck!

    Fuck.

    Fuck.

    Fuck.

    FUCK YOU, LARKING

    FUCK. YOU.

    FUCK. YOU.

HOLLIS *(Soothingly, overlapping at " // ")*: I can see him, Rona. You're so close. You're so close. I can see him.

GREGORY *(Overlapping at " /// ")*: Rona Rona Rona Rona Rona Rona Rona Rona Rona Rona Rona Rona Rona Rona Rona Rona Rona Rona Rona Rona.

LARKING *(Overlapping at " /// ")*: Rona, you stupid mule, don't fuck this up for me—

    God put you on this earth to do one thing and it sure isn't acting. I want a son, Rona, give me a son, Rona //// give me my son ///// give me my son

PHYSIC *(Overlapping at " //// ")*: Push, Rona, push, Rona, push!

RONA *(Overlapping at " ///// ")*: FUCK YOU LARKING IT ISN'T YOURS.

(The baby comes.)

LARKING: What?

(The Physic holds up the baby.)

PHYSIC: It's a girl, Rona! It's a girl!

(Rona doesn't say anything.)

Rona?

(No answer.)

HOLLIS: She wanted a boy.
LARKING: "It isn't yours."
    (To Rona) Whose is it then?
HOLLIS: It isn't crying.
LARKING *(To Rona)*: Answer me, you stupid whore. Was it Brom?
HOLLIS *(To Physic)*: Why isn't she crying?
PHYSIC: She's too early, / I was afraid of this
LARKING *(To Rona)*: Was it Henry?
GREGORY *(To Physic)*: What's wrong what's wrong?
HOLLIS: The poor little— Oh Rona.
LARKING: What.

(Larking looks at the motionless baby in the Physic's arms. They watch, silently, as the Physic wraps it in a cloth.)

GREGORY: Can I hold her?

5

Larking and the Physic are in costume. Hollis sits, only half in her Noah's Wife costume. She looks like she's been through a storm.
    The Major-Domo stands at the door.

MAJOR-DOMO: The Duke is waiting.

LARKING: Yes we know.

MAJOR-DOMO: The Duke never waits.

LARKING *(Referring to Hollis)*: She's almost ready.

(Hollis doesn't move or respond. Not altogether there.)

MAJOR-DOMO: She doesn't look ready.

LARKING *(Sotto voce)*: Put on your shoes, you stupid slag. Don't make me beg.

HOLLIS *(Not looking at him, biting her words)*: Rona lies in the next room, nearly dead.

LARKING: And you think your stubbornness will make her well?

PHYSIC: Even if we push her out of our minds, who will play her part?

LARKING: I will

PHYSIC: You?

LARKING: If the rest of you speak slowly, and add a few long pauses, I can climb down the scaffold, and tear off the God beard, and get into Shem's costume, while throwing my voice onto the stage—

PHYSIC *(Dry)*: Who needs the rest of us? You may as well play all the parts.

LARKING *(Not realizing he was being dry)*: You don't know how long I've considered it.

MAJOR-DOMO: Your answer, sirs.

PHYSIC *(To Larking)*: Face it, there's no one—

GREGORY: There's me.

(The three men look at him.)

I know the lines. I watch every night.

PHYSIC: He knows the lines. He watches every night.

(Larking turns away, disgusted.)

LARKING: Better not to go on at all.

(The Major-Domo starts to go. With a trace of sadistic delight:)

MAJOR-DOMO: I will give His Highness the bad news.
HOLLIS: Stop.

(He stops, hearing the authority in her voice. [For the first time in the scene, it's like she's completely there, woken from her spell.])

(To Larking, a command) We will perform. And Gregory will take her part. And we will be saved.

(Larking takes in Gregory one more time. Capitulating:)

LARKING: It will be a night to remember.

6

The performance for the Duke. We are in the middle of the scene where the animals file onto the Ark. Gregory stands in for Rona, playing Shem and Shem's Wife.

NOAH:

    Here are cocks, kites, crows,
    Rooks and ravens, many rows,
    Storks and spoonbills, heaven knows,
    Each one in his kind.

SHEM:

    And here are doves, digs, drakes,
    Redshanks running through the lakes . . .

(Hollis whispers to the Physic, as Shem continues to narrate the parade of animals:)

HOLLIS *(Sotto voce)*: It isn't going well.

PHYSIC *(Sotto voce)*: At least he knows the words.

SHEM *(Continuous, underneath)*:
> . . . Each fowl that to safety makes
> In this ship men may find.

HOLLIS *(Sotto voce)*: I don't mean Gregory. The crowd is sitting on their hands. They're city people—they've seen effects before.

PHYSIC *(Sotto voce)*: What can we do? We have lines.

SHEM:
> Camels, donkeys trail behind
> Buck and doe, hart and hind
> Beasts of every type and kind
> Have boarded, thinketh me.

NOAH:
> Wife! Why stands thou there?
> Come in, on God's half!
> Time it were,
> For fear lest that we drown.

NOAH'S WIFE: Yea, sir, I will not.

(Beat. The Physic is flummoxed.)

NOAH: Thou will . . . "not"?

(Larking hisses from the wings, sotto voce:)

LARKING: You will! She will!

NOAH'S WIFE: Yea I will not.

NOAH *(Privately; to Hollis, not the audience)*: Why not?

(She kisses him softly on the mouth.)

HOLLIS: I don't feel like it.

(Shifting to Noah's Wife again:)

> Husband dear, set up your sail
> And row forth with evil hail,
> For without any fail,
> I will not out of this town!

NOAH:

> Headstrong wife, the waters rise
> There is no room for . . . *(Reaching for a rhyme)*

NOAH'S WIFE:

> —Compromise?
> Nevertheless it's too unwise
> To leave our friends behind.

NOAH:

> Fine friends to you they'll surely be
> If you, with they, are under the sea.

NOAH'S WIFE:

> Then row forth, Noah, get thee gone
> If you're so deft at moving on—
> Cut old ties, forget old friends
> Dispense with *all*, if it your spiteful God offends!

(Maybe there are murmurs and snorts from the unseen crowd. Larking furiously signals to Gregory to intervene.)

LARKING: Gregory!

SHEM:
> Father, I shall fetch her in, I trow,
> Without any fail!

NOAH: Good lad—

SHEM:
> Mother, look and see the wind,
> For we are set to sail.

NOAH'S WIFE:
> Son, go again to him and say
> I will not come therein today.

SHEM: Brothers, help me fetch her in!

(Shem pulls the cord that releases the wooden cutouts of Ham and Japhet.)

NOAH: Yes, good sons, make haste—
> Which of you can help?
SHEM: I, Shem, the tallest!
HAM: And I, Ham, the strongest!
JAPHET: And I, Japhet, the . . . longest-naméd!
SHEM: We all shall help
HAM *(Echo)*: help
JAPHET *(Echo)*: help.

SHEM:

> Mother we pray you all together
> Come into the ship for fear of the weather.

NOAH'S WIFE:

> How can we trust our maker anymore?
> My will is just as iron as before!

(A furious Larking appears as God—an unplanned intervention.)

GOD:

> Stubborn wife, whose mouth runneth freely
> I, your *God*, commandeth . . . theely.
> Halt this madness and board the ark
> Or *all* of us shall drown.
> (All of you I mean.)

(Hollis delivers the following clear-eyed—on the verge of contemporary, naturalistic acting:)

NOAH'S WIFE:

> For the sake of all the luckless others
> For children lost and for their mothers
> For buried friends and buried brothers
> For those already gone to ill,
> I now submit unto Thy will.

(At last she boards the ark.)

SHEM: Welcome
HAM: Welcome
JAPHET: Welcome, Mother, to this boat
NOAH'S WIFE: Now have thou *that* for thy note!

(She cuffs "Japhet" on the head, and his wooden head goes flying off, into the seats.

From somewhere far off, far above the audience's heads, through an opening in a brick wall, comes a hearty chuckle. The Duke. The actors look up. The chuckle goes on and on. They don't know whether or not to continue.)

7

Larking, Hollis, Gregory and the Physic back in their chamber. They all look down at their feet. A long silence, then:

LARKING: You've condemned us all. You know that?

HOLLIS: I do.

LARKING: You've murdered us all—

PHYSIC: That's / enough—

LARKING *(Continuous)*: And not a word in your defense!

HOLLIS: It felt right, is all.

LARKING: "Felt," always felt. Did you have accomplices? *(Looks at the Physic)* Him?

HOLLIS: What choice did he have?

LARKING: In front of the fucking Duke.

GREGORY: Shouldn't say "fucking Duke."

(The Major-Domo is suddenly in the doorway.)

MAJOR-DOMO: Well then.

(They all stand as he enters the room. He unrolls a little scroll.)

A message from His Excellency, the Duke of Travo.

GREGORY: Does that mean he liked it?

(The Major-Domo ignores this and reads:)

MAJOR-DOMO *(Reading)*: "Players all,
    First, let me congratulate you on a most comic and diverting evening"—
LARKING: "Comic," what's he mean comic?
HOLLIS: Shhh.
MAJOR-DOMO *(Continuing to read)*: "Your 'God' was an enjoyably pompous buffoon, amusingly in love with the sound of his own voice. *(Larking silently fumes)* More wonderful still were the fisticuffs between poor Noah and his saucy spouse. As a married man, I can well appreciate the trials of a disobedient wife.
    Now with thanks I send you on your way—
    And because you have pleased me so well, a new honor:
    You may now call yourselves The Duke of Travo Players.
    We look forward to your return next Christmastime."
    (He looks up from the page)
    Well. I think you've made rather a hit with the Duke.

(Larking looks at his feet. A gathering storm.)

LARKING: Send us on our way?
MAJOR-DOMO: I can't remember hearing kinder words from His Highness.
LARKING: That's it? Thank you and goodbye and have a nice life? Or a nice death, / more like?
PHYSIC: Larking, steady / now—
LARKING: No—not Larking, steady! Don't you understand, we'll die out there!
MAJOR-DOMO: This is not a refuge, it's a working village. Only those with a real purpose in society earn their shelter.

LARKING: Purpose, did you hear that? We don't serve a purpose!

MAJOR-DOMO *(Helpfully)*: Like a butler or a horseman

LARKING: I thought—I told all these souls—

HOLLIS: It will be all right

LARKING: Will it?

PHYSIC: We'll keep moving, we'll outrun the sickness. It's worked so far.

LARKING: Did it work for Brom? Or Henry?

HOLLIS: You're the man who said don't just lie down and die.
"The Duke of Travo Players." *(Not entirely believing this, perhaps)* We'll say that name and doors will open for us. Doors that were shut before.

(Beat.)

LARKING *(To himself, desolate)*: I thought this was the ark.

HOLLIS: What?

LARKING: I thought this was the ark. But there isn't any ark.

8

Rona sits up in her cot. She looks very weak, but she's turned a corner. The cards are spread before her.

RONA: St. Felicitas, I asked you for a son
Not a lemon-faced girl.
St. Felicitas, you don't listen
Or you don't care
Or you don't fucking exist.
(She swipes the cards off the bed)
Now I've got nothing but me
And that's not much.

(A knock on the door.)

What.

(Gregory enters.)

But the quarantine—they say I'm poison for another week.

GREGORY: You're not poison.

RONA: No more than usual.

GREGORY *("You don't understand")*: I prayed for you and it bled. *(He takes the nail out of his pocket)* The Christ-nail bled, like he said it would.

(She just looks at him. Then she starts to pick up the cards. Gregory moves to help.)

RONA: Don't. There's an order.

(In another part of the stage, Hollis and the Physic:)

PHYSIC: You kissed me.

HOLLIS *(Playfully obtuse)*: Did I?

PHYSIC: I wasn't sure if it was just

HOLLIS: A fluke?

PHYSIC: Or for the play.

HOLLIS: I don't think Noah's Wife is much of a kisser

PHYSIC: No

HOLLIS: Efficient at procreation, maybe.

PHYSIC: They had to be doing *some*thing for forty days.

HOLLIS *(A beat)*: "Asher."

PHYSIC: What

HOLLIS: Just seeing how it sounds—I never get to say it.

PHYSIC: You kept my secret.

HOLLIS: Before we even met, someone warned me about you.

PHYSIC: But something changed your mind.

HOLLIS: I think . . . I stopped believing in that kind of magic.

PHYSIC *(Dismissive)*: Ghosts. Spells.
    We are more alone in the world than we thought.

(Just then, Rona finishes picking up the tarot cards. For a moment the scenes intersect:)

GREGORY: I think about that night, all the time. The night you came to me.
RONA *("You think a lot of yourself")*: Oh I came to you did I.
GREGORY: Yes.

> HOLLIS *(To the Physic)*: Are we?
> PHYSIC: ?
> HOLLIS: Alone?

RONA *(To Gregory)*: I think about it too.
GREGORY: You do?
RONA: Don't make me say it again.

> HOLLIS: What if, when we forget magic, we make room for something else?

(Gregory kisses Rona, lightly.
    During the following, the Physic takes Hollis's hand in his.)

GREGORY: Soon as the quarantine is up, we're moving on.
RONA: Where?
GREGORY: The next city, the next square. Mr. Larking says I can play Shem now. So you don't have to be both. You can just be a lady.
RONA: A lady, is that what I am.
GREGORY: Yes. *(Beat)* Do you think you might come to me again, sometime?
RONA: Who can say?

(A feeling that she definitely will.)

Life is long.

(She looks out the window at the coming spring.)

9

Time has passed. Noah and his Wife watch the floodwaters retreating. A miniature Ark is perched atop a forced-perspective Mount Ararat. Rona and Gregory look on from the flies, operating the pulleys and ropes together.

NOAH:

> Now all the sorrows we were in,
> And all our trials, are no more.

NOAH'S WIFE:

> But Noah, where are all our kin
> And company we knew before?

NOAH:

> All are drowned—spare me your din—
> For all their sins they paid, full sore.
> A better life let us begin,
> So that we grieve our God no more.

NOAH'S WIFE:

> But Husband, how shall our lives be led,
> Since none are in this world but we?

NOAH:

> Our children shall each other wed
> And thus shall multiply their seed!

(Maybe Noah's Wife finds this a little questionable.)

> They'll till the soil and bake the bread
> And soon, a world shall begin to be.

(In the wings, the Playwright seems agitated. From across the stage, he locks eyes with Quincy Tyler Bernstine. [As they talk, Noah's Flood continues, mutely. Noah raises the olive branch to the heavens in thanks to God.])

PLAYWRIGHT: What are you thinking, at the end?

QUINCY *(A beat)*: I'm not gonna lie, sometimes I'm thinking about dinner. Or, "Quincy, do your laundry." And then I feel guilty, because everyone in the world just died and I'm thinking about dinner. But—she must've had that moment too.

PLAYWRIGHT: Noah's Wife.

(From the wings, Rona turns a crank and the floodwaters recede.)

QUINCY: And Hollis. At some point you have to think about dinner. The persistence of the normal is strong. And I guess it's sad that we forget so easily, that the people of the future will never understand—

PLAYWRIGHT: But maybe that's how we're able to move forward.

QUINCY: People have always thought the world was about to end. They've been saying it for a thousand years. And yet—

PLAYWRIGHT *(Facile)*: Here we are.

QUINCY: Something's wrong. What's wrong.

(Behind them, Noah looks skyward as God descends from on high. Larking starts to deliver a long and decorous speech that we can't hear. The Playwright takes in the play happening around them.)

PLAYWRIGHT: I just don't know if we deserve it.

(A confused beat.)

QUINCY: Deserve what?

PLAYWRIGHT: The happy ending.

QUINCY: Oh

PLAYWRIGHT: We all know how *Noah's Flood* ends. The water recedes and the sun shines, and rainbows—

QUINCY: What's wrong with that?

PLAYWRIGHT: It says the crisis is over, and I guess that's not the way I feel. It's more like . . .

QUINCY *("I know what you mean")*: The sky is still falling.

RONA *(From the wings, a stage whisper)*: Gregory!

PLAYWRIGHT: I'm worried we're saying the work is done, just by ending the play. When it's just starting.

(In the wings, Rona struggles with the heavy rope that's meant to pull the storm clouds offstage.)

RONA: Gregory I need you!

QUINCY: Uh, I think she's trying to—

PLAYWRIGHT *(Ignoring Rona)*: That's the trouble with catharsis, it's innately complacent.

(Rona comes onstage and physically drags him back into the wings.)

QUINCY: But it's so delicious.

(He and Rona pull the ropes, and the dark clouds track off. Divine sunlight rains down on us. Catharsis.)

PLAYWRIGHT: And then, what's the opposite of catharsis?

(Before she can answer, focus shifts back to Noah's Ark:)

GOD:

> Noah, take thy wife anon,
> And thy children—every one.
> From the ship thou shalt be gone,
> And to a world more free.

(Noah and his Wife exit the ark and enter the bright new world, arm in arm.)

> Beasts and all that cannest fly
> Out anon with you shall they
> On earth to grow and multiply;
> I will that it so be.
> Grow, and multiply, and *live*—
> I will that it so be.

(God looks out at us in the audience:)

> My blessing now I give thee here:
> From now no longer need you fear
> My storm clouds shall no more appear;
> And now farewell, my darlings dear.

END OF PLAY

AUTHOR'S NOTE

In early workshops of the play, Heidi Schreck played the role of Hollis. I commissioned Heidi to write a monologue from the actor's perspective to enhance Act Two, and she responded with the wonderful account of her experience playing Mrs. Cratchit at Actors Theatre of Louisville. Because it isn't realistic for Heidi to play herself at every performance of *The Amateurs*, we devised a solution where the role is named for whichever actor is playing Hollis at the moment. So, in the Vineyard Theatre production, Quincy Tyler Bernstine delivers the Mrs. Cratchit monologue as if the words are her own. This should be the solution for further productions as well.

AFTERWORD

Something I don't remember being taught about plays is that they change, over time, when you aren't looking. I haven't altered a word of these plays since they premiered, and yet—they've changed. I can only assume they'll continue to change.

When I wrote *Maple and Vine*, beginning in 2009, I set out to make a play about people escaping the modern world. Katha and Ryu are running from technology, yes, but also from the paralyzing feeling of having *too* many choices, too much freedom. Developing the play with director Anne Kauffman and the theater company The Civilians, I inherited reams of interviews that The Civilians had conducted with real people who "escape" from the twenty-first century: cloistered nuns, the Amish, Civil War reenactors. In order to free myself from doing a mere book report on these people (which was tempting, they were fascinating), I invented the Society of Dynamic Obsolescence: a community where it is forever 1955.

I couldn't have predicted the ways in which Katha and Ryu's escape has become more resonant in the years since. The idea that a couple would move to the 1950s felt more purely whimsical when the play was first performed at the Humana Festival and Playwrights Horizons. Now, because the far-right movement in this country often invokes the 1950s as some sort of high point of American society, there is a darker edge to Katha and Ryu's wish fulfillment. The play always had darkness, but now its darkness is more tinged with plausibility.

Of course it would be a mistake to draw too close a parallel between the SDO and the current far-right yearning for a mythological 1950s. For one thing, the SDO members know that the '50s held as much darkness and cruelty as it did glamour—especially for women, people of color, and gays (in other words, the characters in the play). They know that the Cleavers were always a fiction, and often an oppressive one. The perverse gravity of their choice (and this is why the SDO is more than a costume party, or a trip to the Ren Faire) comes from the fact that the characters live there despite—and in some cases, because of—the decade's deep injustices.

This is all to say, I invite you to read *Maple and Vine* in both the context I first wrote it in, and the context of today (in which we have perhaps even more reasons to escape the modern world).

The other plays in this collection are also being seen through a new lens. When *The Amateurs* premiered at the Vineyard Theatre in 2018, the Black Death stood for nothing but itself, a centuries-old plague—until Act Two, when the playwright draws an allegory with the AIDS epidemic. Nowadays it doesn't take a poetic mind to read the play and think of Covid. (As Heidi Schreck mentions in her Foreword, Covid literally forced itself onstage when the play was produced in February 2020.) What was once a play about a distant plague now touches on what we experienced first-hand—the durability of live performance during a terrifying pandemic.

From our vantage point in 2024, we know Phil Spector to be a more extreme sort of monster than the comparatively innocuous egomaniac who, back in 2006, inspired the character Vic Watts in *Doris to Darlene*. And now, when I read the scene where Mr. Campani entertains the idea of sleeping with his sixteen-year-old student, I gasp at his moral lapse. I don't remember audiences gasping at this when the play premiered at Playwrights Horizons in 2007, although it was always understood as a deep wrinkle on an otherwise inspirational character.

It would be inaccurate to say that I either regret or embrace the ways the changing world has marked my plays. It just *is*—a mark of time passing, like my clicky right hip joint and the carpal tunnel in my left hand. To the reader picking this book up (god willing) in another ten or twenty years: You are better equipped than I to judge how these plays have resisted, or surrendered to, the changing world.

—JH
October 2024

ACKNOWLEDGMENTS

With thanks to the directors who helped me shape these plays, especially Anne Kauffman, Ken Rus Schmoll, Oliver Butler, Les Waters, and Adam Greenfield.

With thanks to the Artistic Directors who took a chance on me, especially Tim Sanford, Marc Masterson, Maria Striar, Sarah Stern, and Doug Aibel.

With thanks to *(I hope I'm not forgetting you, I'm sure that I am)*—

Heidi Schreck, Kip Fagan, Adrien-Alice Hansel, Amy Wegener, Deborah Stein, the Clubbed Thumb Writers' Group, Bathsheba Doran, Paula Vogel, Rachel Viola, Sarah Ruhl, Sonya Sobieski, Rebecca Wisocky, Robert Quillen Camp, Ruth Margraff, Sawako Nakayasu, Val Day, Mac Wellman, Lucas Hnath, Tanya Palmer, Mark Subias, Steve Cosson and The Civilians, Madeleine Oldham, Kirsten Childs, Meg MacCary, Abby Rosebrock, Christie Evangelisto, Lisa Timmel, Mark Lerman, Sylvan Oswald, Ari Edelson, Darron L West, Sean Daniels, Richard Gray, P. Carl, John L'Heureux, Cherríe Moraga, Aishah Rahman, Britton Rizzio, Susan Glass

ACKNOWLEDGMENTS

Burdick, Allison Narver, John Glore, Megan Monaghan, Bob McAllister, Emilya Cachapero, David Zinn, Kristen Gandrow, Ruby Takanishi, Ben Harrison, Megan Rohrssen, John Snell, Liz Snell, Carey Perloff, Mark Rucker, Marge Betley, Siobhan Glennon, Polly Noonan, Carole Maso, Sage Van Wing, Kelly Gillespie, Alex Barron, Katie Doran, Perry Lorenzo, Emily Morse, Bray Poor, Todd London, New Dramatists, Peter Kim, Jeanine Serralles, Kate Turnbull, Marin Ireland, Jesse Pennington, Paul Niebanck, Pedro Pascal, Trent Dawson, Joel de la Fuente, Rebecca Henderson, Patch Darragh, Brian Sgambati, Gio Perez, Satya Bhabha, Quincy Tyler Bernstine, Michael Cyril Creighton, Kyle Beltran, Jennifer Kim, Thomas Jay Ryan, Greg Keller, De'Adre Aziza, Laura Heisler, David Chandler, Michael Crane, Tom Nelis, and Tobias Segal.

And, above all, thank you to Cynthia and David Harrison.

—*JH*

JORDAN HARRISON grew up on Bainbridge Island, near Seattle. He was a Pulitzer Prize finalist for *Marjorie Prime*, which premiered at the Mark Taper Forum and had its New York premiere at Playwrights Horizons. His play *Maple and Vine* premiered at the Humana Festival at Actors Theatre of Louisville and went on to productions at American Conservatory Theater and Playwrights Horizons, among others. Harrison's other plays include *Kid-Simple*, *The Museum Play*, *Finn in the Underworld*, *Act A Lady*, *Amazons and Their Men*, *Doris to Darlene*, *Futura*, *The Grown-Up*, *The Amateurs*, *Log Cabin*, and, most recently, *The Antiquities*. He has also written a children's musical, *The Flea and the Professor*, with Richard Gray, and a grown-up musical, *Suprema*, with Daniel Zaitchik. Harrison's work has premiered at the Arden Theatre, Berkeley Repertory Theatre, Clubbed Thumb, Goodman Theatre, Humana Festival, Menier Chocolate Factory, Minetta Lane Theatre, National Asian American Theatre Company (NAATCO), Portland Center Stage, Theatre @ Boston Court, and Vincyard Theatre. He is the recipient of Guggenheim and Hodder fellowships, the Horton Foote Prize, the Kesselring Prize, the Roe Green Award, the Theater Masters Visionary Playwright Award, the Heideman Award, the Loewe Award for Musical Theater, a NEA/TCG grant, and Jerome and McKnight Fellowships from The Playwrights' Center. As a screenwriter, Harrison's credits include *Orange Is the New Black*, *GLOW*, and *Dispatches from Elsewhere*, as well as a feature script for Pixar. A film adaptation of *Marjorie Prime*, directed by Michael Almereyda, premiered at the Sundance Film Festival, where it won the Alfred P. Sloan Feature Prize. Harrison is a graduate of Stanford University and the Brown University MFA program, and a proud alumnus of New Dramatists.